Dr Haili Hughes and Sam Gibbs

Love the One You're With

Why teachers stay and what we can learn from them

hachette LEARNING

hachette LEARNING

www.hachettelearning.com

Together we unlock every learner's unique potential

At Hachette Learning (formerly Hodder Education), there's one thing we're certain about. No two students learn the same way. That's why our approach to teaching begins by recognising the needs of individuals first.

Our mission is to allow every learner to fulfil their unique potential by empowering those who teach them. From our expert teaching and learning resources to our digital educational tools that make learning easier and more accessible for all, we provide solutions designed to maximise the impact of learning for every teacher, parent and student.

Aligned to our parent company, Hachette Livre, founded in 1826, we pride ourselves on being a learning solutions provider with a global footprint.

To order, please visit www.HachetteLearning.com or contact Customer Service at education@hachette.co.uk / +44 (0)1235 827827.

ISBN: 978 1 0360 1159 8

First published in 2026 by
Hachette Learning (a trading division of Hodder & Stoughton Limited),
An Hachette UK Company
Carmelite House
50 Victoria Embankment
London EC4Y 0DZ

www.HachetteLearning.com

The authorised representative in the EEA is Hachette Ireland, 8 Castlecourt Centre, Dublin 15, D15 XTP3, Ireland (email: info@hbgi.ie)

Impression number 10 9 8 7 6 5 4 3 2 1
Year 2030 2029 2028 2027 2026

Cover photo © Mary Luts/Shutterstock.com
Illustrations by DC Graphic Design Limited, Hextable, Kent.
Typeset in the UK.
Printed in the UK.

A catalogue record for this title is available from the British Library.

FSC www.fsc.org MIX Paper | Supporting responsible forestry FSC™ C104740

Haili: *Dedicated to my family, whose support and understanding undoubtedly kept me in the teaching profession for over twenty years*

Sam: *For Lucas, Maya and Elliott, who have taught me the true purpose and value of education*

ABOUT THE AUTHORS

Dr Haili Hughes is an Associate Professor and Associate Dean of Educational Innovation and Impact at La Trobe University in Melbourne, Australia. Prior to this, she was the only professor and MAT leader in the UK. She served as a school leader for over 20 years, as well as being an academic and systems leader in education companies. She has written 10 education books and advised the Department for Education on ITT and mentoring. She is an elected councillor at the Chartered College of Teaching and a commissioner at the Teaching Commission.

Sam Gibbs taught and led in UK secondary schools for 12 years and is now Director of Professional Learning at Greater Manchester Education Trust. Prior to this role, she worked for a national teacher education provider, leading training and development in schools across the country. Sam is Deputy Chair of the Trust Wide CPD Leaders Forum, a free national network that advocates for collaboration and professional generosity to drive system-led improvement. She also sits on a number of advisory boards and is a commissioner at the Teaching Commission.

Dr Haili Hughes

Sam Gibbs

ACKNOWLEDGEMENTS

Thank you to all the teachers who shared their stories.

REVIEWS

I absolutely love the deeply personal nature of this book, while still being academically informed and extremely practical. The storytelling approach (including both the authors' fascinating personal narratives) gives life and humanity to the important and widely applicable themes, which have important messages for people working at every level within the school system. The focus on more experienced teachers is particularly important for many reasons that are explored in the book. This is a vital group of experts who are too often overlooked and yet at the absolute heart of securing the best not only for pupils but also for the less experienced teachers who rely on their wisdom and support.

Sam Twiselton, Emeritus Professor and Former Founding Director of Sheffield Institute of Education (SIoE)

Nothing matters more for our schools and pupils than teacher quality: nothing underpins this more than retaining expert motivated professionals in our classrooms. As rates of teacher attrition escalate, it is natural to focus on those who leave; but the real story rests with those who remain and the schools where they work. This book is a valuable contribution to a national priority, as Sam Gibbs and Haili Hughes provide insightful, biographical, practical and vital messages from teachers who have stayed – culminating in their pioneering THRIVE model. We need to hear and heed their voices.

Dr Robin Bevan, Educational Coach, Consultant and Advocate; Former Headteacher; and Commissioner at the Teaching Commission

Love the One You're With: Why teachers stay and what we can learn from them is a rare blend of research and humanity. It's a study that gives voice to the teachers who choose to stay when leaving might be easier. Hughes and Gibbs move beyond data to reveal the emotional intelligence, moral courage and nuance behind long-term commitment. This book reframes retention as integrity in motion: the art of staying aligned with one's purpose in a profession that constantly tests it. Both timely and deeply humane, it's essential reading for anyone who cares about education's future.

Mary Myatt, Education Writer and Speaker

I was absolutely delighted to read this manuscript. What a joy to encounter such a refreshingly positive account of what sustains teachers in the profession. Importantly, the book does not attempt to gloss over the very real challenges facing our sector. Instead, it names them and confronts them directly and thoughtfully. By focusing on the experiences of teachers who have chosen to stay, Haili and Sam provide a powerful and much-needed counterpoint to the prevailing narrative of crisis. Their work highlights the deep sense of purpose, value, community and professional fulfilment that keeps so many teachers committed to the classroom. If you know of anyone considering teaching as a profession, place this book into their hands as it will serve as an honest and realistic account of what they can expect; and as a guide to how they can sustain a long and happy career. It will be equally valuable as a resource for serving teachers, leaders, policymakers and the wider profession to understand how better to support and nurture our wonderful teaching workforce.

Emma Hollis, CEO at NASBTT

Love the One You're With is an excellent premise and beautifully delivered. Instead of focusing solely on why teachers leave, the authors move the conversation on to what helps teachers stay. They blend research, analysis of policy and real experiences to shine a very human light on this issue, as well as providing concrete frameworks for leaders and policymakers to forge a better path.

Sarah Cottinghatt, Research Lead at Steplab! Professional Development Consultant for Schools

Love the One You're With is a compelling reminder that teacher retention is not about individual resilience but about the conditions we create for teachers to thrive. The book is packed full of research about the reasons people leave the profession, and crucially what might help them stay and flourish. Clear, honest and deeply humane, with many illuminating testimonials from teachers and leaders that will have you both nodding and shaking your head, this book sets out not just the problem, but the courage and options required to build a profession worth staying in.

Sam Crome, Headteacher and MAT Director of Education

As Founder of The MTPT Project, I warmly welcome this powerful and nuanced exploration of retention. Gibbs and Hughes recognise the way that gender, parenthood and caring responsibilities interact with issues like workload, wellbeing and autonomy so frequently raised as factors contributing to attrition. This may come as no surprise from authors who have firsthand experience of the intersection of teaching, leadership and motherhood. Gibbs and Hughes draw on broad research, and write with pragmatism but also from the heart, emphasising that when schools truly value teachers' lives beyond the classroom, they create cultures where experienced colleagues can thrive. This book highlights that inclusive, flexible approaches are fundamental to keeping brilliant teachers in the profession and sustaining a diverse, committed workforce.

Emma Shepherd, Founder of The MaternityTeacher PaternityTeacher Project

We know there is a serious problem with teacher retention. We know teachers are leaving in droves. Why? Hughes and Gibbs state, 'We are failing to recognise and reward their worth, and we are expecting them to shoulder the burden of an increasingly stretched and pressurised system'. The authors start with the need to break this cycle, but take us further by asking: Why do teachers STAY? This insightful book weaves the stories of teachers with 20+ years in the classroom, illustrating how leadership, autonomy and community become the bedrocks for retention. I highly recommend it.

Patrice Bain, Teacher, Researcher, Author, Speaker

In this book, Haili and Sam move nuancedly between research and hands-on experience to generate insights relevant for schools across the country. They place vision at the heart of these insights that goes beyond retaining teachers in post, but igniting teaching as a beautiful, joyful vocation that enriches our desire for intellectual curiosity, purpose and belonging.

Dr Neil Gilbride, Honorary Senior Research Fellow,
University of Worcester and Chartered Psychologist

CONTENTS

Foreword xi

Introduction xiii

PART 1: WHAT CAN WE LEARN FROM THE PAST? 1

Chapter 1: Policy and research landscape of teacher retention.... 3

Chapter 2: Why do we need experienced teachers to stay in our classrooms? 21

PART 2: TEACHERS' STORIES 31

Chapter 3: Our teaching stories 33

Chapter 4: In their words 49

Chapter 5: Why teachers stay: a thematic exploration of teacher retention 69

Chapter 6: Retention of teachers from marginalised ethnic groups 123

PART 3: COVID-19 143

Chapter 7: Impact of the Covid-19 pandemic 145

Chapter 8: Portrayal of teachers in the media during the pandemic 152

PART 4: WHAT CAN WE LEARN FROM ELSEWHERE? 161

Chapter 9: What can we learn from other fields? 163

Chapter 10: What can we learn from other countries? 189

PART 5: PUTTING IT ALL TOGETHER 215

Chapter 11: A codified framework for teacher retention 217

PART 6: KEY LEARNINGS 227

Chapter 12: Schools and Trusts that have got it right: case studies 229

Chapter 13: Key findings for leaders 257

Chapter 14: Key findings for policymakers 262

PART 7: CLOSING WORDS 267

Chapter 15: Call to action 269

FOREWORD

Ensuring schools in England have the teachers they need has been a challenge for more than a decade. Prolonged staff shortages create difficulties for hard-pressed senior leaders that come to affect the quality of education pupils experience. The damage is felt most deeply in schools serving the most disadvantaged communities. For many years, policymakers' instincts have been to seek solutions in recruiting more teachers. Recruitment policy has its place but, with the system as it is, this amounts to pouring more water into the metaphorical leaking bucket. With this book, Haili and Sam ask the important question 'What if we looked at closing the holes instead?'

Retention matters for teacher supply just as much as training new teachers does. Indeed, it matters even more, as many trainees do not complete their training nor end up working in a state school. But retention also matters because it means pupils benefiting from their teachers getting better every year and the strong relationships that form from continuity. Trainees and new teachers benefit too, as they develop their practice with guidance from supportive and experienced colleagues.

That's why the focus of this book on retention of experienced teachers is so refreshing for the retention debate. There has been justified focus on supporting early career teacher retention, as they are more likely to leave than their more experienced colleagues. But too many experienced teachers are also leaving, with the extra damage this does to schools' institutional memory and the wisdom they can draw on. The urgency of identifying solutions to this problem is now as important as ever.

Haili and Sam are two highly experienced teachers, who are perfectly placed to tell this story and make this case compellingly. Their accumulated understanding of the stresses and strains of learning the trade of being a teacher, moving school, supporting new teachers on their journeys and themselves leading across teams and schools brings weight to the narrative. They have both worked outside of education, which brings unique external perspectives. They have also experienced all the types of school culture they describe so vividly, from the toxic to the supportive.

The book is underpinned by far more than anecdote and personal experience, as it is grounded in robust evidence from high-quality research. The authors' own qualitative research and analysis brings added rigour to the narrative, while also bringing the points to life with the all-important voices of teachers and leaders working on the ground.

Important messages for school leaders and policymakers emerge from the book, supported by rich and vividly described practical examples. Case studies of leaders putting the ideas into practice in their schools and Trusts, and vignettes of practice in other countries, demonstrate that these are realities that can be implemented, not simply idle suggestions.

Haili and Sam's book comes at a critical time for policymakers and school leaders to assess how we continue improving retention in the system. Seizing the chance to do so could improve teaching quality and create more opportunities for children and young people to thrive.

Jack Worth, Lead Economist at National Foundation for Educational Research

INTRODUCTION

Teacher recruitment and retention have long been recognised as critical issues in the education sector, with direct implications for the quality of teaching and for student outcomes. These challenges, particularly in England, have persisted for decades, marked by periods of crisis, which are often countercyclical with periods of economic downturn being associated with better teacher supply.[1] However, one of the most pressing concerns today is the significant attrition rates among teachers, particularly those who are early in their careers. While much attention has been devoted to understanding why new teachers leave the profession, there is a distinct yet equally important group that requires focused investigation: teachers with over 20 years of experience. This book aims to explore the factors that contribute to the decision of long-serving educators to stay in teaching, offering a critical examination of the complexities of teacher retention in the post-pandemic era.

This introduction outlines the nature of the teacher-retention problem in England, particularly in the context of the challenges exacerbated by the Covid-19 pandemic, and highlights why it is crucial to examine the experiences of teachers who have remained in the profession for over two decades. We also briefly discuss the long-term issues surrounding teacher recruitment and retention, including uncompetitive pay, excessive workload and the difficulty meeting teacher-supply targets, before situating this book within the broader landscape of teacher-retention literature.

The impact of Covid-19: accelerating existing issues

The Covid-19 pandemic, which began in early 2020 in the UK, acted as a significant catalyst, amplifying the teacher recruitment and retention crisis in England. At the onset of the pandemic, there was an initial surge in applications for teacher-training programmes, likely driven by the economic uncertainty in other sectors. The prospect of job stability in teaching, a traditionally secure career path, seemed more appealing

1 Hutchings, M. (2011) 'What impact does the wider economic situation have on teachers' career decisions? A literature review' from Institute for Policy Studies in Education, London Metropolitan University [online] Available at: https://assets.publishing.service.gov.uk/media/5a7b14e140f0b66a2fc05055/DFE-RR136.pdf (Accessed: 7 May 2026).

during the turbulent times of a global health crisis.[2] However, this temporary increase in interest quickly gave way to deeper challenges as the pandemic unfolded.

For many teachers, the pandemic marked the beginning of an era of unprecedented pressures. Teachers were suddenly required to adapt to remote teaching with little preparation, navigate new technology platforms and manage the wellbeing of students who were learning in isolation. These challenges were particularly acute for those in secondary schools, where teaching complex subjects and ensuring student engagement in an online environment were significantly harder.[3] Moreover, schools were forced to implement and constantly revise Covid-19 safety protocols, which added to the already heavy administrative burden that teachers faced.

While the pandemic exacerbated the existing workload crisis, it also introduced new strains. Teachers reported significant emotional burnout due to the constant uncertainty, disrupted learning and the added responsibility of safeguarding their students' mental health during lockdowns.[4] For many, the pressure of managing not only academic outcomes but also the safety and wellbeing of students during a global health crisis became a tipping point. In the years following the pandemic, teacher-retention statistics revealed that many educators, particularly those with less than five years of experience, were leaving the profession at higher rates than before:[5] 11.3% before the pandemic and 11.7% afterwards.[6] We discuss the impact of the pandemic in more depth later on in this book (Chapters 7 and 8).

---

2 Belger, T. (2021) 'UCAS teacher training applications data: 7 things we learned' on *SchoolsWeek* [online] Available at: https://schoolsweek.co.uk/teacher-training-apply-ucas-applications-rise (Accessed: 30 April 2026).

3 Siddiquei, M.I. and Kathpal, S. (2021) 'Challenges of online teaching during COVID-19: An exploratory factor analysis' in *Human Behaviour and Emerging Technologies*, 3(5), pp.811–822.

4 Kim, L.E., Oxley, L. and Asbury, K. (2022) 'My brain feels like a browser with 100 tabs open: A longitudinal study of teachers' mental health and well-being during the COVID-19 pandemic' in *British Journal of Educational Psychology*, 92, pp.299–318.

5 Baker, M. (2022) 'Post-Pandemic Teacher Retention: A National Crisis' in *Educational Review*, 74(2), pp.234–246.

6 UK Government (2025) 'Government evidence to the STRB – data annexes – September 2025' [online] Available at: https://assets.publishing.service.gov.uk/media/6900daff84b816d72cb9aa97/STRB_26_data_annex.xlsx (Accessed: 7 May 2026).

However, what remains less understood is the experience of teachers with over 20 years of service. While it is clear that many teachers were considering leaving after the pandemic, some with decades of experience chose to stay. Understanding why these educators, who have weathered numerous changes in the educational landscape, remain committed to their profession is essential for developing effective strategies to retain this valuable and often underappreciated group of educators.

Long-term challenges in teacher retention

Despite the specific pressures created by Covid-19, long-standing issues have continued to drive teacher turnover and dissatisfaction in England, with no simple solutions on the horizon. The persistent nature of these challenges highlights the complexity of the problem.

One of the most significant and frequently cited factors contributing to the teacher-retention crisis is the disparity in pay between teachers and professionals in other graduate-level occupations. The salary structure for teachers, particularly in the early stages of their careers, has historically been uncompetitive compared to the private sector, despite the considerable responsibility and qualifications required for teaching.[7] While there have been occasional pay rises, these have often failed to keep up with inflation and the increasing cost of living, leaving many teachers feeling undervalued.[8] Additionally, the issue of pay has been compounded by the increase in living costs, particularly in cities such as London, where the cost of housing is prohibitive. Without competitive compensation, retaining experienced teachers becomes even more difficult.

Workload has been another persistent issue affecting teacher retention. Over the years, government reports and teacher surveys have consistently shown that workload, particularly related to administrative duties and marking, is one of the primary reasons that teachers leave the profession.[9] A teacher's workday often extends beyond the classroom, as they are required to prepare lessons, grade assignments, attend meetings

7 Sullivan, A., Johnson, B., Simons, M. and Tippett, N. (2020) 'When performativity meets agency: how early career teachers struggle to reconcile competing agendas to become "quality" teachers' in *Teachers and Teaching*, 27, pp.1–16.

8 Blatchford, P. (2018) 'The Teacher's Salary Dilemma: Why Pay Does Not Reflect the Value of Teaching' in *Teacher Education Quarterly*, 45(3), pp.3–18.

9 Elliott, S., Brown, A. and Jones, H. (2017) 'Teacher Workload: Causes, Consequences, and Solutions' in *Journal of Education Policy*, 32(4), pp.499–512.

and fulfil numerous bureaucratic responsibilities. These pressures are exacerbated by the rise in high-stakes accountability measures and standardised testing, which require teachers to devote additional time to data collection and analysis, leaving little room for professional development or personal time.[10] For teachers who have been in the profession for decades, the cumulative effect of these workload pressures often leads to burnout and dissatisfaction.

Another key challenge in the recruitment and retention of teachers in England is the ongoing difficulty in meeting teacher-supply targets, particularly in subjects including mathematics, physics and computing. These shortages have been a persistent issue, with schools struggling to recruit qualified teachers in shortage subjects.[11] For long-serving teachers, particularly those in specialised subject areas, the pressure of covering gaps in subject-specific teaching due to recruitment shortfalls can be overwhelming. Additionally, teacher-supply problems are compounded by rising student numbers, particularly in secondary schools, where student–teacher ratios have increased, adding further strain on already overburdened educators.

The value of experienced teachers

While the challenges outlined above contribute to the overall teacher-retention problem, the focus of this book is on the experiences of teachers who have stayed in the profession for 20 years or more. These educators have weathered periods of significant change, including shifts in educational policy, curriculum changes and fluctuations in government funding. They have seen the profession evolve and have adapted their teaching methods, sometimes in response to external pressures and sometimes in pursuit of their own professional growth. Their decision to remain in the classroom, despite the challenges, offers valuable insights into the factors that contribute to long-term teacher satisfaction and retention.

Experienced teachers often have deep, intrinsic motivations for staying in the profession, including a sense of purpose, a commitment to their students and a passion for the subject they teach.[12] For some, the decision

10 Bubb, S. and Earley, P. (2020) *The Impact of Educational Accountability on Teachers: A Longitudinal Study*. London: Routledge.

11 Allen, R. (2019) *Teacher Supply in England: A Review of the Evidence*. London: Education Policy Institute.

12 Frenzel, A.C., Daniels, L. and Burić, I. (2021) 'Teacher emotions in the classroom and their implications for students' in *Educational Psychologist*, 56(4), pp.250–264.

to remain in teaching is grounded in a sense of duty to the community or the desire to make a difference in the lives of young people. Others may stay due to the relationships they have built with students, colleagues and their school communities. Understanding these personal and professional motivations is crucial for creating strategies that support and sustain experienced teachers throughout their careers.

Additionally, experienced teachers bring unique strengths to the classroom. They have developed a deep knowledge of pedagogy, classroom management and subject-specific content. Their teaching is informed by years of experience, which allows them to navigate difficult situations with confidence and to offer guidance to younger, less experienced colleagues. Retaining these teachers is not only important for the individual educators themselves but also for the broader educational system, as their expertise plays a key role in improving educational outcomes. This is further explored later on in this book in Chapter 2.

A new perspective on teacher retention

The challenges surrounding teacher recruitment and retention in England are multi-faceted and complex, shaped by long-standing issues such as pay disparities, workload pressures and teacher-supply shortages. However, the impact of the Covid-19 pandemic intensified these challenges, further straining an already under-resourced education system. While much of the focus has been on understanding why new teachers leave the profession, less attention has been given to the factors that keep long-serving educators in the classroom.

As this book went to press, the National Foundation for Educational Research (NFER) published some research with the Nuffield Foundation on what helps to improve teacher retention. School-leadership support is an important factor for retention. The report identified that teachers working in schools with good student behaviour, and support to deal with disruptive behaviour, are more likely to stay. The study also revealed that higher pay satisfaction and the impact of CPD on teachers' practice are significant factors associated with improved retention.[13]

13 Worth, J., Del Pozo Segura, J.M. and Kuhn, L. (2026) 'What helps to improve teacher retention? A pathway analysis of factors affecting retention', Slough: NFER [online] Available at: www.nfer.ac.uk/media/3stjkeac/what_helps_to_improve_teacher_retention.pdf (Accessed: 20 April 2026).

This book seeks to build on some of this early work by exploring why teachers with over 20 years of experience choose to remain in the profession, despite the pressures and challenges they face. By examining their motivations and experiences, and the strategies that have helped them sustain long-term careers in teaching, we aim to contribute to the development of more effective policies and practices that can support teacher retention in the future. Retaining experienced teachers is essential for the future of the education system in England, and understanding their experiences is a crucial step towards addressing the teacher-retention crisis.

Part 1
What can we learn from the past?

CHAPTER ONE:
Policy and research landscape of teacher retention

History of teacher retention

As we discussed in the Introduction, teacher recruitment and retention in England has been a recurring issue, though its severity has varied over time. There have, however, been multiple periods when challenges in recruiting and retaining teachers have been more acute.

In the 1970s, economic instability and high inflation led to widespread public-sector wage freezes, including for teachers (although this was punctuated with some quite substantial pay increases to undo some of the damage).[14] Low pay, combined with difficult working conditions, led to a shortage of teachers, particularly in urban areas and in subjects including maths and science. This led to significant teacher strikes in the 1980s over pay and conditions – particularly after the introduction of Conservative Government policies under Margaret Thatcher. These strikes were partly driven by dissatisfaction with wages and working conditions, and contributed to teacher shortages and low morale.

Although this book's authors, Haili and Sam, are both too young to remember this period, we are sure many who were schooled during the late 80s have vivid memories of this period; as do teachers involved in the strikes, who often describe the experience as a challenging but necessary form of collective action, fuelled by dissatisfaction with pay, working conditions and governmental policies. Many believed that striking was the only way to compel the government to take action on their grievances. According to David Ross,[15] the strikes fundamentally changed the role of the Educational Institute of Scotland (EIS), as teachers from all over

14 Houghton, A. (1974) 'Report of the Committee of Inquiry into the pay of Non-University Teachers' London: HMSO [online] Available at: https://education-uk.org/documents/houghton1974/index.html (Accessed: 7 May 2026).

15 Bloom, A. (2022) 'Improving Teachers' Pay: 1980's Campaign' on 175 Years Strong / The Educational Institute of Scotland [online] Available at: https://175.eis.org.uk/improving-teachers-pay/improving-teachers-pay-1980s-campaign (Accessed: 30 April 2026).

Scotland rallied together, driven by a belief in the power of collective bargaining. The strikes also targeted key political constituencies, focusing efforts to maximise disruption without overstretching individual teachers, who lost only a day's pay per week in many cases.[16]

Many teachers had mixed feelings about the strikes. In one account, a teacher from Edinburgh recalls standing on a picket line for the first time, noting the division it caused among colleagues. While most supported the strikes, others crossed picket lines, leading to heated confrontations and damaged relationships.[17] The strikes did ultimately result in a pay review and improved working conditions, but they also left a lasting impact on teacher morale and relations within schools.

MPs at this time wasted no time in vilifying the teachers who were striking and blaming the National Union of Teachers for rejecting the deals the Conservative government had offered. In some transcripts from the House of Commons, MP for Ealing North, Harry Greenway said:

> Will my right hon. friend accept that the great tragedy of the strike is that the children of this nation are suffering so badly? That includes ordinary children, disabled children and children taking examinations... Will my right hon. friend do all in his power to get the NUT leadership to negotiate, negotiate and negotiate again for the sake of the children of this country and their future?[18]

The strikes in the 1980s were largely over by 1987, but recruitment and retention challenges persisted into the 1990s too. Again, these challenges were mostly due to public-sector pay constraints and funding cuts. Pay for teachers was uncompetitive compared to other professions, and schools struggled to attract and keep staff, especially in subjects including science, maths and languages, where a job in industry often provided better salaries and more flexibility. In addition, during this

16 Macdonald, D. (2022) 'Memories of 1980s pay strikes show why teachers must get a fair deal' on *Tes magazine* [online] Available at: www.tes.com/magazine/analysis/general/memories-1980s-pay-strikes-show-why-teachers-must-get-fair-deal (Accessed: 30 April 2026).

17 Macdonald, D. (2022) 'Memories of 1980s pay strikes show why teachers must get a fair deal' on *Tes magazine* [online] Available at: www.tes.com/magazine/analysis/general/memories-1980s-pay-strikes-show-why-teachers-must-get-fair-deal (Accessed: 30 April 2026).

18 Deb, H.C. (1985) 'Teachers' Dispute (England and Wales)' vol 84 cc150–8 on UK Parliament [online] Available at: https://api.parliament.uk/historic-hansard/commons/1985/oct/22/teachers-dispute-england-and-wales (Accessed 30 April 2026).

time, the introduction of the national curriculum, Ofsted inspections and league tables indicating school performance put increased pressure on schools and teachers. This ended up leading to rising workload concerns and dissatisfaction within the profession, contributing to a high turnover rate among teachers.

John Clifford spoke about this period in the book *Humans in the Classroom* as one of the most challenging periods in his 60-year career in teaching:

> One of the biggest changes I witnessed in teaching was the introduction of the National Curriculum. Of course, it's good for teaching to have some element of containment, as the discipline of a curriculum is important, so nationally we all focus on the same thing. But it hindered me, as I felt I wanted to experiment and was bound.'[19]

Ofsted

The introduction of the Office for Standards in Education, Children's Services and Skills (Ofsted) in the early 1990s in England elicited mixed reactions from teachers, with many feeling both anxious and sceptical about its role and the impact it might have on their profession. The anxiety was caused by the high-stakes nature of Ofsted inspections. Teachers feared that the short, intensive inspection visits could misrepresent the quality of their teaching and schools. A study by Mahony and Hextall[20] found that teachers viewed Ofsted as a form of intense scrutiny that placed significant pressure on them, particularly because inspections could result in negative judgements that had long-term consequences for schools and teachers' careers. Teachers expressed concerns about the emotional strain inspections imposed, as Ofsted judgements often led to feelings of insecurity about their professional abilities.

The introduction of Ofsted inspections prompted a significant increase in teacher workload, as extensive documentation and evidence to demonstrate their effectiveness had to be prepared. Many teachers viewed these added demands as detracting from their ability to focus on teaching and student learning, with Ofsted inspections often focusing on superficial elements rather than meaningful educational quality.[21]

19 Hughes, H. (2022) *Humans in the Classroom*. London: McNidder and Grace, p.195.

20 Mahony, P. and Hextall, I. (2000) *Reconstructing Teaching: Standards, Performance, and Accountability*. Falmer: Routledge.

21 Gillborn, D. and Youdell, D. (2000) *Rationing Education: Policy, Practice, Reform and Equity*. London: Open University Press.

The rigidity of the inspection framework was a frequent complaint from teachers during this period. They felt that inspectors focused too much on narrow, predetermined criteria, which didn't always reflect the unique context or challenges of their schools. According to Jeffrey and Woods, teachers felt that Ofsted inspections promoted a 'one-size-fits-all' approach, ignoring the complex realities of different schools and undermining teachers' professional autonomy.[22] This led to a general feeling of disillusionment with the broader education system, viewing Ofsted as part of a trend towards marketisation and managerialism in education,[23] where the focus shifted to measurable outcomes rather than holistic educational values.[24]

Education policy under labour

When the Labour Party was elected in 1997 under Tony Blair, they placed education at the heart of their agenda. The party's campaign famously focused on the phrase 'education, education, education', reflecting their commitment to make it a top priority. Upon election, Labour articulated several key objectives for education, emphasising improvements in standards, investment and equality. These included the introduction of National Literacy and Numeracy Strategies to ensure that primary-school students received better support in these crucial areas. Blair described education as 'the best economic policy' and saw improving educational attainment as essential for ensuring social mobility and preparing the workforce for the challenges of a globalised economy.[25]

Labour recognised that schools needed greater investment to raise standards, and promised increased funding to address years of underinvestment. Their manifesto committed to reducing class sizes, especially in primary schools, by recruiting more teachers and improving school infrastructure. They also introduced initiatives including Building Schools for the Future (BSF), which aimed to refurbish or

22 Jeffrey, B. and Woods, P. (1998) *Testing Teachers: The Effects of Inspections on Primary Teachers*. London: Routledge.

23 Ball, S. (1993) 'Education Markets, Choice and Social Class: The Market as a Class Strategy in the UK and the USA' in *British Journal of Sociology of Education*, 14, pp.3–19.

24 Fielding, M. (2001) 'OFSTED, Inspection and the Betrayal of Democracy' in *Journal of Philosophy of Education*, 35, pp.695–709.

25 Blair, T. (2005) 'Speech on Education to City of London Academy, 12 September, Downing Street' [online] Available at: www.pm.gov.uk/output/Page8181.asp

rebuild secondary schools across the country, improving the learning environment for students.

Many teachers reacted positively to the increased investment in education. For the first time in years, schools saw substantial funding increases, allowing for improvements in resources, infrastructure and teacher recruitment – particularly teaching assistants – which helped alleviate workload pressures and improve classroom environments.[26] As free-school-meals students during this time period, both Haili and Sam remember the opportunities they were given to attend trips and engage in music lessons due to increased resources and funding.

Addressing educational inequality was a key driver for the Labour government as, during their campaign, Blair had emphasised the importance of social inclusion, particularly for children from disadvantaged backgrounds. They introduced the Sure Start programme to provide early years support to families in disadvantaged areas, ensuring that all children had access to education, health and childcare services from a young age. They also aimed to increase the number of students from disadvantaged backgrounds entering higher education, setting a target of 50% participation by the end of the 2000s – another scheme both Haili and Sam benefited from.

This period from 1996 to the mid-2000s is often described as a golden time in education in England, due to that combination of increased investment, policy reforms and a focus on improving outcomes for both teachers and students that we have discussed. Not only did there seem to be more funding, there was also a heavy investment in recruiting and training new teachers. For example, when Teach First was introduced in 2003, which was backed by the government, it brought highly qualified graduates into the profession, while also improving teacher-training and professional-development opportunities. During this time, teacher salaries saw steady increases. The introduction of the Performance-Related Pay scheme and the Teaching and Learning Responsibility (TLR) payments allowed schools to reward teachers for taking on additional responsibilities. This, combined with increased job security, helped improve morale and retain more experienced educators.

26 Furlong, J. (2022) 'Universities, Research, and Initial Teacher Education in England and Wales: Taking the Long View' in *The Palgrave Handbook of Teacher Education Research*. Cham: Palgrave Macmillan [online] Available at: https://doi.org/10.1007/978-3-030-59533-3_12-1 (Accessed: 30 April 2026).

Attempts to alleviate workload pressures were also introduced, with initiatives aimed at reducing excessive administrative burdens on teachers, allowing them to focus more on classroom teaching. This resulted in an increase in PGCE (Postgraduate Certificate in Education) applications, making teaching a desirable and competitive field to get into.[27] Indeed, Haili did not even manage to gain a place on a PGCE after her first application during this time period and had to complete more work experience before applying a year later!

The post-Blair period

However, it did not take long for teacher numbers to fall again. By the late 2000s and into the early 2010s, following the 2008 global financial crisis, the UK government imposed austerity measures that affected education budgets. A public-sector pay freeze and cuts to school funding led to worsening working conditions and increased class sizes, causing recruitment and retention issues. Teachers reported growing frustration with administrative tasks, paperwork and data-driven accountability measures. A 2014 report by the National Audit Office (NAO) warned that teacher shortages were worsening, particularly in secondary schools.[28]

This is the time in teaching that both Haili and Sam are most familiar with, having qualified and taught throughout this whole period. It was a time of sweeping changes. In the early 2000s, both of us had a huge amount of freedom and autonomy in our classrooms. Within the confines of the national curriculum, we were both able to teach what we wanted, how we wanted. Observation tended to be high stakes, with one observation taking place per year linked to performance management. Sam has spoken about the Ofsted 'Outstanding' lesson on Sherbert Lemons she had procured from *Tes magazine* for these occasions, which she kept in her top desk and wheeled out for these observations. Professional development focused more on operational parts of teaching and was often based around fads such as learning styles or thinking hats.

27 Worton 'The role of capital in the field of initial teacher education in England' [online] Available at: https://discovery.ucl.ac.uk/id/eprint/10110984/1/Worton_The_role_of_capital_in_the_field_of_initial_teacher_education_in_England_Main_FINAL.pdf (Accessed: 30 April 2026).

28 National Audit Office (2014) 'Training new teachers' [online] Available at: www.nao.org.uk/wp-content/uploads/2016/02/Training-new-teachers-Summary.pdf

However, towards the mid-2010s, the pendulum started to swing. Evidence-informed teaching became the new buzz-word and professional development centred around the principles of the science of learning – a realm that had previously been more for psychologists than teachers. This movement reignited both our passions, but it also led to perhaps the over-codification and prescription of teaching techniques, with teacher agency being somewhat eroded.

Undoubtedly, the engagement with evidence improved our practice but teaching was also facing a new challenge – the graduate-recruitment competition. As the economy recovered, professions including finance and technology became more competitive in attracting graduates, making teaching a less attractive option for new university leavers. The late 2010s to early 2020s were characterised by this squeeze in terms of teacher recruitment and retention. There were chronic shortages of teachers in certain subjects, particularly in science, technology, engineering and mathematics (STEM), modern foreign languages and geography. This issue continues to be a significant challenge in secondary schools even today, with the Royal Society of Chemistry (RSC) highlighting that some students may never be taught by a chemistry specialist until they reach undergraduate level.[29]

The continued austerity and funding cuts during this time period by successive Conservative governments have meant that efforts to address pay and retention have remained challenging. This has led to high levels of teacher turnover. A report by the Education Policy Institute in 2019 highlighted that the rate of teachers leaving the profession within five years of qualifying was alarmingly high. Nearly a third of newly qualified teachers were leaving within this period.[30] Experienced teachers are also voting with their feet, as 43,500 teachers left the state-funded sector in 2022–23. This represents 1 in 10 (9.6%) of all qualified teachers. The majority left due to leaving the state-funded sector in England for a change of career.[31] Anecdotally, when speaking to hundreds of school

29 Roberts, K. (2007) 'Non-specialist teachers on course' on Royal Society of Chemistry [online] Available at: https://edu.rsc.org/news/non-specialist-teachers-on-course/2020716.article (Accessed: 30 April 2026).

30 Fullard, J. (2021) 'Local pay and teacher retention in England' on Education Policy Institute [online] Available at: https://epi.org.uk/publications-and-research/local-pay-and-teacher-retention-in-england (Accessed 30 April 2026).

31 Department for Education (2024) 'School workforce in England' on Gov.uk [online] Available at: https://explore-education-statistics.service.gov.uk/find-statistics/school-workforce-in-england (Accessed: 30 April 2024).

leaders, this is a trend that is also being followed by teaching assistants, as they seek out better-paid and less stressful employment.

Covid-19

Of course, one of the main reasons cited for teacher attrition most recently is workload, with teachers spending excessive time on administrative tasks, marking and planning. A 2019 survey by the Department for Education showed that over 80% of teachers found their workload unmanageable.[32] Since 2020, anecdotal evidence from colleagues would indicate that this has seemed to worsen, with Covid-19 and its associated impacts only seeking to exacerbate the issues. This is despite some evidence to the contrary in the 'Working lives of teachers and leaders: wave 4' survey.[33]

The Covid-19 pandemic almost certainly intensified teacher recruitment and retention issues. While there was an initial spike in applications to teacher-training in 2020 due to economic uncertainty in other sectors, the pandemic also increased the workload crisis. Teachers faced significant challenges in adapting to remote teaching, managing student wellbeing and dealing with Covid-related disruptions in schools. During this period, both Haili and Sam had never worked harder, and the burnout due to the emotional strain of managing student learning and safety under unprecedented conditions was exhausting. Post-pandemic, many teachers reported reconsidering their career, further fuelling retention issues. This may be due to the lack of flexibility teaching offers; teachers may have enjoyed the opportunity to work in a more hybrid environment during this time.

The years 2020 to 2021 were such an unprecedented time in teaching that Haili chose to write her Doctoral thesis on teacher identity during this period. After suffering her own crisis of teacher identity, she was curious about whether other experienced teachers had also felt a shift. The experienced teachers she interviewed all spoke about how

32 Walker, M., Worth, J. and Van den Brande, J.: National Foundation for Educational Research (2019) 'Teacher workload survey 2019' on Department for Education [online] Available at: https://assets.publishing.service.gov.uk/media/5e12fcb7e5274a0f9e82e4fd/teacher_workload_survey_2019_main_report_amended.pdf (Accessed: 30 April 2026).

33 Department for Education (2025) 'Working lives of teachers and leaders: wave 4' on Gov.uk [online] Available at: www.gov.uk/government/publications/working-lives-of-teachers-and-leaders-wave-4 (Accessed: 7 May 2026).

challenging the partial school closures had been, but also stressed the immense amount of pride they had felt in the profession as a whole. A major theme that was highlighted in the research was the lack of support teachers felt they had received from the government and, by extension, from the general public. Teachers who were interviewed spoke about the negative media headlines about teachers during this time and the effect they had on their love for their profession.

When the then Prime Minister, Boris Johnson, announced that primary schools would reopen to students in the Early Years Foundation Stage (EYFS, ages 4–5), Year 1 (ages 5–6) and Year 6 (ages 10–11) from 1 June 2020 and that secondary schools should open to up to one-quarter of students in Years 10 and 12 (ages 14–15 and 16–17) for 'some contact' from 15 June, the National Education Union initiated an appeal to the government to delay school reopenings for teachers' safety. This led to the profession being widely denigrated as 'lazy' and 'scaremongers'.[34] Even before the negative depiction of teachers in the national press during the pandemic, many teachers already believed that society did not value their profession[35] and the pandemic, and the way in which teachers were portrayed during it, may have exacerbated these pre-existing negative beliefs.

A column by journalist Rod Liddle stated 'Covid has made heroes of many of our frontline workers… but not teachers'.[36] In the column, Liddle juxtaposed the behaviour of teachers and schools against NHS staff, criticising school closures and intimating that cancelling exams let our children down – a decision, of course, that had nothing to do with the nation's teachers. He prompted readers to consider 'is there any profession in the country which has had an easier, stress-free nine months than the teaching profession?' The role of the press has often reflected the concerns of society, but has also often shaped them. This means that negative coverage in the press about teachers' work during

34 Dabrowski, A. (2020) 'Teacher Wellbeing During a Pandemic: Surviving or Thriving?' in *Social Education Research*, 2(1), pp.35–40.

35 OECD (2020) 'TALIS 2018 Results (Volume II): Teachers and School Leaders as Valued Professionals' from TALIS. OECD Publishing: Paris [online] Available at: www.oecd.org/en/publications/talis-2018-results-volume-ii_19cf08df-en.html (Accessed: 12 May 2026).

36 Liddle, R. (2020) 'Covid has made heroes of many of our frontline workers… but not teachers' on *The Sun* [online] Available at: www.thesun.co.uk/news/13432637/covid-frontline-heroes-not-teachers-rod-liddle (Accessed: 12 May 2026).

the pandemic may have led to a decline in public opinion about teachers, which could lead them to feel like they are not valued. Teachers who feel underappreciated and disrespected may lose the motivation to work, especially in times of difficulty, which leads to lower occupational commitment, job performance and potentially attrition.[37] The portrayal of teachers in the media is explored in more depth later on in this book in Chapter 8.

With these kinds of derogatory comments and opinions being modelled by those in positions of power in society, it followed that members of the public also jumped on the bandwagon of teacher-bashing too. Stories shared on X during school closures, often by tabloid newspapers such as the *Daily Mail*, were frequently accompanied by rude and negative comments about teachers, such as the interaction below:

> **Daily Mail headline 26 June 2020:**
>
> Suspended for telling the truth – Star primary school head is suspended for saying some lazy teachers were 'sat at home doing nothing'
>
> **Comments include:**
>
> For some it's just a paid long holiday
>
> Why should lazy teachers have to work if they can stay at home, or head to the beach, on full pay.
>
> Start cutting their pay, see if they're happy to stay at home then[38]

This is one such comment thread of thousands that were popular on X during school closures, when many teachers felt that they had never worked harder, planning both online lessons and face-to-face lessons for vulnerable students. It is easy to see why reading such negative comments when teachers were feeling under a great amount of stress may have had an impact on the way they felt about their jobs.

Stephen Ball suggests that performativity is a culture and a form of regulation that judges teachers, while providing incentives and control by using rewards and sanctions. This positions teachers as being

37 Kim, L.E., Owusu, K. and Asbury, K. (2024) 'The ups and downs in perceived societal appreciation of the teaching profession during Covid-19: A longitudinal trajectory analysis' in *British Educational Research Journal*, 50, pp.93–111.

38 *Daily Mail* (2020) 'Suspended for telling the truth' on X [online] Available at: trib.al/TwMQUxa (Accessed: 13 May 2026).

encapsulated by their performative worth, through measures of output and productivity.[39] The people who judge may be politicians, school leaders or, in these examples, journalists and members of the public. Ball refers to this as a 'discourse of derision', where teachers appear to be held culpable by the popular press and in the rhetoric of government policy for a number of national problems, such as a high proportion of unskilled, unqualified school-leavers and high levels of national unemployment.[40]

Governmental views of teachers

This negative view of teachers is not a recent phenomenon; indeed, it perhaps began as far back as the late 1960s, with the so-called Black Papers.[41] But, New Labour also promoted a discourse of derision in its academisation project, which focused on the need for change and modernisation, implying that schools were old-fashioned and providing a substandard education. In his speech at Bexley Business Academy, Tony Blair stated that Labour was aiming for '… not just better facilities, but a wholly new and better way of delivering education, developing the potential and aspirations of each individual child'.[42] This focus on innovation rather than stagnation suggested that teachers needed to up their game and make education more tailored and bespoke for the students they served.

The mantle for the derision of teachers' work was taken up by the Conservative-led administration in 2010, who continued to provide critiques against educators, focusing particularly on their view that schools represented a particular type of progressivism. Sir Michael Wilshaw, who was Her Majesty's Chief Inspector, spoke about his own experiences working in schools and gave a damning critique about the education provided in schools, particularly his old school in Hackney, claiming '… there would have been many others just as bad that never

39 Ball, S.J. (2003) 'The teacher's soul and the terrors of performativity' in *Journal of Education Policy*, 18(2), pp.215–228.

40 Ball, S.J. (1990) *Politics and Policy Making in Education: Explorations in Sociology*. London: Routledge.

41 Slater, E. (2018) 'Fight for Education: A Black Paper. Edited by C.B. Cox and A.E. Dyson. London: The Critical Quarterly Society. 1969. P.80. Price 5s' in *British Journal of Psychiatry*, 115(526), pp.1082–1083.

42 Blair, A. (2002) *The courage of our convictions: why reform of the public services is the route to social justice*. London: Fabian Society.

hit the headlines and got away with blue murder'.[43] This claim, that without Ofsted to drive up standards, schools would be failing children, is a theme that has featured prominently in national newspaper stories and speeches by politicians including Michael Gove, who has been the architect of many of the changes in English education alongside Nick Gibb.

Among Gove's derisive comments about teachers was a labelling of them as 'Enemies of Promise'[44] who exercise 'the soft bigotry of low expectations'.[45] These speeches were followed by negative press coverage of teachers, which supported this rhetoric and circulated negative representations of teachers out to the masses. At times, it seems like the government and the press have worked together to popularise and promote a particular view of teachers, which means that the public more freely support their attempts to seem to control and subjugate what goes on in schools. It is no wonder then that the government has continued to fall short of its recruitment targets for new entrants to the profession, particularly in key subject areas.

Recruitment and retention initiatives from the 1980s to present day

Throughout these periods, it is clear that there have been several recurring issues impacting on teacher recruitment and retention in England. Pay disparities, workload and competition from other graduate professions are all challenges that do not seem to go away. It would be unfair to say, however, that this is a crisis the government have walked into, as during each decade they have implemented various strategies to address teacher retention. These are outlined in the following table.

43 Wilshaw, M. (2012) 'High expectations, no excuses' (a speech to the London Leadership Strategy's Good to Great conference) [online] Available at: https://webarchive.nationalarchives.gov.uk/ukgwa/20141107034501/http://www.ofsted.gov.uk/news/high-expectation-no-excuses-sir-michael-wilshaw-hmci-outlines-changes-ofsted-inspection-drive-delive-0 (Accessed: 12 May 2026).

44 Gove, M. (2013) 'Michael Gove speech on academies' [online] Available at: www.gov.uk/government/speeches/michael-gove-speech-on-academies (Accessed: 12 May 2026).

45 Gove, M. (2013) 'Michael Gove: The civil rights struggle of our time' [online] Available at: www.gov.uk/government/speeches/the-civil-rights-struggle-of-our-time (Accessed: 12 May 2026).

Time period	Measures put in place
1980s–1990s	• Performance-related pay schemes • Induction and support programmes, with structured programmes to help NQTs transition into the profession smoothly
2000s	• Workforce remodelling under the National Agreement in 2003, aimed at reducing teacher workloads, including limiting administrative tasks; providing planning, preparation and assessment (PPA) time; and introducing teaching assistants to support classroom management • Introduction of financial incentives such as 'golden hellos' (financial bonuses for teachers in shortage subjects including science and mathematics) and retention bonuses • To improve teacher career pathways, the DfE established the National College for Teaching and Leadership (NCTL) in 2013, focusing on leadership development and advanced training

2010s	• The Department for Education (DfE) introduced the Workload Reduction Toolkit in 2018, aiming to help schools reduce unnecessary administrative burdens
	• The DfE launched the Teacher Recruitment and Retention Strategy in 2019 with several key measures:
	  • **Early Career Framework (ECF):** Introduced a two-year induction for new teachers, providing them with extra mentoring, training and development, aimed at ensuring early-career support and reducing the high attrition rates in the first five years of teaching
	  • **Flexible Working:** A focus on increasing flexible-working opportunities in schools, encouraging parttime roles and job-sharing to support work–life balance
	  • **Leadership Support:** Strengthened leadership training, so school leaders could effectively manage their staff and create positive working environments that retained teachers
	• The DfE committed to raising starting salaries for teachers to £30,000 by 2022–23, a significant increase aimed at making teaching more competitive with other professions
	• The DfE expanded National Professional Qualifications (NPQs), offering teachers a range of leadership and specialist qualifications to enhance their careers and job satisfaction, to aid career progression and retention

Time period	Measures put in place
2020s	• The DfE introduced initiatives focused on mental health and wellbeing support, including easier access to mental-health services and improved pastoral care for teachers • The DfE provided teachers with training in digital technologies and remote-learning tools to help them manage the new demands of online teaching, ensuring they were better supported during the transition • Financial incentives continued in the form of retention bonuses for teachers in shortage subjects (e.g. STEM) and underserved areas, aiming to maintain teacher numbers where they were most needed

As is evident from the table above, the late 2010s was a period of many incentives aimed at both attracting teachers to the profession and retaining them. Many of the strategies outlined were informed by the 'Factors affecting teacher retention: qualitative investigation Research report' conducted by CooperGibson Research in 2018 for the DfE. Key findings of the research were that, despite previous efforts, workload remained the most important factor influencing teachers' decisions to leave. The report also highlighted that early career teachers made the decision to leave the profession quickly, typically within three months of when they first started to consider leaving, whereas more experienced teachers were more likely to consider their decision over one to two years. Teachers' decisions to leave the profession were generally driven by the accumulation of a number of factors, over a sustained period of time, and included factors such as a lack of in-school support, few progression opportunities and low recognition and autonomy.

Current teacher-retention challenges

In-school support is a factor that has been raised more recently in discussions with teachers – particularly when it comes to managing student behaviour. Research and surveys conducted in the years following the Covid-19 pandemic have indicated that student behaviour has worsened in schools across England. Many teachers have reported an increase in disruptive behaviour. A survey by Teacher Tapp in collaboration with Save the Children UK found that nearly 90% of teachers observed emotional and social delays in students, which they attributed to the extended school closures during the pandemic. These issues have manifested in increased behavioural problems, including difficulties with focus and interaction, especially among disadvantaged students.[46] Schools have also reported significant rises in suspensions and exclusions since students returned to in-person learning, suggesting an increase in violent or aggressive behaviours. In 2022, suspensions reached their highest recorded levels, indicating the depth of the behavioural crisis in many schools.[47] Teachers are calling for more government support and funding to help tackle these issues, particularly to address the growing attainment gaps and the social–emotional needs of students that have been exacerbated by the pandemic.[48] This will definitely need to be a focus of any work the Labour government does on teacher recruitment and retention, as it is making an already challenging job almost impossible to sustain.

In 2024, a Labour government was elected, and the Secretary of State for Education, Bridget Philipson MP, made it clear that rebuilding the teaching workforce is one of her main priorities. In a letter to the profession, she stated:

> We will work urgently to recruit thousands of brilliant new teachers and reset the relationship between government and the education workforce. For too long the teaching profession has been talked down, side-lined and denigrated. I have made it my first priority to write today to the people at the centre of making change happen: our workforces.'[49]

There has also been an ongoing emphasis on high-quality CPD for teachers to ensure that they feel professionally fulfilled and to help to

46 Maisey, R. (2024) 'A deep dive into behaviour in schools' on Nuffield Foundation [online] Available at: www.nuffieldfoundation.org/news/a-deep-dive-into-behaviour-in-schools (Accessed: 30 April 2026).

47 Save the Children (2024) 'Thousands of teachers reveal "deep problems" in classrooms four years on from school lockdown' [online] Available at: www.savethechildren.org.uk/news/media-centre/press-releases/2024/teachers-reveal-deep-problems-in-schools-4-years-on-from-covid-lockdown (Accessed: 30 April 2026).

48 Save the Children (2024) 'Thousands of teachers reveal "deep problems" in classrooms four years on from school lockdown' [online] Available at: www.savethechildren.org.uk/news/media-centre/press-releases/2024/teachers-reveal-deep-problems-in-schools-4-years-on-from-covid-lockdown (Accessed: 30 April 2026).

49 Department for Education (2024) 'Education Secretary begins push to recruit 6,500 new teachers' on Gov.uk [online] Available at: www.gov.uk/government/news/education-secretary-begins-push-to-recruit-6500-new-teachers (Accessed: 30 April 2026).

enhance retention. During the election campaign, Labour committed to introducing a 'CPD entitlement' for teachers, which would mean that they had autonomy over their own professional development.[50]

Conclusion

So, have we learned anything from the retention and recruitment strategies already put in place? It is difficult to say. As outlined in this chapter, there is evidence that teachers are largely still citing the same reasons for wanting to leave the profession as they were in the 1980s – especially workload and pay. It is perhaps too soon to judge whether the DfE's recruitment and retention strategy has done anything to counteract the loss of teachers. According to *Tes magazine's* Matilda Martin, early indications are that the ECF may not have made a massive difference. One-fifth of teachers who undertake the ECF still leave after two years, with only 79.3% of early career teachers still teaching in state schools in 2023, two years after beginning the ECF.[51] This retention rate is similar to the pre-ECF figures published in the school workforce census, when 78.3% of teachers were still in the profession in 2019, two years after qualifying.[52] Hardly a huge change.

In 2025, the Teaching Commission produced a report that diagnosed the teacher recruitment and retention crisis in England as severe and systemic, not a short-term problem. It emphasised that teacher shortages and high exit rates threaten educational quality and equality, particularly for disadvantaged students who are most likely to be taught by inexperienced or unqualified staff. The report's key findings on teacher retention highlighted that teacher attrition is alarmingly high, with about 40% of teachers leaving the profession within 10 years of qualifying. This attrition pattern has essentially weakened the workforce: it takes around 10 newly qualified teachers to replace every 7 experienced teachers

50 Scutt, C. and Peacock, A. (2024) 'Today's proposals are crucial for a CPD entitlement that works' on *SchoolsWeek* [online] Available at: https://schoolsweek.co.uk/todays-proposals-are-crucial-for-a-cpd-entitlement-that-works (Accessed: 30 April 2026).

51 Department for Education (2025) 'Teacher and leader development: ECF and NPQs' on Gov.uk [online] Available at: https://explore-education-statistics.service.gov.uk/find-statistics/teacher-and-leader-development-ecf-and-npqs (Accessed: 30 April 2026).

52 Martin, M. (2024) 'Have new teacher training reforms helped retention?' on *Tes magazine* [online] Available at: www.tes.com/magazine/news/general/have-new-teacher-training-reforms-upped-retention (Accessed: 30 April 2026).

who exit. This erodes levels of expertise in schools and leaves fewer mentors for early career teachers. Indeed, losses are particularly severe in the middle of teachers' careers (5–15 years' experience), the cohort historically vital for leadership and mentorship. A shrinking middle tier undermines institutional memory and professional support structures within schools.

The report also underscored structural issues that contribute to retention problems: workload intensity, barriers to flexible working and inequalities in progression and retention that affect key groups including people of colour and mothers returning to the profession. Like this book, the Commission frames teacher retention not just as a workforce or economic concern but as a social-justice issue: students in deprived contexts are disproportionately affected by high turnover, non-specialist teaching and shortages of experienced educators.[53]

There is a whole section in the report on early-career departures that Haili wrote. Although we truly believe that the ECF has many positive elements, the impact on experienced teachers has not been wholly positive. Indeed, mentors are buckling under the workload, something that former Schools Minister Damian Hinds acknowledged as he unveiled a package of measures to improve training – including combining the ECF and Core Content Framework (CCF).[54] This workload has been added to significantly by the compulsory 20 hours of training Initial Teacher Training (ITT) mentors now have to undertake, as part of the ITT Market Review recommendations implemented in September 2024.[55] Many ITT providers are struggling to find willing schools and mentors to work with their students, as schools are stretched to full capacity.[56] This is a real shame, as many experienced teachers enjoy contributing to the

53 Teaching Commission (2025) 'Shaping the future of teaching' [online] Available at: https://teachingcommission.co.uk/report (Accessed: 30 April 2026).

54 Cumiskey, L. (2024) 'Hinds admits mentor workload "too high" as ECF reforms unveiled' on *SchoolsWeek* [online] Available at: https://schoolsweek.co.uk/hinds-admits-mentor-workload-too-high-as-ecf-reforms-unveiled (Accessed: 30 April 2026).

55 Gov.uk (2024) 'What is a mentor?' [online] Available at: https://becoming-a-teacher.design-history.education.gov.uk/manage-school-placements/what-is-a-mentor (Accessed: 30 April 2026).

56 Cumiskey, L. (2024) 'School teacher trainers reveal ITTECF mentor workload doubts' on *SchoolsWeek* [online] Available at: https://schoolsweek.co.uk/school-teacher-trainers-reveal-ittecf-mentor-workload-doubts (Accessed: 30 April 2026).

development of new teachers, but their increased workload means that they just can't manage it. Of course, working with new teachers is not the only thing we need experienced teachers for. The next chapter explores the importance of experienced teachers and why we desperately need to keep them in the profession.

CHAPTER TWO:

Why do we need experienced teachers to stay in our classrooms?

Introduction: personal experience

The reasons we need to retain experienced teachers may seem, at first thought, instinctively obvious. It goes without saying that we need great teachers in front of students, and we can probably assume that more experienced practitioners are broadly more skilled. But the quality of their practice is just one important aspect of the value of their years in the classroom.

When one of this book's authors, Sam, started her teaching career, she was almost entirely dependent on the support of experienced colleagues. As the first NQT the school had taken on in several years, she was more fortunate than she knew to be surrounded by teachers who already knew the school, the students and the curriculum.

On receiving her timetable for the year ahead, one of her department colleagues sat down with her and helped her write seating plans for her classes, working through the registers and pointing out combinations of students who might work best together, as well as those who definitely would not. Recognising that her top-set Year 11 class might have the potential to be challenging for a brand-new teacher, that same colleague made sure to visit her classroom regularly in those first few weeks – a clear sign to her students that they were accountable for their behaviour; that she was 'one of the team'.

Over the next four years, as she navigated her way from novice teacher to one who was at least proficient and occasionally very good in the classroom, the daily conversations, shared resources and answers to her endless questions from her more experienced colleagues made the job not just possible, but enjoyable. In the workspace they shared at the back of the staffroom, there was always someone to cast an eye over her lesson plans, check the accuracy of her marking or just reassure her that the class she found so challenging would eventually get easier, and her planning quicker.

The support and the camaraderie she found at her first school sustained her in the early years of her career and she has never forgotten it. It is so much easier as a new teacher to feel that you can succeed and belong when an established school community already exists.

Every new teacher deserves to be welcomed into a warm, supportive school as Sam was. And this is why experienced teachers are so important. Their years of classroom practice, their deep understanding of the school community and their expertise are crucial to supporting the development of novice teachers. But, perhaps more important, their longevity shows to those beginning their career in the profession that sustaining it is possible, and desirable.

But, as we know, we are losing our most experienced teachers at alarming rates.

As the pinch of the recruitment and retention crisis tightens, they are most likely to shoulder the burden of additional cover, take on more challenging classes under increased pressure to achieve results and be asked to provide support to new or struggling teachers. For many women, this is likely to coincide with a time in their lives when they have a young family or additional caring responsibilities. We are in danger of burning these colleagues out and fuelling the unvirtuous cycle of retention. Both this book's authors, Haili and Sam, had this experience, as we explain in our own teaching stories in the next chapter.

So, let's look at the very significant benefits of retaining our most experienced teachers.

Experienced teachers achieve better outcomes for students

We know that effective teachers have a significant impact on student achievement. Research from the Sutton Trust found that the quality of teaching is the most significant factor in students' academic success, with the most effective teachers contributing an additional year's worth of progress for students when compared to poorly performing teachers.[57]

57 The Sutton Trust (2011) 'Improving the impact of teachers on pupil achievement in the UK – interim findings' [online] Available at: www.suttontrust.com/our-research/improving-impact-teachers-pupil-achievement-uk-interim-findings (Accessed: 27 May 2025).

The Sutton Trust also found that the effects of high-quality teaching are especially strong for students from low-income backgrounds. They conclude that, if all students had access to teachers in the top 25% of effectiveness, the achievement gap between disadvantaged and more affluent students could be significantly reduced.

We know that teachers become more effective the longer they are in the classroom. There is now a broad research base that shows that teachers continue to develop their effectiveness throughout their careers. For example, in their paper 'Does Teaching Experience Increase Effectiveness?', the Learning Policy Institute found that, taken as a whole, the large and growing body of research applying the teacher fixed-effects analyses demonstrates that teachers become better able to support student learning as their experience increases. The gains from experience are highest in teachers' early years, but continue in the second and often third decades of their careers.[58] This busts the myth that teachers 'plateau' after a few years in the classroom, and that additional experience from that point has no benefit for student attainment. In an even more recent study, the same researchers suggest that teacher effectiveness increases throughout a teacher's career; after a steep initial incline upon entering the profession, teachers tend to follow an upwards trajectory of effectiveness that continues into the second and, at times, third decade of teaching.[59]

Of course, there is variation in effectiveness: not every inexperienced teacher is less effective, and not every experienced teacher is more effective. But, on average, the most effective 20th-year teachers are significantly more effective than the most effective first-year teachers. It is not the passing of time that makes all teachers better, or poor teachers competent – but, in general, most teachers do improve with experience. Early training experiences matter, as we best realise those benefits when teachers start from a strong foundation of preparation and mentoring; of course, this is where we need a virtuous cycle of experienced teachers.

---

58 Kini, T. and Podolsky, A. (2016) 'Does Teaching Experience Increase Teacher Effectiveness? A Review of the Research' [online] Available at: https://learningpolicyinstitute.org/product/does-teaching-experience-increase-teacher-effectiveness-review-research (Accessed: 30 April 2026).

59 Podolsky, A., Kini, T. and Darling-Hammond, L. (2019) 'Does Teaching Experience Increase Teacher Effectiveness? A Review of US Research' in *Journal of Professional Capital and Community*, 4 (4): 286–308.

Much of the focus on retaining teachers recently has been on early career teachers. Yet, if early-career attrition rises and teacher turnover of experienced teachers continues, a larger relative share of the workforce has shorter tenure now than would be the case if retention were stronger. This means that the system may increasingly depend on early career teachers, due both to recruitment shortages and lower retention. These patterns would, over time, change the experience composition of the profession.

International data shows that teachers in England are relatively young (average age 39), which tends to correlate with a higher proportion of less experienced teachers in the workforce.[60] More concerningly perhaps, more experienced teachers could be more unevenly distributed across schools in terms of the socio-economic backgrounds of the students they serve, increasing the risk of a 'double disadvantage' for young people who need great teachers the most. This means that the cost of losing our most experienced teachers is more than just economic: it is a social-justice issue.

Experienced teachers hold invaluable knowledge and expertise based on years of learning and practice

Every teacher will remember how it feels to stand in front of a class for the very first time, the eyes of 30-or-so young people upon you, the mixture of excitement and nerves. Many teachers will have experienced the same emotions we did... an overwhelming sense of responsibility, tinged with panic that we simply wouldn't be able to get them to behave, let alone teach them anything.

A few weeks into Sam's training year, her mentor asked her to deliver her first starter activity to a Year 7 group. She must have spent at least three hours preparing and scripting what was a five-minute task. When she gave the class her carefully prepared instructions, her notes wobbled in her shaking hands. Like most new teachers, she had put a lot more thought into what she needed to say than what the students would learn.

Twelve years later, she could plan most of her week's lessons in that three-hour slot, and they were significantly more effective. During those years, she had accumulated a vast amount of pedagogical expertise, content

60 Cambridge (2016) 'The average age of teachers in secondary schools' [online] Available at: www.cambridgeassessment.org.uk/our-research/data-bytes/the-average-age-of-teachers-in-secondary-schools (Accessed: 30 April 2026).

knowledge and experience working in different school contexts. She had taught some subject content several times, honed her resources and knew how best to convey curriculum content that students often found difficult. She had worked as an examiner, led departments and overseen the design and implementation of new curricula. Most important, she had worked with hundreds of other teachers, observed their practice and had opportunities to be involved in coaching and mentoring. There was no doubt that she was a much more effective teacher, and that her students benefited.

Research bears out Sam's experiences. Studies have shown that experienced teachers improve student achievement at a greater rate because they tend to have better classroom-management skills, deeper curriculum-content knowledge and more refined instructional strategies. This is because they become more adept at delivering content in ways that are accessible and engaging for students. They also become skilled at differentiating instruction to meet the diverse needs of their students, and at designing assessments that accurately measure learning and providing meaningful feedback.

Research reinforces these experiences. John Hattie's synthesis of research on teacher effects indicates that teachers differ substantially in impact on student learning, and that experienced teachers tend to develop more effective instructional and management practices that contribute to those differences. Hattie pointed out that expert teachers have positive influences on students' achievement and engage students in challenging tasks more often compared with less experienced teachers.[61]

Even the highest-quality Initial Teacher Training (ITT) and induction cannot fast-track a teacher to the level of expertise gained over years of practice. In fact, supplementing the professional development of those newest to the profession is another significant benefit offered by experienced teachers.

Experienced teachers support and develop others

The ways experienced teachers support and develop others often go unnoticed but are absolutely crucial. Their impact often reaches far beyond their own classrooms, benefiting colleagues, the wider school community and, ultimately, students. Research tells us that teachers

61 Hattie, J. (2003) 'Teachers Make a Difference: What is the research evidence?' from Australian Council for Educational Research.

who work alongside more experienced peers become more effective themselves. In fact, novice teachers gain the most from having seasoned colleagues nearby, and this influence extends beyond the current school year, improving student outcomes over time.[62]

The Learning Policy Institute (LPI) highlights the link between teacher collaboration and student achievement. Schools where teachers work closely together see faster improvements in teaching and better results for students.[63] This makes a strong case for policies that encourage inexperienced teachers to collaborate with and learn from their more experienced colleagues. It also means we need to avoid clustering novice teachers in certain schools, subjects or year groups, because spreading experience more evenly leads to better outcomes for all students.

The LPI also found that schools with lower rates of teacher turnover, which tend to have more experienced staff, often enjoy a strong, collegial culture.[64] This culture is built on shared knowledge and consistent teaching practice. On the other hand, schools with high attrition rates and fewer experienced teachers struggle with a fragmented knowledge base and less coherent instruction.[65] High turnover has a damaging effect on student achievement that ripples well beyond the classrooms of students whose teachers have left. This is particularly true in schools serving large numbers of low-performing and black students.[66]

---

62 Keese, J., Thompson, C.G., Waxman, H.C., McIntush, K. and Svajda-Hardy, M. (2023) 'A Worthwhile Endeavor? A meta-analysis of research on formalized novice teacher induction programs' in *Educational Research Review*, 38, p.100505.

63 Kini, T. and Podolsky, A. (2016) 'Does Teaching Experience Increase Teacher Effectiveness? A Review of the Research' on Learning Policy Institute [online] Available at: https://learningpolicyinstitute.org/product/does-teaching-experience-increase-teacher-effectiveness-review-research (Accessed: 30 April 2026).

64 Kini, T. and Podolsky, A. (2016) 'Does Teaching Experience Increase Teacher Effectiveness? A Review of the Research' on Learning Policy Institute [online] Available at: https://learningpolicyinstitute.org/product/does-teaching-experience-increase-teacher-effectiveness-review-research (Accessed: 30 April 2026).

65 Ronfeldt, M., Loeb, S. and Wyckoff, J. (2012) 'How Teacher Turnover Harms Student Achievement' from National Center for Analysis of Longitudinal Data in Education Research [online] Available at: https://caldercenter.org/sites/default/files/2024-11/Ronfeldt-et-al.pdf (Accessed: 30 April 2026).

66 Ronfeldt, M., Loeb, S. and Wyckoff, J. (2013) 'How Teacher Turnover Harms Student Achievement' in *American Educational Research Journal*, 50(1), pp.4–36.

When schools collaborate across networks or Trusts, experienced teachers can share their expertise more widely, mentoring peers and strengthening professional practice beyond their own school walls. This kind of collaboration can help ensure that no teacher or school feels isolated and that the benefits of experienced teachers are felt across the system.

Experienced teachers and professional development

In addition, experienced teachers play a central role in shaping meaningful professional development within and across schools. Their deep understanding both of the craft of teaching and the context in which it happens allow them to offer insight that is not only relevant, but immediately applicable. These are teachers who are still in the classroom, close to the ground, who understand the real challenges their colleagues face and can adapt professional learning accordingly.

Because they hold organisational knowledge and understand the rhythms, needs and pressures of the school, experienced teachers are often best placed to lead or contribute to CPD that truly resonates. They can bridge the gap between theory and practice, drawing on their own experience to bring new ideas to life in ways that feel manageable and worthwhile. Crucially, they can follow up. Their ongoing presence means they can support colleagues to embed changes in practice, provide informal coaching and offer encouragement long after the training session has ended.

In many schools, these teachers act as internal teacher educators: mobilising knowledge, modelling reflective practice and guiding others through professional growth. Their contributions aren't confined to scheduled training days. Often, it's the quiet conversations after school, the shared resources or the advice offered during a planning session that shape teacher learning the most.

When schools create space for experienced teachers to lead and influence professional learning, it benefits everyone. Newer teachers gain access to rich, situated knowledge and the school strengthens its internal capacity. This creates a virtuous cycle, in which retention improves; not just because the professional development is better, but because the culture feels more collaborative and sustaining. These are the kinds of environments where we feel experienced teachers want to stay and where others are more likely to thrive.

Experienced teachers are integral to building strong school communities

Of course, academic outcomes are not the only measure of success. More experienced teachers are valuable to the profession for other reasons, which can be harder to quantify but matter a great deal. More experienced teachers can support greater student learning for their colleagues and the school as a whole, as well as for their own students.

Research from the LPI finds that, as teachers gain experience, their students are more likely to do better on broader outcomes beyond test scores, such as school attendance.[67] Why might this be?

We have likely all known or worked with teachers who seem to have a gift for relating to young people, who can build relationships with children who are the most challenging to get into classrooms and to engage in learning. In part, this ability can seem 'unteachable', and perhaps some teachers do possess that special, intangible quality. But you need only spend 10 minutes in the classroom of a very experienced teacher to see the obvious benefit of years of classroom-management experience on working with students with varying behaviours and dynamics.

Experienced teachers are very often significantly more skilled in managing behaviour.[68] Over the years, they develop strong skills in relational practice and understand the importance of building relationships for achievement. Their continued presence can provide stability and continuity – qualities that help build trust and strong relationships across generations, such as when they have taught multiple siblings. In doing so, they shape the school's reputation and often become trusted figures within the community. Often, more experienced teachers are skilled in building relationships with the children who are hardest to reach – another reason why retention is key to many of the current challenges we face.

67 Kini, T. and Podolsky, A. (2016) 'Does Teaching Experience Increase Teacher Effectiveness? A Review of the Research' on Learning Policy Institute [online] Available at: https://learningpolicyinstitute.org/product/does-teaching-experience-increase-teacher-effectiveness-review-research (Accessed: 30 April 2026).

68 Karasova, J. and Nehyba, J. (2025) 'Novice teachers' classroom behaviour management: Situations, responses and impact on student behaviour' in *British Educational Research Journal*, 51, pp.2116–2141.

Importantly, experienced teachers carry tacit knowledge: an understanding of the school's history, values and culture that is rarely written down but essential to how the school functions. They are the ones who 'tell the story of the school'; who know why things are done a certain way and how the informal systems work. When they leave and schools lack the structures to retain and pass on this knowledge, that cultural and relational capital is often lost. Retaining experienced teachers is therefore not only about maintaining staffing levels, but also about preserving the identity, memory and cohesion of the school itself.

Experienced teachers may be better equipped to handle challenges

Despite the way teaching is so often portrayed in the media and mirrored in the ways those outside education perceive the job, those of us who have lived it know the demands it places on our professional and personal lives. It can be physically and emotionally demanding. Current pressures in the system seem to be further exacerbating the demands of the job. From new Ofsted frameworks, an increasing special educational needs and disabilities (SEND) crisis in schools and teachers and leaders being expected to do more with fewer resources than ever before, teaching is not an easy lifestyle to maintain long-term.

Experienced teachers have developed the behaviours and competencies for longevity and may be better equipped to handle these growing challenges. Over time, they have learned how to manage their workload with greater efficiency and have cultivated the resilience needed to navigate difficult periods. With less sense of overwhelm, they remain focused on their students' needs, often bringing a stability and consistency to the classroom that is both grounding and reassuring.

This presence is not only valuable to their students but also vital for supporting early career teachers. As anchors in the school community, experienced teachers provide mentorship, model calmness under pressure and offer practical strategies that newer teachers may not yet have had the chance to develop. Their ability to keep perspective and maintain high standards amidst systemic strain can be a lifeline for colleagues who are still finding their footing.

Moreover, adaptability becomes a hallmark of experience. Having encountered a wide range of classroom scenarios over the years, seasoned teachers are typically more agile when faced with unexpected developments, be that a curriculum overhaul, a shift in policy or the introduction of new technologies. They possess 'adaptive expertise': the ability to apply professional judgement in fluid contexts and to problem-solve effectively on the go. As we have discussed, this makes them not only resilient practitioners but also key contributors to the development and retention of others.

For all these reasons, experienced teachers have immeasurable value – not just to the students they teach, but to their colleagues, the school community, the sector and wider society. These are the colleagues who show up every day, every week, chalking up the months and years in classrooms up and down the country. They are the lifeblood of our schools. But, as we have outlined already in this book, we face the current reality that we are losing our experienced teachers at an unsustainable rate. We are failing to recognise and reward their worth, and we are expecting them to shoulder the burden of an increasingly stretched and pressurised system. This is an unvirtuous cycle we must break.

We have historically tried many tactics to retain our teachers. Some have been successful, others not so much. But we live now in a different world, post-pandemic, and we are facing new and pressing challenges. Experienced teachers will be crucial to the government's ability to deliver its planned reforms effectively and sustainably. In the changing landscape of professional development, for example, where less available funding will require greater in-house provision, schools will increasingly rely on the expertise of their most experienced staff to support and develop colleagues. The 6500 teachers Keir Starmer's Labour government has committed to recruiting in this parliament will depend on those teachers to mentor and guide them through their early years.

The imperative to focus on teacher retention is clear. Now that we have outlined the extent of the challenges we face, our focus for the rest of this book is on those experienced colleagues who have stayed in the profession. But before we hear their stories, we will share ours.

Part 2
Teachers' stories

CHAPTER THREE: Our teaching stories

Haili

Pre-teaching

Unlike many people who go into teaching as a career, I never had a deep intrinsic calling to teach. Indeed, embarrassingly, I used to think that teaching was a career choice people fell back on after they could not think of what to do with an English degree. As an angry teenager from a disadvantaged background, I was often at loggerheads with my own teachers. I had a deep-seated hatred of authority and regularly took out my frustration with the world on my hard-working teachers, who were just trying to do their best for me. Nevertheless, there were some teachers who stood out to me as they never gave up on me. My geography teacher and my German teacher somehow managed to see past my gruff exterior, realising that there was a diamond underneath, waiting to be discovered. Despite this, I commenced my English degree in Leeds wanting to be a tabloid-newspaper journalist – nothing could have been further from my ambitions than becoming a teacher at this point.

It has been a favourite pastime of mine to prove people wrong, and a careers advisor at my secondary school once questioned how I might become a national newspaper journalist when people from my background just didn't do jobs like that. So, I was delighted to win a scholarship at News International in London and become a graduate-trainee reporter at the *News of the World* while in my final year at university. At age 21, I found myself living the dream in London, as the youngest staff reporter on 'Fleet Street'.

Except, it wasn't really a dream; it was a nightmare. As has been widely documented now, the *News of the World* was a hideous environment to work in. Misogyny and toxic behaviours were rife, and I spent my days watching *Big Brother* and trawling *Friends Reunited*, trying to get ex-school friends to sell stories about contestants, and my night-times chasing Prince Harry around exclusive nightclubs. Hardly Pulitzer Prize-winning stuff. When the newspaper was closed down for phone hacking, I saw my chance to do something different, so I moved back to the North West and took some time to reassess what I really wanted.

Work experience

While I was in between jobs, I was given the opportunity to do some volunteering at my old secondary school in Warrington. I observed lots of English lessons and was even afforded the opportunity to work with some small groups of students on some writing interventions. I noticed kids like me who came from socially and economically disadvantaged backgrounds and seemed to have the odds stacked against them; something seemed to click, and I realised that teaching could be a great career choice for me.

The next week, I applied for a PGCE at Liverpool Hope, but it was late in the application process and, even though my interview went well, there were two applicants and one place left and I didn't make the cut. The other candidate had more school experience; I was encouraged to go away, complete more work experience and apply in September for the year after. I did and was accepted and I have since been eternally grateful.

Teacher training

My PGCE course was run by an eccentric academic and teacher who was really engaging and inspirational. He encouraged us to be creative and passionate, as well as motivating us to take calculated risks in our teaching during this period of experimentation. Part of my course involved completing two placements. My first placement was wonderful. It took place at an 'Outstanding' school, and my mentor was wonderful. She struck the ideal balance between support and challenge, and I left the school thinking I might just be a good teacher.

The second placement was awful. It was at a large girl's school and I joined lots of other trainees in different subjects. The culture of the school was brilliant; the wellbeing of staff was really looked after and staff were given autonomy to teach in their own style. However, the Head of English was a known bully and, after my first lesson she observed, she informed me that I needed 'elocution lessons' and that 'the best I could hope for was to be a perfectly adequate teacher'. I burst into tears of anger and left the school, determined not to return the next day. University staff came to support me the next day and chaired a mediation session between myself and the Head of Department. We agreed that I would no longer teach her class and that she would have no further involvement in my placement. The rest of the placement went well but, bizarrely, she did approach me on another occasion to tell me that I shouldn't bother attending a job interview I had, as her friend was the middle leader who would be interviewing me and she had told her all about the way I dressed and my tattoos and that I wouldn't fit into that school. I was flabbergasted and it is still a great story to tell colleagues today.

In a way, this colleague did me a favour. I realised at this moment that the behaviour of mentors really matters and that they can make or break a new teacher's career. It was here my passion for mentoring was born so, in a way, I owe this terrible mentor my thanks.

Starting to teach

My first teaching role was in a wonderful Church of England school in a deprived area of Warrington. Here I cut my teeth, working with some of the most inspirational colleagues. The headteacher was a brilliant, principled head who really cared about his colleagues and the children in his care. My Head of Department was amazing and saw a potential in me to become a leader very quickly. I was not an easy person to line-manage however as, due to my previous experience, I thought I knew it all. Yet, she was an expert at handling me and, when the opportunity came in my third year to become Second in English, I was encouraged to apply. I was pleased to get the job and enjoyed this role immensely, learning lots, with relative stability.

Teaching career

Over the next few years, there were lots of changes happening nationally. Changes in the curriculum, alterations in weightings for speaking and listening and the rules being changed for what schools could count in their percentages for results if students were to sit a GCSE in Year 10 and then resit in Year 11. Unwise decisions were made about the strategic direction to take, and that summer results in English plummeted, as well as all other subjects, and the dreaded Ofsted visit loomed in early September.

For years, the school had languished on a 'Satisfactory' judgement, and everybody knew there was a very real danger of the school moving a category after the inspection. Our worst fears were realised and the school was judged as 'Inadequate'. I can look at it objectively now and see that it was indeed inadequate, as many students at the school were failing to reach their academic potential because behaviour and teaching were not consistent. However, at the time, it seemed very personal... a hideous blow when I knew how hard we all worked. The Head of English packed up her belongings that evening and was never seen again, catapulting me into a middle-leadership position that I didn't want, in incredibly stressful circumstances.

Leadership

For anyone who has never been in a special-measures school, you cannot begin to understand the pressures it brings – particularly for senior leaders and heads of English and maths. Almost monthly Ofsted monitoring visits, 'support' from the Local Education Authority (LEA) and weekly governor's meetings where every student's data was pored over are only a few of the delights I was facing. I was also grappling with long-term sickness of staff, so an endless round of supply teachers were supporting and I was mostly having to provide the cover work. Behaviour was so bad in the school it was almost like a revolving door and I often found myself having to teach several classes at the same time, with doors open.

On top of this, I had been bullied for years by a toxic leader in the school and, now they were my direct line manager, the Machiavellian behaviour became unmanageable. I wrote about this in my book *Preserving Positivity*.[69] This happens far too often in education, where toxic behaviours are swept under the carpet and perpetrators are often promoted out for other schools to deal with.

Things all became a bit too much for me and, after breaking down on a lovely colleague, I went home to speak to my husband about what my options were. I really felt suicidal and, as far as I could see, I had two options: change school and see whether it helped, or quit teaching and go back to journalism. I chose the former and applied for a job 50 miles away. It was a huge gamble, as I would be uprooting my family and giving up my leadership role to return to the classroom, but I had to take the chance.

Teaching again

So it transpired that, in 2013, I was using my Christmas holidays to move to a small village in Saddleworth, a beautiful area on the edge of the Peak District, to take up the post of Teacher of English. What followed were probably the best years of my career. My department was wonderful, the kids were great and, for the first time in a long while, I felt I was great at my job. I enjoyed mentoring new teachers and engaging in my own CPD outside of the school, such as attending researchED conferences

69 Hughes, H. (2021) *Preserving Positivity*. Woodbridge: John Catt Educational.

and getting involved with events in the local area. For a while, this sustained me.

However, I remembered a friend and ex-colleague telling me when I stepped back to become a classroom teacher again, that it would be only a matter of time before I was frustrated at the leaders above me. This was proved to be the case when I worked under a succession of terrible Heads of Department and I began to wonder whether I should give it another shot. Instead, I took on a whole-school role looking after the most able students and supported the local authority in a range of projects, including working with the exam boards and the Department for Education in some teacher focus groups. With this and studying for my third Master's degree, I felt reasonably fulfilled and like I was still learning and improving.

Media and publishing

In 2018, just after giving birth, I commenced a Doctorate in Education at the University of Glasgow, and one of my course mates recommended I join X (then called Twitter). I created an account and was totally confused by the way it worked, so I didn't log on again until a year later. What prompted it was an article written by Caroline Spalding in *Tes magazine* about how she hid her tattoos and thought that this was the right thing for teachers to do.[70] As a very tattooed teacher, who has almost a full body suit, I inherently disagreed and typed out an article in response, sending it off to Ann Mroz, the then *Tes magazine* editor.

Little did I know how much this article would change my life. They accepted it and published it the next day and the article went viral, sparking debate, agreement and disagreement in equal measure. What followed was a bit of a whirlwind: requests to go on radio and contact from journalists. A friend recommended I go back on X to have a look at what people were saying, and that's when my engagement with the wider education community really began. I quickly amassed followers and began to blog and share resources.

In 2019, with the help of some X (then Twitter) contacts, I pitched my first book ideas to publishers, and was flabbergasted when I was accepted. Another colleague helped me to become involved with some Department

70 Spalding, C. (2016) 'I have seven tattoos, but I agree with my school policy that says you should hide them in class' on *Tes magazine* [online] Available at: www.tes.com/magazine/archive/i-have-seven-tattoos-i-agree-my-school-policy-says-you-should-hide-them-class (Accessed: 30 April 2026).

for Education work, and opportunities to speak at conferences were appearing. By 2020, during the Covid-19 pandemic, I was still teaching fulltime, but was increasingly supporting other schools and Trusts and was also a published author of three books – including one on mentoring, which was a big focus of the national education agenda.

Unfortunately, there were no senior leadership teaching and learning opportunities at my school and I was becoming increasingly frustrated at my lack of voice and prospects and the lack of recognition of my expertise. So, when I was offered jobs at professional development company IRIS Connect and the University of Sunderland, I was sorely tempted.

Outside the classroom

At first, I decided against it and told the CEO of IRIS Connect that I would miss teaching too much. However, after another frustrating week of generic CPD that I didn't think was moving my teaching forwards, I decided to go for it and accepted the positions, handing in my resignation to the Headteacher. In July 2021, I left my school with a real sense of sadness. I spent most of the day crying at the beautiful gifts I received from students and colleagues alike and despaired I would regret my decision.

Over the next three years, I had the most unbelievable opportunities, from travelling the world speaking, to signing eight more book deals and working with the DfE in Initial Teacher Training (ITT) policy, as well as being elected for the Chartered College of Teaching's Council. I spoke in around 500 schools, trained thousands of teachers worldwide and passed my Doctorate.

However, all of it felt a little hollow when I compared it to the impact and sense of moral purpose I had felt as a teacher. I also allowed some loud and prominent X 'edu-celebs', who constantly posted about the lack of credibility of those working outside schools, to make me feel that I had to get back as a matter of urgency.

Back to school

Do I regret leaving school? No. It was a great opportunity and I am glad I took it… but the lure of school was calling me back. I had learned so much about system leadership, teacher development and what great teaching looks like over those years that I thought I was ready to give it another go. Ian Brown once said 'for everything a reason',[71] and I am a

71 Brown, I. (2001) 'F.E.A.R.' from *Music of the Spheres*. London: Polydor.

great believer in this. All my experiences in my teaching career and over the last few years have created a rich tapestry of experience and I looked forward to returning to school to put it into good use.

In June 2025, I went back to school. I had toyed with the idea of being a Head and, indeed, even completed my National Professional Qualification for Headship (NPQH) in preparation. However, I had decided that I needed more of a flexible role because of the nature of some of my national work, and instead went back as a Director of Professional Development at a Multi-Academy Trust in Merseyside.

Returning to school, despite not being a teacher or leader on the shop-floor, has been quite a shock. I was only 'out' for three years, but the nature of the job has changed beyond all recognition. When people talk about consultants not understanding the reality of the challenges that schools are facing, they are absolutely right. Leaders and teachers are under more strain than I think they ever have been. Teaching has morphed from being a job to a lifestyle choice... and I quickly realised that I am not willing to dedicate my life to this job. That does not make me a bad person, but when your personal identity is so tied up with your professional identity of being a teacher, it is a difficult pill to swallow.

The future

Therefore, I find myself about to leave the profession again. I have been offered an incredible opportunity to move to Australia and become an Associate Professor of Educational Innovation and Impact, which I have to take. I will continue to be dedicated to raising the status and profile of classroom teachers from my place in the wider education eco-system.

Sam

Loving literature

Similarly to Haili, I was an 'accidental' teacher. Having spent my teenage years planning to become a hot-shot journalist, unlike Haili I quickly gave up on the idea of Fleet Street, when I realised it would probably bear no relation to my favourite 80s TV show, *Press Gang*.

While I had little idea of what career path I should follow, I knew from a young age that a love of literature was in my blood. My dad still reminds me of the hours he spent reading my favourite stories to me, and how I would crossly point out any words he missed and make him repeat the page. I was never without a book in my hands.

But despite my love of reading and writing, I mostly found English lessons at school uninspiring. For igniting my passion for studying the subject, which eventually led me to teaching, I have one person to thank – and that is my A-level literature teacher.

Inspiring teacher

So many teachers can trace their journey into the profession back to one inspiring teacher of their own, and this too is my story. Like many of the very best teachers, mine may not have considered himself remarkable, and he may well be unaware of the life-changing impact he had on an under-confident young student from a working-class family who had never considered herself capable of going to university.

Being taught by this teacher gave me three things. First, a love of Shakespeare, inspired by his lessons on *Hamlet* (my geekery for the play was so well known at sixth-form college, my friends gave me the nickname 'Samlet'…). It led me to my MA in Renaissance Studies and has been a source of joy and literary sustenance throughout my life.

Secondly, he showed me that great teachers don't just teach the content of the curriculum – they teach their students to think. I vividly recall genuine lightbulb moments in his lessons, as we read and discussed in response to his thought-provoking questions and provocations. There were no PowerPoint slides or worksheets – just a copy of the text and a pen in our hands. We were completely immersed in the characters, the themes and the language, sharing our unfolding ideas, making notes in the margins. Everything was centred around the text, layering our understanding of it, moving us towards critical analysis – everything good English teaching should be. It gave me a model I always tried to emulate in my own classroom.

And thirdly, my A-level teacher gave me belief in myself and my potential – and that belief opened the door to university, a degree in English literature and, eventually, a career in education. For all these things, I will forever be grateful to him. As a teacher, I remained profoundly aware that building students' confidence was as important as building their knowledge – especially for those who, like me, needed someone to help them see what they were capable of. I have always felt an affinity for young people whose backgrounds might pose barriers to fulfilling their potential and I wanted my students to know how much I believed in them, as my teacher had believed in me. That is the true, life-changing power of great teachers that goes way beyond academic outcomes.

For those colleagues who are the subject of this book, it is humbling to imagine how many students' lives have been changed by their work in over 20 years of service to our profession.

Entering education

While it took me several more years after college to find my way back to the classroom, I was drawn towards education and, after university, I spent several years in the charity sector working with adult learners. One such charity supported ex-miners to become community leaders, teaching them literacy skills they needed to access funding to improve their local areas, and giving them the confidence to find paid work after years of unemployment. The programme included a trip to the European Parliament in Brussels, taking participants directly to the seat of power where decisions affecting their own communities were made – but, most important, showing them how they could use their voices to make change. My work for the project reminded me starkly of the real-world importance of my subject – without literacy skills, these men could not move forwards in their lives. But most of all I saw, with the closure of the mines, how much had been stripped from them – their self-belief, their pride, their feelings of value in what they had to offer in their communities. I saw the power of education not just to teach skills, but to empower, to leverage social justice, to humanise. I knew then that education was the sector where I wanted to make a difference.

I will admit that the thought of teaching young people filled me more with horror than enthusiasm at this point. How on earth would I ever get a room full of teenagers to do what I asked them?! I began my PGCE with a view to teaching in Further Education, having been advised to take that route to 'cover all bases'. But as soon as I stood in front of my first class – a delightfully enthusiastic and funny Year 7 group at my first training school in Calderdale, West Yorkshire – I knew I had found my path.

My first experiences of professional development did not make me quite so certain of the likelihood of my future success. In an early CPD session at my second placement school, I entered the classroom to find the teacher-facilitator spooning large lumps of dog food into her mouth from a can on her desk. It turned out not to be dog food – just a ploy to make us think as much. Strangely, it was a proposed behaviour-management technique – her foolproof method of making the kids pay attention in her lessons, apparently because they were so impressed by her hardiness. Suffice to say, it was not a technique I chose to emulate when I started teaching.

Teaching as an NQT

I began my NQT year in 2007 at a lovely secondary school in Horsforth, North Leeds. Almost unbelievably now, I was not in the luxury position of choosing the school I wanted to work in, because there was huge competition for English teaching jobs. Fortunately, the school did choose me. I later found out they had received nearly 200 applications for two posts. In the midst of our current recruitment and retention crisis, we have to reflect on what has happened to make the profession so much less attractive to new graduates if we are to have any chance of meeting the current government's pledge to recruit 6500 more practitioners and ensuring a great teacher in every classroom.

I spent four very happy years in Horsforth, a time I now often think of as my 'golden years' of teaching. The students were delightful – well-behaved, engaged, full of humour. I adored them. I have a huge folder full of their letters and cards from when I left the school, and keep in touch with many of them still. This was a time before target grades, before toxic accountability took hold. Staff morale was good and retention was high. I was the first NQT the English department had taken on in years, and so I was surrounded by experience and support.

I became firm friends with two colleagues who were similar ages, both exceptional teachers. We worked incredibly hard, but there was so much fun, friendship and collaborative working. We would pop in and out of each other's classrooms, share resources, cover for one another when we needed to. As a new teacher, I never once felt isolated or alone. At the times of the year when the workload increased and the pile of marking grew, we would sit together in the library and plough through books, coloured pens to one side, mugs of tea and chocolate to the other. It was a happy department and the students benefited hugely. They could see how much we loved our subject, enjoyed our work; how much we cared about them and their success.

Those four years of classroom teaching were joyous, and I was able to develop my practice rapidly. My unofficial mentor was the Head of Key Stage 4 at the time, and we shared GCSE and A-level classes. The value of her support in the early years of my career was enormous. She was a superb practitioner and a model of professionalism. We sat next to one another in the staff workroom, which meant we could plan and mark together, and she was endlessly patient with my constant questions and requests to 'just take a quick look at the mark I've given this one, please?'

I learned everything I know as a teacher from her: how to plan lessons, how to apply assessment criteria, how to give feedback constructively and kindly – and, thanks to her generosity, my inexperience was never exposed to our students. But, most important, from observing daily the ways she worked, I learned how to *be* a teacher. I saw the way she interacted with students, how she dealt calmly with conflict, how she led department meetings, how she treated colleagues with understanding and empathy. She had two young children, and I was in awe of how she balanced her work and her life outside school. I didn't know it at the time, but I remembered years later, when I had my own children, how she created boundaries between her personal and professional life in ways that made the job manageable and enjoyable. This is the true value of experienced teachers, who do more than we could ever quantify to mentor, encourage and uplift new practitioners. When we look after these colleagues and retain them in our schools, our whole profession is immeasurably richer.

It was incredibly difficult to leave a school I loved so much, but increasingly I felt the students there – middle-class, largely affluent – would do well in spite of my teaching, and I sought greater challenge. I remembered a teacher in my first placement school telling me I shouldn't stay at the same place for too long if I wanted to progress, and I was keenly ambitious. In my final year there I had my first child, and was told by the Head of Department that he 'didn't expect as much' from me now: I think he thought he was being kind, but I was thoroughly annoyed at what I felt were limitations being placed on my career progression. It fuelled me to move on and prove that I could be successful at work as well as be a good mother to my new baby.

The next step

If it was challenge I sought, it was challenge I certainly got. In 2011, I took up a post as an Advanced Skills Teacher at a school that was the polar opposite of where I began my career. Situated in inner-city Leeds, the school served not only one of the most deprived wards in the country, but one of the most diverse, with nearly 80 different languages spoken in the community. It had a troubled history, and the constant changes in leadership had done nothing to move it out of special measures, where it had remained stuck for years.

On my first day, the contrast with the leafy lanes of my previous school became abundantly clear when a police officer arrived in my classroom to take the register. While a part of me wondered what on earth I had done, it didn't take me long to fall in love with the school and the children there. But the contrast was never lost on me. These young people – 20 minutes' drive away from my previous school – had nowhere near the same advantages. They often lacked the basics – enough food, clothes, a warm home, supportive families – and that played out in my classroom every day. It was the toughest time of my teaching career to date.

In my first year, we had three different Heads of Department, and more than once I found myself having to step into the position, as well as constantly covering for absent colleagues and picking up GCSE classes. I quickly realised I dramatically needed to change the way I taught because, unlike in my previous school, the life chances of these students were not a given. Relationships were absolutely everything. I had a particularly tough Year 10 class who regularly drove me to tears. An experienced colleague, comforting me after an awful lesson, told me I needed to crack the most challenging student and the rest would follow. This turned out to be excellent advice; the sort of wisdom earned only through doing the hard yards. That particular student, it turned out, was living in supported accommodation at the age of 15, and what I had interpreted as 'attitude' in my lessons masked the reality of a young person struggling with neglect, abuse and a lack of hope for her future. When she invited me to watch her perform at a local youth club and assess her for the speaking and listening component of her English GCSE, I realised that she had asked me because she had no other adult in her life who could, or would, attend, to see her do something of which she was incredibly proud. It was my privilege to be that adult for her on that night. She taught me a great deal – far more than I could ever have taught her – and my small contribution to her eventual success in English is one of the things I am proudest of in my career.

In teaching at that school, I made a choice to try to change the lives of children who need great teachers the most, and I have carried on making that choice every day since. I have the deepest respect for all teachers, but those colleagues who serve schools in the most challenging circumstances deserve our utmost admiration. Until you have taught or led in such a school, it is impossible to understand the pressure and the sheer exhaustion. But there is also so much fulfilment to be found, and so much camaraderie among staff. Where leadership is strong and teachers are well supported, it is more than possible for even the most difficult school to improve rapidly and for teachers to want to stay.

Until that point in my career, I had been more fortunate than I knew to work for good leaders, who treated staff well and led with integrity. Unfortunately, the next few years of my fulltime teaching career were marked by an imperfect storm of toxic accountability and leadership. When the Head in the inner-city school moved on and new leaders took over, I became frustrated by the lack of urgency in tackling a decline in behaviour, feeling that the school for many children now mirrored the chaos of their lives rather than being a safe space. I was expecting my second child, I had no flexibility in my work and I was exhausted.

A new challenge

Just before I was due to return from maternity leave, I decided to move schools and took up a post in a high-performing secondary, which was the flagship school in a small Multi-Academy Trust. The Trust system was relatively new at that point and, sadly, I did not experience what I now consider to be the many benefits of working in a family of schools. In my first week, I was pulled aside by the Chief Executive Officer (CEO) and the Head of School and warned against 'criticising' their use of controlled assessment, which was the method of summative assessment the government had brought in to replace written coursework. While I had not criticised practice – I had not even yet been there long enough to see any – I had been heard expressing surprise that students were being allowed to redraft pieces at home that they were supposed to write in controlled conditions. It was made very clear that I would need to comply with the school's methods, which seemed to me to be to achieve results at any cost.

My fulltime teaching career eventually ended abruptly but, in truth, I had become increasingly disillusioned at how the job had changed. It felt less and less about doing what was right for children, and more and more about hoop-jumping. In the early years of my career, I had a great deal of autonomy – perhaps too much – but, as my experience and expertise grew, I felt it was valued less, perhaps even seen as threatening to some. When asked to write a new GCSE curriculum for English when the specifications changed in 2015, I saw an opportunity to galvanise the department around fresh, innovative ideas; a return to what I saw as 'proper' English teaching, the kind that I had so benefited from myself. However, the Head heavily criticised our concept-led approach, deeming it too risky in a results-focused culture and wanted more exam-question practice and mocks. Her criticism stung, and it further fuelled my disillusionment with the job I had once loved, which felt like it was becoming about churning children through exam factories. Accountability in schools is, of course, necessary and, when it is done sensibly, it drives standards. But when it distorts teaching and learning, it drives teachers from the profession.

I wanted to teach because I am passionate about my subject, about its potential to open up the world for young people, to teach them about humanity and their place in the world. That might sound lofty and idealistic – and the Head of that school told me I was both those things. But I never did, and never will, apologise for holding firm to the belief that education is about far more than just grades, and that when leaders chase results at the expense of integrity, they are serving their own egos, and not children. Later, my colleague Zoe and I used our experiences to write our book *The Trouble With English and How To Address It: A Practical Guide to Designing and Delivering a Concept-Led Curriculum*.[72]

The lowest point

The school where I spent my final year teaching, on secondment within the same Trust, was soon after taken over by a larger Multi-Academy Trust, who immediately replaced the outgoing Head with a leader from their own organisation. I first met her when she came to my classroom during my planning, preparation and assessment (PPA) time and she told me to follow her to her office. Without introducing herself, she motioned me to sit down and pointed to the screen showing a spreadsheet of predicted Year 11 results. 'Are your class going to get these results you're saying they will?' she asked. I replied that I hoped so; that I had made my predictions after marking their most recent mock exam papers. 'Well, you'd better hope so,' she responded, 'because people's mortgages depend on it.' Then, she motioned for me to leave.

Within six months, around a third of the teaching staff had left the school, most of them very experienced teachers. In many ways it was hardly a surprise when I was called to the Head's office one day and issued with disciplinary proceedings. The allegation put to me was that I had made an incorrect mark on a register during a cover lesson. That day, I left her office, walked out of the school in tears, and never returned.

It is hard to convey the impact that leader had on me, and perhaps in isolation I would have borne the brunt of her behaviour with greater resilience and stoicism. But the preceding years of similar experiences

72 Helman, Z. and Gibbs, S. (2022) *The Trouble With English and How To Address It: A Practical Guide to Designing and Delivering a Concept-Led Curriculum*. London: Routledge.

with leadership had slowly eroded my sense of value, my confidence and my joy in the job. I have not, and could not, state all the things that happened there. Some of them I have never shared. But the cumulative effect of working in a toxic culture, where bullying of staff was rife, watching colleagues struggle and eventually break down, knowing it would eventually be my turn, took its toll. At the worst point, I remember driving to work one day and thinking it would be easier to crash my car, because then I wouldn't have to face another day in school. It is still difficult to revisit that time in my life.

While leaving the job I had loved in the way I did was not what I had wanted, there was at least a sense of liberation in it being over. But every experienced teacher knows how much teaching can become a part of your identity, and how it happened was so humiliating it took me a long time to get over, if I ever have completely. It impacted my feelings of self-worth, my confidence and my relationships and, like Haili, I was left struggling with suicidal thoughts. It was, without doubt, the lowest point in my life. In interviewing teachers for this book, we have found too many with similar stories of their treatment at the hands of toxic leaders. We have to end the stigma and shame many feel in sharing their stories and – if we want to retain more teachers – we need to address why toxic cultures are a reality in too many schools. No initiatives – CPD, flexible working, AI-powered marking – will make a single bit of difference if the lived experience of teachers is not defined by trust and psychological safety.

Paying it forward

Life has a funny way of unravelling exactly as it should and, in my next job, at the Institute for Teaching (now Ambition Institute) I gained not only the professional learning I had craved my whole career, working with some of the best educational minds in the system, but the healing I needed too. I was beyond privileged to work with schools across the country on leadership development, curriculum and teacher education, to travel and to be immersed in research and reading. After being in the classroom for so many years, I relished the opportunities to gain a broad perspective on education and meet so many new people. My team, based in the North West, were a brilliant group of ex-teachers, and we were led by a wonderful colleague, a former Headteacher, who restored my faith in leaders. After three years, I was itching to go back into schools, and took up my current role, leading teacher development and curriculum for a Trust in Greater Manchester.

In a way, I feel I have come full circle, now being in a position to shape the lived experience of teachers in our Trust. My deep, unshakeable respect for them fuels everything I try to do. I feel a particular affinity with experienced colleagues, some of whom are featured in this book, and I prioritise work that will make a difference to them: quality, subject-specific CPD; policies that support family life; empowering women into leadership; and providing opportunities to mentor others and share expertise. Mostly, I aspire to create a culture where our teachers feel trusted and respected, and want to stay in our schools.

Experienced teachers have shaped my career. They have mentored me, guided me, lifted me up, supported me through the toughest times and celebrated my successes. I am immeasurably grateful to them, and I try to pay it forward. But too many of our teachers work in schools and Trusts where their experience and expertise are not valued, and this has to change. Our most experienced colleagues have given their working lives in service of children and their futures. They deserve better. Through this book, we want to give them a voice. To them, we say – thank you. We hope you will stay.

CHAPTER FOUR:
In their words

Teacher perspective

Ian Grove

Ian Grove is a secondary design and technology and engineering teacher in his 28th year of teaching. He works at a secondary school in East Sussex and has spent most of his career in the same regional area across several schools, including long service in one school over two decades. Across his career, he has held roles including Subject Leader, Second in Department, Deputy Head of Year and Assistant Principal, before later returning to classroom teaching with additional curriculum and operational responsibilities.

I didn't originally plan to be a teacher. I trained in industrial design and, when I finished my degree in the mid-90s, most of the jobs were overseas. I applied across Europe and got nowhere. One of my tutors suggested teaching. It wasn't a calling, more a practical alternative, but once I started my PGCE and went into schools on placement, I realised I genuinely enjoyed it. The first placement especially – the department culture, the subject passion, the way staff talked about their work – that's what sold me on teaching as more than a stopgap.

Very early on, I learned that teaching is learned from people, not courses. The university side mattered, but the real learning was in departments, watching experienced teachers, being given space to observe others and being guided towards colleagues who were strong in particular areas. My induction year included deliberate opportunities to observe skilled practitioners, and that helped build my foundations.

My early career was intense. Within my second year, I was effectively running a department because of illness and absence around me. I was planning, marking, organising – everything – while still new to teaching. I applied for the Head of Department role and wasn't even shortlisted, partly because senior leaders didn't realise I'd already been doing most of the job. That was my first lesson in how leadership visibility and advocacy matter. I left for promotion elsewhere – and later returned when circumstances and leadership changed.

Across nearly three decades, I've moved between classroom teaching and leadership several times. I've been Curriculum Leader, Pastoral Leader, Assistant Principal, and then later returned to classroom roles with additional operational responsibilities. That variety has helped me stay. I like challenge. I like building things – systems, courses, facilities, logistics – not just lessons. Having additional responsibilities beyond pure classroom teaching has often kept the job fresh for me.

I've also seen firsthand how leadership culture can either sustain or destroy a school's staff body. I've worked under leaders who built trust, optimism and shared purpose, where the mood of the staffroom was buoyant and people felt they were going somewhere together. I've also worked under leaders whose approach changed the atmosphere within weeks, where distrust, fear and favouritism took hold, and good people started leaving quickly. You can feel that shift almost immediately. Staff don't leave schools lightly – but they do leave leadership cultures that make them feel undervalued or unsafe.

I've seen favourites culture up close – small inner circles who receive disproportionate recognition while others' work goes unseen. That corrodes morale faster than workload. Recognition doesn't have to be grand, but it does have to be fair.

Twice in my career I came very close to leaving teaching altogether. The closest point was when I was made redundant during a Trust restructure that cut subject areas and posts. That was the first time I genuinely stopped and asked myself whether this was the moment to leave the profession. I applied for both teaching and non-teaching roles. I attended several interviews that, frankly, lacked dignity and transparency, processes where outcomes were clearly predetermined or where candidates were not treated with professional respect. That experience nearly pushed me out.

What kept me in, in the end, was the classroom itself.

I love my subject. I enjoy making and designing and solving practical problems. I enjoy helping pupils discover that they can make something real, something functional, something they didn't think they could do. I'm good at building relationships with pupils and encouraging them. Young people know when you care and when you're just performing care. They know when you're faking it. When they see genuine subject passion and genuine interest in their progress, they respond.

The small daily moments matter more than the big initiatives. Pupils saying 'thank you' at the end of a lesson. Pupils coming at breaktime to keep working on a project. Pupils asking what they'll be learning next. That steady stream of small affirmations is what anchors me to the work.

Over time, I've also learned how to make the job sustainable for myself. Earlier in my career I spent huge amounts of time on written marking and detailed individual feedback. Now I work much more with whole-class feedback and live verbal feedback. I plan more efficiently. I set boundaries around working time. These days I arrive early, work hard during the day, and generally leave work at work. I rarely work weekends outside of unavoidable peak periods like exam marking. That shift has been essential to longevity.

Professional trust makes a difference here. In the schools where I've been treated as a professional – trusted to manage my work, not micromanaged – I've thrived. Where trust is low and surveillance is high, energy drains quickly. Performance management, in my experience, often becomes a tick-box exercise: its impact depends entirely on how leaders use it. It can be developmental or punitive. The difference is leadership intent.

I also think subject community used to be stronger. Earlier in my career, there were more subject networks, advisory structures and cross-school meetings. Those reduced over time. When you are a sole subject specialist in a school, isolation is a real risk. External subject networks help retention more than leaders sometimes realise.

Financially, I've never stayed or considered leaving because of pay alone. Teaching isn't badly paid compared to many professions, but if you calculated hourly rates honestly, the picture would look different. For me, it has never been the main driver. Leadership culture, professional respect, subject passion and pupil relationships matter more.

At this stage of my career, I'm more conscious of time – how many working years remain and how to keep them meaningful without burning out. Teaching is all-consuming if you let it be. You have to build space for your own interests and creativity. I built a workshop at home and use it to keep my own subject practice alive, and that feeds back into my teaching.

I've stayed because I still enjoy the core work: the subject, the pupils, the craft of teaching. I've stayed because I've learned how to adapt my working patterns. And I've stayed because, at key moments, enough good leaders and good schools made it possible to continue.

If those elements disappeared – subject joy, pupil connection, professional trust – I would not stay. That, more than anything, is what retention depends on.

Teacher perspective

Isabelle Jones

Isabelle Jones is an experienced secondary languages teacher and Associate Assistant Headteacher with over 30 years in the profession. She teaches French and Spanish, and has worked across seven schools in different phases and contexts, including sixth form, comprehensive, faith and independent sectors. She has served as a Head of Department for 18 years and now leads on research, Initial Teacher Training (ITT) and educational visits.

I didn't come into teaching through the usual route, and I didn't grow up in the English education system. I was educated in France, and there the model is very different. Teaching is much more solitary: no departments, no collaborative planning, very little sense of team. When I first worked in an English school as an assistant before training, I realised teaching here was much more of a team profession than I'd expected. That appealed to me immediately. I'm not someone who enjoys working alone. I had originally considered translation and interpreting, but that felt too isolated. Teaching felt collective and purposeful.

I trained through a bespoke in-school route before those became common. It was highly tailored to my needs and strengths. I was supported closely by my department and a mentor, and I built a large evidence portfolio over two years. In many ways, that personalised start was better than much of the generic CPD that followed later. After qualification, development often became fad-driven and whole-school generic. I sat through years of trends that came and went. What sustained me instead was subject community. I became deeply involved in my subject association and built my own professional learning through reading, networking and contributing to CPD myself. That sense of ownership over my development has been a major reason I stayed.

You do need certain dispositions to last in teaching, but they're often misunderstood. People talk about resilience as if it means simply enduring everything. I don't think that's right. You need reflective resilience – the ability to ask what can be changed, what cannot, and not to take every difficulty as a personal failure. Teaching is emotionally personal work. When things go wrong, people think they are wrong. That's why early career teachers sometimes leave, because they interpret a difficult class or a poor lesson as proof they are not good enough. Experienced teachers can help reframe that. I still tell trainees now: a bad lesson does not make you a bad teacher.

You also need to be intellectually critical. Not cynical, but questioning. Education produces a steady stream of silver bullets. If you don't develop the habit of asking 'why would this work here?', you get exhausted chasing every initiative. Engaging with research helped me enormously with that. It gave me language and confidence to question approaches constructively, not defensively. It strengthens your professional self-belief. It means, when you disagree, you're not just saying 'I don't like this'; you're saying 'the evidence suggests otherwise'. That changes the conversation.

There are phases of life that are genuine pressure points for retention. Having young children was the hardest period for me. The exhaustion is physical and mental, and the guilt culture around presence in school can be intense. There is still too much presenteeism in teaching – the sense that if you are not visibly there late, you are less committed. That is particularly punishing for young mothers and carers. You rearrange your work to cope, but you feel judged anyway. That's an inflection point where many people question whether they can continue.

I did briefly consider leaving at that stage but, when I examined it seriously, I realised I still loved the work itself. I enjoy teaching. I enjoy working with young people. I enjoy building subject understanding and confidence. I didn't want a job that was only about paying the mortgage. That sense of purpose mattered. Teaching is never finished, unlike some professions where you complete a task and it is done. With teaching, improvement is ongoing and impact is often delayed. Sometimes you only discover years later that you made a difference. Former students write to you out of the blue. Often they are the ones you worried about most. That unpredictability is bewildering but also sustaining.

Experienced teachers bring perspective that cannot be fast-tracked. We help newer colleagues see that difficulty is normal, that setbacks are survivable, that cycles repeat. We can say, calmly, this has happened before and we will get through it. We also bring honesty. Anyone who claims never to have had behaviour issues or difficult classes is not being truthful. Normalising struggle protects people from unnecessary self-doubt.

Leadership makes an enormous difference to whether experienced teachers stay. I have worked in schools that were the best places to work, but later became the worst, purely because leadership changed. In the best environments, you are trusted as a professional, your subject expertise is respected, systems are supportive and your contribution is recognised. In the worst, you are micromanaged, often by non-specialists, and required to follow neat but irrelevant systems that do not fit your subject. There is no time for professional dialogue. You become a number. Culture shifts faster than people realise when leadership shifts.

The best leaders I have worked with combined challenge with genuine listening. They ask you to explain your thinking. They facilitate meaningful professional conversation. They recognise you as both a professional and a person. They sometimes say no, but they explain why. That builds trust and reflection rather than compliance.

Workload remains the structural issue that threatens retention the most, especially for experienced staff with complex lives. Preparation time is not realistic for the number of groups teachers teach. Expectations around individual adaptation for every pupil can become impossible in classes of 30. Managing expectations – from policy, from parents, from the public – is essential. Many people still believe teachers work short days and long holidays. That persistent misunderstanding damages morale. A more honest public narrative about the real scope and complexity of teaching would help retention more than many small policy tweaks.

Flexibility is the other major pressure point. Since the pandemic, many professions have embraced remote and hybrid work. Teaching remains one of the least flexible graduate careers. That comparison is increasingly visible to younger teachers. Even small flexibility – occasional later starts, clustered meetings, protected remote planning time – can make a disproportionate difference. I see this clearly in further education, where limited hybrid models are already improving recruitment and retention.

Pay and portability also matter, especially later in a career. When pay is not portable between schools or Trusts, experience becomes a liability rather than an asset. That sends a damaging signal about how experience is valued. Some older teachers feel they are seen as expensive inconveniences rather than professional resources. That perception pushes people out.

I have stayed because teaching remains intellectually and humanly rich. It is varied, relational and purposeful. I have stayed because I built my own professional learning networks and did not rely solely on institutional CPD. I have stayed because good leaders, at key moments, treated me as a professional and a person. And I have stayed because, even after 30 years, I am still learning. The day you think you have nailed teaching completely is the day you should probably stop.

Teacher perspective

Adam Robbins

Adam Robbins is a secondary science teacher and whole-school Lead Practitioner based at The Regis School in Bognor Regis. He has been teaching for 21 years, spending almost his entire career in the same school through multiple phases of change, including special measures, rebuilding, academisation and Trust development. Over that time, he has served as Head of Department and now works in a cross-school improvement role alongside classroom teaching. He is also an author and national contributor to professional learning conversations.

I didn't go into teaching as a calling. I finished a biochemistry degree with fairly average results and needed something to do next. Teacher-training was funded, so it seemed like a sensible one-year plan. I thought at worst I'd understand schools better when I became a parent. At best, it might be interesting. I didn't expect to stay.

My training was very old-school. A lot of it was about performance and control – keep them busy, make it fun, if they're not engaged it's your fault. Some of it was useful, some of it wasn't. My first proper job was in the school I'd attended as a pupil. Within six weeks we were in special measures. I was one of 30 new teachers. It was chaotic and stressful, but strangely it didn't feel professionally devastating at that stage because I didn't know any different. Inspectors came in, gave very precise feedback, and I improved quickly. In some ways, that level of clarity helped me early on.

I've now been through multiple headteachers, multiple school identities and several system resets without leaving. People often ask why. Partly it's temperament. I'm quite good at compartmentalising. When I leave the building, I can switch off. I don't carry everything home. I also have a fairly stoic belief that teachers have to focus on what is within their control and accept what isn't. You can't fix every social factor in a child's life. You can control the quality of your teaching, your routines, your relationships. That mindset protects you.

There's also a slightly less noble truth: teaching suits certain personality types. If you're a bit of an attention-seeker, it's a perfect job. You have an audience all day. Early in my career, I leaned heavily into the performance side – big demonstrations, high entertainment, constant activity. Over time, I've shifted towards quieter, more disciplined classrooms where pupils do more of the thinking. That was a hard transition – stepping back from being the centre – but it improved outcomes and reduced exhaustion.

The period when I came closest to leaving the profession was when I became Head of Science and results didn't improve fast enough. I'd worked incredibly hard to turn the department around. Senior leaders were supportive in words but, when outcomes came in below target, the message shifted to 'do more'. I developed stress-related health symptoms. I remember sitting at home looking at the mortgage and thinking: I don't know how to fix this. That sense of professional helplessness is dangerous.

What pulled me through was finding the wider professional community. Reading, engaging with research-informed practice, connecting with people outside my school. One book in particular gave me reassurance that my instincts weren't wrong and that I needed to stay the course rather than chase every new initiative. That external validation mattered enormously. It recalibrated my confidence. Soon after, my Trust's direction of travel aligned with that evidence-informed approach, and the tide turned. Results improved. My sense of professional control returned.

That experience taught me something important about retention. Teachers leave when they feel isolated inside their own building and uncertain whether what they believe about good teaching is valid. External professional networks, subject communities and research engagement are not luxuries – they are retention mechanisms.

Professional development across my career has been mixed. I've had some excellent CPD and some truly poor CPD. The frustrating part, when you become more experienced, is that bad CPD becomes harder to sit through because you can see the flaws immediately. For experienced teachers especially, development has to create space for reflection, contribution and testing ideas – not just delivery. Coaching models and experiential cycles work better than top-down instruction. Experienced teachers carry a lot of tacit knowledge. Good CPD draws that out and refines it rather than ignoring it.

School culture matters enormously. Behaviour systems matter enormously. If behaviour is poor, everything else becomes heavier – planning, marking, relationships, energy. I see experienced teachers going parttime not because they want leisure, but because they need recovery time from constant low-level disruption. That is a retention warning sign. Where behaviour is calm and predictable, teaching is joyful. Where it is not, even strong teachers erode.

I've been fortunate that when major life events happened – family health scares, personal crises – my school was deeply humane. Colleagues told me not to come in, to take the time needed, that they would cover. Schools are often very good at responding to acute crisis. Where the system is weaker is in handling longer-term adjustments – health conditions, sustained workload strain, disability accommodations. We still lose experienced teachers there through inflexibility or procedural clumsiness.

Later in my career, when I began contributing beyond my school – publishing, speaking, supporting other teachers – my leaders created a hybrid role so I could stay while expanding my work. That flexibility retained me. Without it, I might have left for a different pathway. Retention is sometimes about redesigning roles around people, not forcing people into fixed roles.

I have considered leaving at several points. Early on, financial incentives like training bursaries and loan repayment kept me in long enough to become competent. Later, professional community and intellectual renewal kept me in long enough to become effective. More recently, role flexibility and trust from leaders have kept me in long enough to remain energised.

When experienced teachers leave, what we lose most is nuance. Experience builds judgement – about people, about timing, about which problems are real and which are noise. It builds perspective across cycles of reform. It builds conversational skill with parents and colleagues. It helps younger teachers calibrate their instincts. You lose that quiet stabilising influence when experienced staff disappear.

I've stayed because I still find the classroom meaningful, because I've been allowed to grow, because I've found professional community beyond my school and because, at key moments, leaders chose flexibility over rigidity. Teaching is still hard. But when the culture, behaviour and professional learning are right, it is still one of the most worthwhile jobs there is.

Teacher perspective

Janine Carter

Janine Carter is an English teacher at The East Manchester Academy and has been teaching since 2000. Across 25 years in the classroom, she has worked in multiple secondary schools and contexts, including periods of parttime teaching, one-to-one tutoring and departmental leadership. She has navigated major life transitions alongside her career, including motherhood, divorce and mid-career change. She is also a union representative.

I came into teaching for two reasons, and I'm quite honest about both. One was practical – I thought it would work well with family life because I expected to become a mother and I liked the idea of school holidays aligning with children's holidays. The other was more personal. I've always felt I had a strength in communicating with people without judging them, and I wanted to help young people prosper in the way education helped me. It felt like a good use of what I'm naturally good at.

I had a very strong induction. My first school was supportive, structured and relational. I felt looked after and taken seriously. That matters more than people realise. Early professional experiences shape how long you stay. I liked being an NQT – as it was then – because I felt I was growing and being guided, not inspected.

What has kept me in teaching longest is relationships with students. That's the anchor. Whatever noise sits around the job – policy, accountability, pressure – the classroom relationship is the daily reality. Over time, life experience deepens that. Becoming a mother, getting older, going through difficulty – all of that builds empathy and perspective. I've always approached students from a place of celebration and development rather than judgement. That was once seen as unusual. Now we have the language for it, but it was instinctive for me from the beginning.

Experience also builds emotional regulation. When you're newer, everything feels like a verdict on you. Later, you understand that a bad lesson is a bad lesson, not a bad teacher. That distinction is protective. I try to pass that on to early career teachers now because I see how quickly self-doubt can push people out.

There were periods when my career undulated quite sharply. I was flying early on, then I hit a very difficult school in serious difficulty and left. I went parttime in a quieter school, had my daughter and stepped back from career progression for several years. I don't regret that at all. I do think some women feel pressure to make career decisions based only on maternity timing. That's too narrow. That period with young children is precious and it changes your priorities. I chose home first for a while. Later, when I was ready, I wrote to a former headteacher and asked for parttime work. He welcomed me back for one-to-one tutoring. That flexibility – and that leader – kept me connected to the profession.

Flexibility at re-entry points is critical for retention, especially for women. One Head later offered me a contract and said he would not overload my timetable even though he could have. I asked if I could have first period free so I could drop my daughter at school. He said yes. That single act of flexibility made the job sustainable at that stage of my life. Those decisions matter more than many formal retention policies.

Leadership culture has had the biggest impact on whether my work felt sustainable or punishing. I've worked under leaders who built trust, optimism and shared endeavour, and under leaders whose fear and control damaged morale quickly. When Ofsted pressure intensified over the years, I saw fear move down through leadership layers into audit culture – checking, monitoring, proving – and that fear changes how schools feel to work in. Earlier in my career, inspection sometimes felt like validation of good teaching. Later, it felt like a threat hanging over leaders, and that anxiety filtered down.

I do think the profession became too driven by external judgement and compliance. Teachers are encouraged to be reflective early in their career – then later treated as if they cannot reflect without being told what to fix. That undermines professional identity. I've never met a curious teacher who didn't want to improve. What we need is inquiry-based leadership – leaders who ask what's really going on, what support is needed, what the constraints are – rather than assuming the solution in advance.

There are predictable vulnerability points in a teaching career. New motherhood is one. Midlife and menopause is another, and we don't talk about that enough. Confidence and energy can dip sharply. External judgement hits harder at those times. Women in particular can internalise professional criticism more deeply, especially when combined with social messages that teaching is 'just a job' or not high status. The erosion of public respect for teachers has had a real emotional impact. That used to be a quiet source of professional pride and stability. Its loss is felt.

I have never seriously wanted another career. Even in hard periods, I didn't want to do something else – I just wanted teaching to be more humane. I'm proud of my 25 years. I still go home with what I call golden moments – small interactions that remind me the work matters. No profession is easy. Teaching is hard, but it is meaningful.

Professional development helps retention when it is thoughtful and respectful. The most powerful development I've experienced has been subject-specific, dialogic and chosen – not generic, fad-driven or imposed. Conversations between teachers solving real classroom problems together are more valuable than many formal sessions. But that requires leaders confident enough to host open professional dialogue rather than control it.

In very challenging schools, like the one I work in now, the emotional load is heavier – but so is the sense of purpose. That has kept me in rather than pushed me out. The work feels worthwhile. The camaraderie among staff is strong. Pressure can also create negative dynamics – blame, fear, defensiveness – but where leadership brings clarity, stability and authenticity, those effects reduce over time.

If I think about what would most improve retention, especially for women in their 30s, it would be flexibility across the life course. The ability to step back temporarily without losing your professional place. Sabbaticals. Parttime transitions. Role redesign. The message that you can leave for a period and come back without penalty. Life is not linear, and teaching careers shouldn't have to be either.

I've stayed because I still believe in the work, because relationships with students still matter to me, because good leaders at key moments made it possible to continue and because I've learned to protect my professional identity from passing judgement cycles. Teaching is not easy, but it is still, for me, the right place to be.

Teacher perspective

Jessica Austin-Burdett

Jessica Austin-Burdett is Head of Art and Community at Deptford Green School in London, and is in her 29th year of teaching. A trained fine artist, she entered teaching through an art PGCE in Manchester. She has worked across five secondary schools, including long service in a highly arts-rich comprehensive where she stayed for 14 years. Alongside departmental leadership, she leads community partnerships linking students with creative industries, higher education and practising artists.

I didn't grow up knowing I wanted to be a teacher. I was doing my art degree and helping my younger brother and his friends prepare their portfolios when they were applying for post-16 courses. I was giving them feedback and helping them talk about their work, and they said, 'We wish you were our teacher'. Around the same time, one of my tutors, who also trained teachers, told me I was strong at helping others improve but poor at talking about my own work, and suggested teaching might suit me. Two separate people saying similar things made me pay attention. Teaching moved from a vague idea to a real option.

My PGCE experience was excellent and very broad. I trained across very different schools – private, faith and highly challenging – and that variety helped confirm my values. I've always believed education should be for everyone, not only the advantaged, and I've consistently chosen to work in schools serving diverse and often deprived communities. Arts education, in particular, should not be reserved for the privileged. That belief has anchored many of my career decisions.

What shaped me most early on was working alongside experienced teachers who were still positive, still passionate, still evolving their practice. One of them told me never to teach the same scheme of work unchanged year after year, but to keep refining, keep responding to context, keep it alive. Another told me that behaviour is rarely about you personally: students are often reacting to what you represent, not who you are. That single idea probably kept me in the profession. I've passed it on to every trainee and early career teacher I've mentored since.

I am resilient, but that resilience has been tested. About five years ago, after a school was taken over, I was effectively pushed out through a process that made experienced staff feel incompetent and unwanted. It was emotionally coercive and deeply damaging. Several colleagues left teaching entirely at that point. I nearly did. What troubled me most was the sense that experience was being treated as a cost problem rather than a professional asset. Experienced teachers are less malleable – we ask questions, we challenge weak ideas – and some leadership cultures don't welcome that. I think that is a serious retention issue across the system.

What brought me back, and kept me in, was the work itself and the impact I can see through creative education. In my longest-serving school, arts were genuinely valued. We had strong leadership support, rich partnerships and extraordinary opportunities for students: international projects, artist collaborations, design-industry placements, major exhibitions, residential trips. I saw students go on to real creative careers – fashion houses, design studios, independent practice – and I could trace a line from school experience to adult outcome. That kind of visible impact is incredibly sustaining. It turns teaching from routine delivery into life-shaping work.

Those outwards-facing partnerships matter enormously for teacher retention too. If you never leave your classroom, never connect with the real creative world, never bring live practice back into your teaching, the job becomes dry and repetitive. I could not stay in teaching if it meant being permanently classroom-bound. My current role includes community and industry links, working with universities, studios and cultural organisations, and that keeps my professional thinking alive.

Subject value is central. Teachers stay where their subject is respected. In schools where creative subjects are squeezed, marginalised or treated as timetable filler, morale drops quickly. In my current school, leaders actively protect creative subjects. Students must choose creative options at GCSE. Trips, exhibitions and collaborations are built into the yearly plan. That takes leadership courage in an accountability system that pushes in the opposite direction, but it makes a huge difference to staff commitment.

Recognition also matters – not just pay, though pay must be sufficient – but regular, visible recognition that your work matters. Knowing your contribution is seen and valued day to day is more powerful than occasional grand gestures.

Motherhood was a significant inflection point. I had my daughter at 40 and was studying for a master's at the same time. My headteacher then was not supportive of maternity or returners, and I was later passed over for promotion more than once. That experience showed me how vulnerable teachers can be at life-transition points. Later leaders were more humane, allowing flexibility for key moments, assemblies, transition events, and that made a real difference. Flexibility at these stages is not a perk; it is a retention necessity, especially for women.

Professional development has kept me engaged when it is subject-specific and practitioner-driven. Generic, fad-driven CPD is rarely useful for experienced teachers. Subject networks, research engagement and professional associations have been far more sustaining for me. They build intellectual confidence and protect against initiative fatigue. They also help teachers distinguish between genuinely new thinking and recycled fashion – something experienced colleagues are often best placed to see.

Looking system-wide, workload and curriculum overload are major drivers of attrition. Too much content, too little time, too much assessment. Teachers never feel finished, never feel on top of the work. Depth is sacrificed for coverage. That is exhausting and demoralising. I would like to see curriculum and assessment slimmed down to core knowledge and skills, with more opportunity to revisit and embed learning.

Flexibility in working patterns would also help – even small structural flexibilities. Earlier in my career, schools sometimes built in small humane gestures – half days, protected time, seasonal flexibility. Those have largely disappeared. Teaching has become more rigid just as other professions have become more flexible. That comparison is increasingly visible to younger teachers.

I have stayed because I still believe in creative education, still value working with young people and still find the work meaningful when done in the right culture. I have stayed because I found schools where leadership had the courage to value subjects like mine. I have stayed because partnerships, community links and real-world creative work kept the profession alive for me.

If you strip out subject value, professional dignity and creative opportunity, you strip out the reasons many experienced teachers remain. That is the risk the system needs to take seriously.

Teacher perspective

Paul Wade

Paul Wade is an Assistant Principal, SENCo and teacher of English and drama in a secondary school in north-east Lincolnshire. He has been teaching since 2002, entering through the Graduate Teacher Programme, and has held a range of pastoral and leadership roles alongside classroom teaching.

Teaching was never the grand plan. I think you'll hear that from a lot of people of my generation. I came into it because I needed a job and it seemed like something I could try. I'd seen a television drama about teaching that made it look lively and purposeful, and I'd been working in a mentoring-type role already. A teaching opportunity came up with training attached, and I took it. That was in 2002, which sounds slightly unreal when I say it out loud.

The training route I took threw you straight in. I started teaching Year 9 poetry with no real preparation. I was dreadful. I remember thinking: I can't stay dreadful at this – that's not fair on the students and it's not fair on me. So I worked at it until I became competent, then more than competent, and somewhere along the way I realised I actually liked it. You build pride in getting better at something difficult.

One of the reasons I've stayed is that the job keeps changing if you let it. Roughly every four or five years I've shifted emphasis – pastoral work, SEN, leadership, now drama alongside English. A year ago, I wasn't teaching drama at all. Now I'm rehearsing GCSE performances and sitting there thinking, 'how on earth did I end up here?' – and actually enjoying it. That variety matters. Doing exactly the same thing for decades would have driven me out.

The daily intellectual unpredictability is a huge retention factor. You can walk into a lesson with one plan and come out having had a completely different –

and better – conversation. I taught a lesson on *A Christmas Carol* that turned into a debate about the afterlife, and one student said, 'Sir, I just refuse to believe in the existence of nothing'. That line has stayed with me. Moments like that are gold. You come out with a story and a thought, not just a completed task.

Professional development has been mixed across my career. Some has been transformative, especially early work around positive reinforcement and behaviour, which completely changed how I saw classroom relationships. Highlighting what students are doing right instead of only correcting what they're doing wrong was powerful learning. Some CPD, though, has been frankly pointless. I've sat through sessions where someone reads quotations off slides and asks you to 'reflect quietly'. Experienced teachers can tell the difference instantly. Good development respects your professionalism and gives you something usable. Poor development wastes the one thing teachers never have enough of – time.

One thing that becomes more important as you get more experienced is recognition. Not flattery, just professional acknowledgement. We're quite bad at that in education. New teachers often get encouragement and coaching. Later on, there's an assumption you'll just get on with it. But experienced teachers still need to be told, occasionally and sincerely, that what they're doing matters and is done well. There are colleagues delivering five excellent lessons a day, shaping lives quietly, and nobody says 'thank you'. That wears people down over time.

I've come close to leaving at a few points. Once, when workload became physically dangerous – I was so exhausted from marking that I fell down the stairs at home. A colleague had done the same. That should have been a warning sign to the system, not just to us. Another time was when workload and marking expectations became completely unrealistic – multiple exam classes, mountains of scripts, no adjustment when you said it was too much. The response was essentially: it still needs doing. That's when people start to think seriously about leaving.

Workload is not just about hours, it's about headspace. The job lives in your mind all the time. You walk around supermarkets spotting texts you could use in lessons. You pick up leaflets for language analysis. You buy props for drama rehearsals out of your own pocket. You help run breakfast clubs because students are hungry, then worry because they don't have coats. All of that is morally right but mentally heavy. Teaching has absorbed more and more social responsibility, and that accumulation is exhausting.

Leadership makes a decisive difference. The best leaders listen – genuinely listen – and act on what they hear. One of the best retention moves I've seen was a Headteacher who capped email sending times. No emails after late afternoon, none at weekends. It sounds small. It was transformational. Suddenly Sunday evenings were yours again. That's what real wellbeing leadership looks like – structural, not slogan-based.

The worst leadership trait is learned harshness – leaders who were treated badly and repeat the pattern. You can see it happen. Good leaders communicate, invite expertise and understand that schools are collective enterprises, not one-person shows. There's no point hiring experienced people and then refusing to hear their experience.

Personal survival strategies matter too. I've learned to put stress in a box when I go home, most of the time. I've learned you cannot do everything tonight. I've learned to talk to people outside my subject bubble and build relationships across the school. Staffroom culture matters more than policy documents. The characters, the storytellers, the experienced voices – they helped me stay. I worry we're losing them because there is no longer time or space to be a character. Everything is standardised, scripted, PowerPointed. Some consistency is good, but total uniformity drains personality and joy.

If experienced teachers leave in large numbers, what we lose is perspective, culture and wisdom. We lose the people who can say, calmly, this has happened before and here's how we handled it. We lose the storytellers, the subject obsessives, the staffroom mentors. We risk creating a workforce of efficient but interchangeable operators. That might look tidy, but it's a loss for young people.

I've stayed because the classroom is still intellectually alive, because students still surprise me, because variety still exists in the role and because, at key moments, some leaders chose to listen and act. But the pressures are real, and unless workload, autonomy and professional dignity are taken seriously, more experienced teachers will decide it's no longer sustainable.

Teacher perspective

Chris Barnes

Chris Barnes is a classroom teacher in his 26th year of teaching. He has worked across UK state and independent schools and spent nearly a decade teaching internationally in Moscow, followed by further experience in Malaysia. Originally trained in speech and language therapy, he entered teaching through a PGCE with the intention of moving into educational psychology, but chose to remain in the classroom. Over his career, he has held both classroom and senior leadership roles, including deputy headship.

I didn't set out to become a teacher for life. I originally trained in speech and language therapy and planned to move into educational psychology. Teaching was meant to be something I did for a couple of years along the way. But once I was in the classroom, working directly with children, I realised this was the part of the work I loved most – the guiding, the explaining, the helping people understand things. That's what kept me there.

My early experience very nearly pushed me out. My induction year was, honestly, awful. The school didn't really understand how to support a new teacher, and I felt like I was in the way more than anything else. At the end of the year, my contract wasn't renewed. I seriously considered leaving the profession altogether. What stopped me was being encouraged to try supply teaching instead. I spent two years moving between schools, year groups and contexts. That turned out to be one of the most important phases of my development. It built my confidence and made me more adaptable. It also showed me that one bad fit doesn't mean you're in the wrong profession.

Supply teaching pushed me out of my comfort zone in a good way. I worked with different colleagues, different approaches, different expectations. I learned to adjust quickly and not assume there is only one right way to do things. That flexibility has stayed with me ever since.

The biggest turning point came when someone suggested teaching overseas. I hadn't seriously considered it before, but I took the chance and ended up in Moscow – and stayed for nearly nine years. International teaching changed my perspective completely. You're still teaching – still doing what you love – but in a different cultural setting, with different viewpoints and different approaches to learning. You might teach a maths method and have three children from three different countries show you three different valid ways of solving the same problem. That keeps you intellectually alive as a teacher.

It also gave me a very strong sense of belonging. Staff communities overseas can be incredibly close because you're all adapting to a new place together. That sense of shared purpose and mutual support is powerful. For me, belonging is a big part of retention. If you feel you belong – with the people and in the culture – you stay.

One of the things that's kept me in teaching is the long memory of it. Pupils I taught years ago still get in touch. They find you and say, do you remember me, you taught me in Moscow. That tells you the work mattered. Even if you were part of their life for only a short time, it counted. That sustains you more than any metric.

Adaptability is probably the quality that's helped me most to stay. Working internationally, especially, you can't be rigid. You can't say, 'this is how I've always done it'. You have to adjust, rethink, respond to what's in front of you. People talk about growth mindset – overseas, you actually have to live it. You learn not to stand on pride about methods. You change what needs changing and move forwards.

I've also had setbacks. After several years as a deputy head, I was suddenly let go when a school group changed ownership. No real explanation. That was a shock. Shortly afterwards, during Covid, I moved again internationally for work. Later, trying to return to the UK system, I found the recruitment process incredibly difficult from overseas. The UK interview model is very heavy – multiple tasks, lesson observations, full days – whereas international recruitment is often based on CV, conversation and professional track record. I do think overly complex recruitment processes can push experienced teachers away.

Professional development has mattered to me, but much of it I've had to drive myself. I've done coaching training, leadership courses and specialist programmes, but often through my own initiative. I've wanted to pursue further qualifications, including a master's, but haven't often found schools willing to invest at that level. A lot of what I bring comes from outside interests – languages, outdoor education, leadership through scouting. Experienced teachers often still want to grow, but the system doesn't always make that easy.

The leaders who made the biggest difference to me were the ones who showed trust. They said – I believe in you, I trust your judgement, here are the resources, go and do the job well. That kind of leadership keeps people. Control-heavy cultures don't.

I've stayed in teaching because it has remained purposeful, because I've been able to grow and change and because, at my best moments in schools, I've felt trusted and valued. But if I had to reduce it to one thing, it would be this: I stayed where I felt I belonged.

Across these examples, the common thread is not a programme but a pattern of choices. Leaders notice where the work is unnecessarily hard, and they change it. They build trust where they can, flexibility where it is possible and professional growth into the normal flow of work.

That does not remove the difficulty of teaching. But it does make staying more possible – and more likely.

CHAPTER FIVE:

Why teachers stay: a thematic exploration of teacher retention

Teacher interviews and analysis

It is clear from the research set out in this book that teacher retention remains a critical issue globally, with attrition contributing to recruitment crises and educational inequality.[73, 74] While much literature focuses on why teachers leave, we want this study to explore why experienced teachers remain, and to privilege the voice and experiences of veteran teachers – those who have dedicated their whole professional lives to working in schools. These voices are often sidelined, so we conducted over 100 interviews with teachers in England who have spent over 20 years teaching or leading in schools. We then drew on this extensive data to conduct a thematic analysis. There were many threads and commonalities, so we have structured this narrative around 12 core, recurring themes, which we have illuminated with peer-reviewed research. The 12 themes are:

- relationships and belonging
- moral purpose
- resilience and personal growth
- flexible human-centred leadership and culture
- professional identity and self-efficacy
- accountability and toxic leadership
- women, motherhood and family life
- professional development

73 Ingersoll, R. (2001) 'Teacher turnover and teacher shortages' in *American Educational Research Journal*, 38(3), pp.499–534.

74 Worth, J. and Van den Brande, J. (2020) 'Teacher autonomy: how does it relate to job satisfaction and retention?', Slough: NFER [online] Available at: www.nfer.ac.uk/publications/teacher-autonomy-how-does-it-relate-to-job-satisfaction-and-retention (Accessed: 30 April 2026).

- love of subject
- professional agency
- systems and routines
- deliberate recruitment and retention strategies.

Recent neuroscience research reveals that our brains are inherently attuned to stories, making narratives more engaging, memorable and influential than isolated facts or data.[75] Therefore, we begin each theme with the case study of a teacher who has remained in the profession and then link their experiences thematically to the other teachers who we interviewed.

Relationships and belonging

Sarah has worked at the same school for 26 years. She stays as she feels part of the community. She has seen other teachers come and go, but she enjoys the camaraderie she feels with a fairly stable staff. She enjoys the banter in the staffroom at lunch and has enjoyed taking part in staff activities such as the staff band and choir. She also enjoys building relationships with students. Due to being at the school so long, she has often taught family members of students she teaches – including their parents! This gives Sarah and her students a shared history to draw upon.

Community

Sarah is not alone. Relationships with students and colleagues are repeatedly cited as central to teachers' commitment.[76] Participants in all our interviews described teaching as an inherently relational profession, where trust, laughter and shared human experiences reinforce their professional identity and sense of purpose. This aligns

75 Very Big Brain (2025) 'The Neuroscience of Storytelling: Why Your Brain Loves a Good Plot' [online] Available at: https://verybigbrain.com/professions-interests/the-neuroscience-of-storytelling-why-your-brain-loves-a-good-plot (Accessed: 30 April 2026).

76 Day, C. and Gu, Q. (2010) *The New Lives of Teachers*. London: Routledge.

with Kelchtermans, who argues that collegial relationships are a key factor in teacher resilience and satisfaction.[77]

The teachers we interviewed consistently identified relationships with students and colleagues as the bedrock of their professional satisfaction and motivation. They frequently highlighted the joy and fulfilment of making a difference to young people's lives: 'When a child says thank you... that's priceless.' Many described watching students grow into adulthood as a source of profound satisfaction.

The teachers commented on the deep joy they feel from building relationships with students: 'They make me laugh every day... they challenge me... they make me reflect.' This student-centred purpose is a consistent anchor keeping this teacher in the profession. They added: 'The day-to-day with the kids... I love it.' This emphasises that, even after decades of teaching, no day is the same, and highlights the constant novelty, human engagement and challenge that keeps this teacher energised.

This enjoyment of building relationships with students is a strong motivator for many of the teachers we interviewed. One stated: 'It brings me great joy to be in the classroom... I've never got bored of it.' This emotional and intellectual satisfaction they draw from their classroom interactions fulfils them as they get to watch their students grow, not just academically, but personally, and they value the opportunity to learn alongside them.

Relationships with students are not the only ones that create a sense of belonging. Strong bonds with colleagues create essential emotional support networks. Such phrases as 'We lean on each other. We laugh. We cry.' illustrate the depth of these relationships. Some teachers recalled funny moments with their colleagues: 'We used to play hide and seek around the school... We'd have a proper laugh.' They also remembered staff nights out and social activities: 'Every Friday, 70 to 80 of them go to the pub together.' These shared rituals, humour and a culture of informal bonding foster deep loyalty. It seems clear that teachers stay when they feel part of something that values fun, friendship and being known beyond their professional role.

One of the teachers we interviewed came from France and felt that teaching in the UK, with its culture of departments and collaboration, has

77 Kelchtermans, G. (2005) 'Teachers' emotions in educational reforms' in *Journal of Educational Change*, 6(4), pp.287–303.

offered them a sense of belonging that their home system didn't: 'I came from France where there are no departments or teams. The team spirit here was a huge positive. Working as part of a team has kept me going.'

Teachers also described valuing camaraderie not only with fellow teachers but also with non-teaching staff, highlighting a culture of inclusivity: 'It is wonderful to know you can say "you'll never guess what happened today" to any colleague.' This teacher spoke warmly about the cross-subject collegiality and humour as an essential part of what has sustained them in the role. They warned against siloed departments and emphasised the role of informal staffroom relationships in providing catharsis, perspective and joy – especially in difficult times. This was a thread that was enthusiastically repeated by many of the teachers we questioned: 'It's relationships. It's not just in meetings. It's saying good morning, sharing stories, listening to people.'

The importance of collegial relationships, informal conversations and shared positivity seems crucial to professional satisfaction for teachers, so much so that, when these relationships are removed, teachers notice: 'Our staffroom is like a ghostship, everyone's too busy, it's silent.' This teacher mourned the demise of staffroom culture. This loss of informal support structures has weakened professional bonds and retention: 'We used to have things like county advisers and regular subject meetups. That's what kept you going.' This teacher spoke about the erosion of local professional networks and support systems. As a sole practitioner, at times they had to rely on self-directed learning and external relationships to stay motivated and connected. The loss of these systems contributed to teacher isolation, especially in practical subjects such as design and technology (DT).

Some teachers we interviewed found it challenging to feel a sense of belonging at points in their career. For example, the people of colour we interviewed highlighted the emotional toll of the lack of representation in leadership: 'The amount of women of colour who are headteachers at secondary is just shocking... I could probably fit them in my office.' Teachers spoke candidly about the emotional weight of being a black leader in a predominantly white leadership landscape. They recalled entering leadership spaces where they were the only person of colour, and how this undermined their sense of belonging. However, networks of support and mentors were crucial to their confidence and progression, but they had to seek these actively outside of their school. This reveals that teachers feel that representation, inclusion and identity safety are often overlooked factors in retention discussions.

Another teacher felt that they struggled to feel a sense of belonging as their teaching approach and philosophy is incongruent with colleagues'. To help with this, they sought a sense of belonging in wider teacher networks: 'Reading Sherrington's *The Learning Rainforest* reassured me that I wasn't crazy. I went to researchED and it helped me calibrate my instincts.' Due to feeling isolated within school, they instead turned outwards to professional networks for affirmation and development. The wider edu-community has been vital in keeping this teacher in the profession.

Watching growth

Teachers spoke about the satisfaction they feel from helping students develop: 'Helping someone to understand something is golden… I can go into a room and come out with a story.' All the teachers shared moving and humorous anecdotes about the memories they have made with their classes, including philosophical discussions with previously disengaged students, which reaffirmed their beliefs in the transformative power of teaching.

Staying in the same school also helped with this: 'We've stayed very much in the same area, the same community… We will sometimes be the most stable point in [students'] lives.' The long tenures have allowed this teacher to see students develop over time, reinforcing their investment in teaching and the school's broader social fabric. This sense of being part of the wider school community for a long period of time was also a key thread in most interviews: 'I'm teaching children whose parents I taught… it brings it home to the children that you're a person.' The power of this school-based community has created a profound sense of psychological safety. This teacher spoke fondly of early-career experiences with collegial rituals: Friday pub visits, staffroom laughter, informal mentoring. However, they also mourned the erosion of these communal spaces, particularly post-Covid, and warned that the decline of the staffroom culture has reduced informal support and cross-departmental bonding.

Professional support

Secondary teachers spoke about the support they receive from their faculties: 'English departments have always been very supportive. We just threw our arms around each other.' This teacher felt their department had acted as a buffer against external pressures and negative leadership experiences.

Teachers also appreciated the intentional crafting of this culture of belonging by leaders: 'We celebrate with golden tickets and lunch appreciations every day. Belonging is central; everyone's part of something bigger.' This ritualised appreciation – both informal and formal – cultivates staff morale. All teachers felt that they were more likely to stay when they felt noticed and celebrated as part of a purposeful team.

Other interviewees spoke about the little things leaders do to promote belonging: 'All staff get free breakfast and lunch and we finish early on Fridays, when we are encouraged to get out of the building!' Respecting the physical and emotional needs of staff helps create a culture of care. It also normalises rest and self-care, which are crucial to long-term retention. One teacher stated: 'It's tribal... belonging matters here. We purposely have traditions that are ours, like Bing Bong Bingo.' These shared rituals, warm language and tradition create a culture of 'the way we do things round here'. It is this emotional grounding that helps teachers feel secure, connected and invested in their school. This feeling was described in different terms by another teacher: 'It's just a big family, the world's craziest family, but it's ours.'

It seems clear that leadership emerges as one of the most decisive themes in many teachers' stories, both for good and ill. Trusted, relational leadership creates flourishing environments: 'The feel of the place, the mood of the place was buoyant, upbeat. We were going places. Those things collectively are what keep me going.' Therefore, 'protecting the joy, carving out time to laugh together' can be a major retention factor.

Relational leadership and structured mentoring are pivotal. Mentorship was universally described as 'totally invaluable', especially during career transitions. Trusted, relational leadership creates flourishing environments, while toxic leadership erodes teacher morale and commitment: 'I think that's one of the reasons why I'm still here, because I had that mentoring. That support was totally invaluable. It could have been really difficult if I didn't have someone on my side.' The structured mentoring this teacher received through the now-defunct 'Fast Track' programme provided both technical guidance and emotional support, particularly during early leadership roles. They repeatedly emphasised that having a mentor when entering new roles, not just as a trainee, is vital for long-term success in the profession.

Teachers we interviewed stressed the importance of building emotional bonds among staff through events including residentials, shared lunches and concerts. Community rituals and social traditions create belonging, loyalty and emotional resilience among staff: 'Always plant your hyacinths. You have to protect the joy.' Making school joyful and memorable is vital not just for children, but for staff. Teachers need to see and feel the impact of their work on children's happiness and success to sustain their own morale. It is this purposeful crafting of culture that has made it impossible for some teachers to imagine working at another school: 'I find it so hard to leave because it's just a brilliant space.' A defining feature of this teacher's career is a deep attachment to the school community. They speak of a school culture where former students return to teach and staff supported one another through the tragic loss of a student. This relational glue, built over years of shared hardship and joy, forms a core retention driver.

This teacher was not the only participant who had been in the same school for their whole career. Another teacher added: 'My kids have always been at school with me. I've only ever worked at this school.' They describe school as an extension of their family and personal identity, and this blending of their personal and professional life has contributed to their sense of belonging and purpose. Although they sometimes fantasise about leaving, fear of change and deep-rooted place attachment keep them grounded.

Overcoming challenges

Of course, there was an acknowledgement that teaching can be hard and exhausting, but that colleagues often help overcome these challenges: 'We lean on each other. We laugh. We cry. That's what keeps you going.' This recurring theme of the importance of human connection, with both students and colleagues, highlighted the staffroom and camaraderie with peers as crucial support systems that offer emotional sustenance and shared purpose.

Even in particularly tough schools, these collegial relationships can help teachers. One teacher recalled that, in their first school, despite the extreme challenges of behaviour and safeguarding, the collective solidarity, social cohesion and regular breaks reinforced their emotional wellbeing and professional motivation. When these conditions eroded, particularly after academisation, so too did their desire to remain.

Conclusion

These narratives consistently show that relationships, community, shared purpose and psychological safety are at the core of why teachers stay in the profession. While systemic changes and external pressures have threatened these conditions, many teachers remain due to the deep fulfilment they find in human connection and belonging. Yet, what about people's motivation to become teachers? A key driver seems to be a sense of moral purpose.

Moral purpose

Nigel initially worked in finance in London but, after the first few years of his career, he began to feel disillusioned with his job and wanted to pursue a career where he felt he could make a difference. His parents had been teachers and he remembered the way his father spoke with pride about the professional rugby players he had taught in PE. Now 28 years later, Nigel has his own stories about the children whose lives he has positively impacted.

Social change

Teachers enter the profession for a variety of reasons, but many teachers we interviewed are driven by a deep moral purpose: the belief in education as a vehicle for social change and empowerment.[78] This resonates with research suggesting that moral purpose sustains motivation despite systemic challenges.[79] Teachers spoke of the privilege of shaping young lives and of contributing to social justice.

Many of the teachers we interviewed believe that their sustained commitment to teaching is anchored in a belief in education as a transformative force, both in their own lives and in the lives of students:

78 Fullan, M. (2001) *Leading in a Culture of Change*. San Francisco: Jossey-Bass.

79 Day, C., Sammons, P., Stobart, G., Kington, A. and Gu, Q. (2007) *Teachers Matter: Connecting Work, Lives and Effectiveness*. Maidenhead: Open University Press.

'I wanted to empower young people to prosper in a way I think education has done for me.'

Teaching as an opportunity to influence lives positively and help students explore ideas came up in many teachers' narratives, as did the idea of challenging injustice by using education as a platform for critical thinking: 'Education is political. More so in English than any other subject. It really annoys me that nobody has the guts to stand up and say this isn't right.'

A vocation

The concept of teaching being more than just a job came up repeatedly: 'We can't run schools like shops. Education isn't transactional.' This teacher views teaching as a civic, ethical and humanistic mission. Staying is about being part of something meaningful, not just efficient. Others view teaching as a public service and value their role as part of a larger social system. This sense of mission keeps them committed despite systemic frustrations: 'You can't overcome years of social deprivation overnight… you have to play your role.'

This was emphasised by others, who feel teachers are more likely to stay when they feel their work is meaningful and aligned with a bigger purpose: 'We are about transforming lives… you need to be all in to do that as it is a vocation.'

This view of teaching as a vocation, driven by a deep commitment to make a difference, saw many teachers describe education as a transformative tool, which fortified their resolve to remain in teaching, even under pressure: 'If you want to make a difference, if you want to make things better, then this is the job for you.' This lasting desire to contribute meaningfully to society is rooted in deep purpose and calling: 'It felt like a career rather than a job… something that made a difference.'

For some teachers, moral purpose and intrinsic motivation, as well as a lifelong passion for their subject, stem from childhood inspirations: 'It's something I've always dreamed of. I always grew up playing being the teacher and that made me want to go into the profession and put history into stories.'

For a few teachers, their motivation stems from personal transformation inspired by a teacher: 'He made me into a musician; I wasn't one when I started. I ended up performing across the world. He gave me the passion to do what he did for others.' Their teaching is driven by a moral purpose to offer students the same life-changing opportunities.

For others, teaching was not their original career or their natural first choice for a career. One teacher transitioned from journalism and PR to teaching to have a more direct, meaningful impact on students' futures. Their sense of gratitude and duty underpin their dedication to social justice and student outcomes: 'It'd be much easier to influence children and influence their futures being in the classroom.' Others' entry into teaching was pragmatic and accidental, but they found purpose and capability within the profession: 'It was never ever a plan but I quite enjoyed it, and that's how I fell into it.'

Entering teaching to impart knowledge and inspire lifelong learning helps teachers develop a strong intrinsic motivation and intellectual passion. These underpin their resilience to remain in school: 'I knew that I wanted to teach. I knew that I wanted to impart knowledge and inspire and just keep researching for the rest of my life.'

Inclusivity

Teachers we interviewed connected their leadership progression to a desire to expand their positive impact on students: 'You always know you're doing the right thing for kids. I don't see how you do it otherwise.' This moral purpose was a common route into teaching and was driven by a desire to do something socially useful and work with young people. Their emotional and ethical connection to the community sustains their motivation.

For others, the moral purpose was joined by an ethical stance on equality and inclusion. Remaining in schools serving disadvantaged communities gives teachers' work enduring meaning: 'Personally, I don't think private schools should exist. Education should be for everybody. It aligns with my more socialist values.' They are also motivated by the long-term successes of their students and the visible legacy of their influence: 'Students I taught now work for Burberry, Prada. They would never have done that without our work. We are creating citizens, not just training kids for jobs.'

Those teachers who are also now leaders spoke about how articulating a values-led vision creates emotional and moral alignment for their teams. Their teachers stay because they believe in the purpose of the work: 'We're part of something bigger, helping children belong to us, not something else. We value students having rich memories of school.'

This idea of values-driven leadership being a key retention-driver was reiterated by teachers also. Their motivation is guided by a desire to solve problems and support students rather than personal career advancement. This strong vocational identity and internalised commitment to teaching have sustained their careers, as well as a political awareness of social-class inequalities, which have guided efforts to ensure equity and access: 'The inequality that shrieked at me was social class. We had everyone from politicians' children to absolute poverty.'

Identity

These teachers' stories show that a strong professional identity can develop over time. It is clear that a strong start is vital, but what about remaining long-term through all the challenges?

Resilience and personal growth

Amira trained as a teacher straight out of university, full of certainty about who she wanted to be in the classroom. The first few years, however, tested that certainty daily. Behaviour was challenging, self-doubt crept in quietly and there were evenings when she questioned whether she was cut out for the profession at all. What kept her going were small moments she almost missed at the time: a reluctant reader staying behind to finish a paragraph, a class finally grasping a concept she had retaught three different ways, a 'thank you' scribbled at the bottom of an exercise book.

Over time, Amira learned that resilience wasn't about coping silently or pushing through alone. It was about seeking support, reflecting honestly and allowing herself to grow: 22 years on, she speaks with calm confidence about her practice, not because teaching became easier, but because of what she herself had learned.

Personal resilience and professional growth have emerged as critical protective factors that support teachers to remain in the profession. This does not mean teachers enduring conditions at all costs and putting up with a bad deal, but by enabling adaptation, agency and sustained professional identity for them.

Resilience

Resilience in teaching is best understood not as an individual trait that some teachers possess and others lack, but as a dynamic process shaped by personal resources, professional learning and organisational conditions. Research consistently shows that teachers who are able to reflect on challenges, regulate emotional responses and reframe setbacks as opportunities for learning are more likely to sustain commitment to the profession.[80]

However, one teacher did warn against becoming an island and being too self-reliant: 'You've got to be reasonably self-reliant and resilient, but not so much that you isolate yourself.' This teacher's career narrative features multiple leadership disappointments, redundancies and systemic changes, yet he consistently demonstrates resilience, adaptability and reflection. He recounts incidents of being overlooked for leadership due to misinformation, losing leadership roles in restructures and experiencing toxic leadership cultures and favouritism. Yet, despite these setbacks, he continues to seek out opportunities and reinvent his professional role, often reframing setbacks as chances for change – all supported by other colleagues.

Yet, of course, teaching can be immensely challenging. So when challenges also happen at the same time in their personal life, teachers really have to dig deep to continue being resilient. One teacher spoke emotionally about going back to work after maternity leave and recalled her journeys into work: 'I remember being stuck in traffic just crying because I wanted to be at home with my baby.' Like many long-serving teachers, this teacher spoke about how resilience had to become a foundational trait, especially in balancing school leadership with motherhood. Her reflections on returning to fulltime work just three months after giving birth, without flexibility, highlight systemic issues that push many women out of the profession. She notes that retention is often about 'benefits outweighing the difficulties', a balance that isn't guaranteed.

Both The MaternityTeacher / PaternityTeacher (MTPT) Project's research and the 2024 'Missing Mothers' report highlight that women in their 30s, many of whom are mothers, are the largest demographic to leave

80 Gu, Q. and Day, C. (2007) 'Teachers' resilience: A necessary condition for effectiveness' in *Teaching and Teacher Education*, 23(8), pp.1302–1316.

the teaching profession in England each year.[81] One of the core findings of this report is that workload stress, lack of flexibility and inadequate support for mothers returning to work after maternity leave are major drivers of attrition. Around only 27% of those who left reported being satisfied with the support they received on return to work, while most felt unsupported during a critical phase, exacerbating stress and making the emotional and practical demands of teaching harder to manage.[82] They recommend that greater workplace flexibility and structured support, such as coaching during and after maternity leave, are among the most feasible and high-impact strategies to retain parent-teachers. These align with the idea that growth and resilience are supported by intentional organisational practices, not left to individual grit alone. Other teachers talked about additional challenges, such as ill parents or children and bereavements in the family: 'How I got through that was I'm a stubborn person. I've run a marathon, so I'll keep coming to school.'

School-based challenges can also be an enormous test of resilience. A teacher recalled how he'd worked in a tough school, where children didn't seem to want to learn: 'Challenging classes for me was a problem-solving exercise. I had to really dig deep to harvest my resilience and think, what can I do to improve this?' By framing teaching as a continual problem-solving challenge, particularly in his early years with difficult classes, he highlighted the importance of resilience, flexibility and a growth mindset in dealing with difficult behaviour and navigating demanding school environments.

Another teacher identified resilience and adaptability as essential traits for long-term survival in education. He framed policy shifts, curriculum reform and school transitions as opportunities to develop rather than as threats: 'You don't see challenges as challenges – you see them as opportunities to learn and grow.'

However, another teacher made an important contribution when she said: 'You need to be resilient, but not to the point of self-destruction. Some students will not engage, and that's not always your fault.' Her nuanced understanding of resilience includes knowing when to persist and when to let go. She doesn't romanticise teaching, and accepts its limitations without personalising every challenge. This ability to

81 The New Britain Project (2024) 'Missing Mothers' [online] Available at: www.newbritain.org.uk/missing-mothers (Accessed: 30 April 2026).

82 The New Britain Project (2024) 'Missing Mothers' [online] Available at: www.newbritain.org.uk/missing-mothers (Accessed: 30 April 2026).

maintain perspective and, indeed, to compartmentalise stress helped another teacher have longevity in his career: 'I'm very, very good at not thinking about certain things when I'm not in that environment. I think I have a relatively stoic belief system: teachers need to recognise what they can and can't control.' These skills have protected him from burnout in high-pressure environments.

Personal growth

Importantly, this form of resilience is closely linked to growth. Personal growth plays a crucial role in how teachers interpret and respond to the inevitable difficulties of the role. Studies on teacher motivation suggest that when teachers perceive themselves as developing – becoming more skilled, more confident and more effective – the emotional demands of teaching are more manageable.[83]

The same study by Li et al. found that self-efficacy predicted resilience, which itself is associated with lower levels of burnout (emotional and motivational strain). This suggests that teachers who develop confidence and resilience – both linked to professional growth – are better equipped to regulate emotion and handle job demands.[84] What is more, reviews of teacher-wellbeing literature show that teachers' psychological wellbeing, emotional regulation and job engagement are interrelated with perceptions of competence and growth. While not always causal, studies consistently report that teachers who feel supported in developing their skills, including emotional and professional growth, report higher job satisfaction and intentions to stay in the profession.[85] This growth provides a sense of trajectory. Rather than seeing challenges as evidence of failure, teachers who experience growth are more likely to view them as part of a longer professional journey.

83 Shanshan, L. (2023) 'The effect of teacher self-efficacy, teacher resilience, and emotion regulation on teacher burnout: a mediation model' in *Frontiers in Psychology*, 14 [online] Available at: www.frontiersin.org/journals/psychology/articles/10.3389/fpsyg.2023.1185079 (Accessed: 30 April 2026).

84 Shanshan, L. (2023) 'The effect of teacher self-efficacy, teacher resilience, and emotion regulation on teacher burnout: a mediation model' in *Frontiers in Psychology*, 14 [online] Available at: www.frontiersin.org/journals/psychology/articles/10.3389/fpsyg.2023.1185079 (Accessed: 30 April 2026).

85 Worth, J. and Van den Brande, J. (2020) 'Teacher autonomy: how does it relate to job satisfaction and retention?', Slough: NFER [online] Available at: www.nfer.ac.uk/publications/teacher-autonomy-how-does-it-relate-to-job-satisfaction-and-retention (Accessed: 30 April 2026).

Culture

Where teachers talked about their school culture and how it helps them be more resilient, they understood that the leaders they were working under had really spent careful time crafting a culture where staff were able to be resilient. One teacher spoke about the need for staff wellbeing, for example, to be lived not laminated: 'We don't do yoga. We buy into counselling and create space to laugh. But we do always finish the term with a silly raffle and we all leave smiling.' They felt that this avoids superficial wellbeing practices and instead integrates care, humour and mental-health support into the culture in authentic, non-patronising ways.

Another teacher spoke about how as well as a commitment from leaders, it also takes a commitment from teachers themselves to manage their own resilience: 'The work is the planning and the presenting and the engaging with the kids... The job is the grind. But, I've shaved away the stuff that is draining and kept the parts of the job that give me joy.' One of the most powerful strategies this teacher credits for her retention is her conscious mental separation between the 'work' (teaching, learning, planning, student relationships) and the 'job' (bureaucracy, admin, performance-tracking). This psychological boundary allows her to find fulfilment even in challenging contexts, including toxic school environments. It reflects a sophisticated emotional-resilience strategy and a refusal to let institutional noise erode her love of teaching.

Coping with tragedy and trauma

Experiencing a tragedy at school can be a source of emotional turmoil, and one teacher recalled experiencing student suicide early in her career, a traumatic event that deepened her empathy and strengthened her resolve to support young people. She said: 'That experience massively shaped how I went forward... education is about more than outcomes.' A study in Australia explored how teachers are affected by the suicide of a student. Understandably, exposure to at least one student suicide was associated with high levels of distress in both personal and professional domains. Many teachers reported that the event impacted their emotional life, professional thinking and coping needs, highlighting that such tragedies can leave lasting emotional and reflective impacts on teachers' perspectives.[86] An experience like this can blur boundaries between personal and professional roles and prompt teachers to reflect on their teaching identity and values; equally, experiencing the loss of a student can deepen commitment and shift how teachers conceptualise their purpose beyond academic outcomes.[87] Luckily, this experience is not widespread, but sadly is more common than it should be.

However, it is not just the death of a student that can be traumatic for a teacher. With increasing levels of poverty in England and students having access to inappropriate materials online, upsetting safeguarding issues are something that every teacher will have to deal with at some point in their career. The name for this is *secondary traumatic stress (STS)*, which is trauma experienced indirectly through exposure to others' traumatic events. This term helps to explain how working with traumatised children and severe student distress affects teachers' emotional states. A study shows that teachers can experience symptoms similar to trauma reactions (anxiety, emotional exhaustion) when regularly confronted with students' traumatic situations.[88] Here, a great deal of resilience is needed from teachers to help them navigate their work. As a teacher added: 'It's not just a job. That's why people leave. They feel like failures. The impact of what we do isn't always visible – it can take years.'

Workload

Workload is a common factor cited for teachers leaving the profession, so it is no surprise that this also came up in the interviews: 'The workload cannot be done in the time we're given. People think we work 9 to 3. It's insulting.' Yet, despite these challenges, this teacher's continued presence in the classroom is not due to a lack of awareness of these problems; rather, she stays in spite of them, due to strong internal motivation and self-belief. She also spoke about ways of working smarter to manage workloads and also the importance of sensible marking policies and strong systems from leaders.

86 Kõlves, K., Ross, V., Hawgood, J., Spence, S.H. and De Leo, D. (2017) 'The impact of a student's suicide: Teachers' perspectives' in *Journal of Affective Disorders*, 207, pp.276–281.

87 Arksey, A.M. and Greidanus, E.J. (2022) '"I Could Hardly Breathe": Teachers' Lived Experiences of Bereavement After the Violent Death of a Student' in *Canadian Journal of Counselling and Psychotherapy*, 56(1), pp.47–69.

88 Sam, C.H. and Gupton, J. (2024) 'Reconceptualizing Teachers as First Responders' in *Practitioner & Theoretical Perspectives Journal of Trauma Studies in Education*, 3(2), pp.152–168.

Versatility

Other teachers manage to deal with workload by having boundaries and thinking practically about what is possible: 'I've learned you can't do everything... you've got to leave some things for tomorrow.' This attitude, coupled with a thirst for learning, was what many teachers cited as positive influences on their resilience. This perseverance, adaptability and a thirst for continuous learning was cited by many as critical to their longevity. One teacher spoke about having taught across a wide range of subjects, sometimes out of necessity, demonstrating his versatility. He tried to embrace new challenges and use professional setbacks as learning opportunities, while his reflective practice and capacity to evolve professionally have sustained his enthusiasm.

Burnout

However, staying in the classroom is not as simple as just constantly being resilient. Early research positioned resilience as a buffer against stress, where teachers who could adapt, cope and persevere were shown to manage emotional demands more effectively in the short-term. However, more recent research complicates this picture. Studies now distinguish between:

- adaptive resilience (supported, growth-oriented, sustainable)
- endurance resilience (continuous coping without relief).

It is the latter that is strongly associated with burnout. Gu and Day found that teachers who remained committed over time did not simply cope better; they had access to relational, organisational and professional resources. Where those resources were absent, resilience became emotional self-management, not renewal. This can be a key precursor to burnout.[89]

In addition, other research highlights that constant emotional regulation is a major risk factor. Maslach and Leiter's model[90] identifies burnout as arising when:

- emotional demands are high
- recovery is insufficient
- personal resources are repeatedly drawn upon without replenishment.

89 Day, C. and Gu, Q. (2014) *Resilient teachers, resilient schools*. London: Routledge.
90 Maslach, C. and Leiter, M.P. (2016) 'Burnout' in *Stress: Concepts, cognition, emotion, and behaviour*. Cambridge: Academic Press, pp.351–357.

Teachers who are repeatedly required to be resilient often engage in suppressing emotional responses, absorbing organisational stress and maintaining performance despite misalignment or overload. Over time, this leads to emotional exhaustion, the strongest predictor of burnout and attrition. In other words, resilience without recovery becomes depletion. This was really evident when one teacher told us: 'I was trying so hard to do everything... there was nothing left to give.' She was later signed off with stress as she struggled to cope with the emotional toll of working with increasingly complex, vulnerable students. Her story shows that retention is not just about staying, but about learning how to stay, by developing sustainable working habits, setting boundaries and managing emotional labour over time. This is essentially the essence of resilience and personal growth.

When that burnout hits, it can be hard to recover from. Burnout is typically characterised by emotional exhaustion, depersonalisation and reduced sense of personal accomplishment.[91] Of these dimensions, reduced personal accomplishment is most directly related to attrition. Teachers who feel they are no longer growing, improving or making an impact are significantly more likely to leave the profession. A teacher described her experiences glibly: 'Teaching has almost broken me at times. And yet here I am.' She described herself as having grit and perseverance in the face of systemic and personal hardship, referring to herself as 'bloody minded' and repeatedly referring to the determination required to stay. This mental resilience is underpinned by her role as a trailblazer in her family – being one of the first to attend university – and a deep pressure not to fail.

Control and a growth mindset

Crucially, resilience is strengthened when teachers feel a degree of control over their professional learning and decision-making. Self-determination theory emphasises the importance of autonomy, competence and relatedness for motivation and wellbeing.[92] In schools where teachers are trusted as professionals, supported to develop expertise and encouraged to reflect on practice, resilience is more likely to flourish. This, in turn,

91 Maslach, C. and Leiter, M.P. (2016) 'Understanding the burnout experience: recent research and its implications for psychiatry' in *World Psychiatry*, 15(2), pp.103–11.

92 Ryan, R.M. and Deci, E.L. (2000) 'Self-determination theory and the facilitation of intrinsic motivation, social development, and well-being' in *American Psychologist*, 55(1), pp.68–78.

supports retention by aligning teachers' psychological needs with their professional environment.

Growth mindset can also strengthen self-efficacy and become a core resilience resource. This is because growth mindset supports self-efficacy by framing competence as developing, not fixed. Research shows that:

- teachers with higher self-efficacy report lower emotional exhaustion
- self-efficacy mediates the relationship between stress and burnout.

Skaalvik & Skaalvik[93] found that teachers who believe they can grow in effectiveness are better able to manage emotional demands, as long as working conditions are reasonable. This ability to remain positive and, at the same time, build resilience was also a common thread from the teachers we interviewed. One teacher said: 'You have to have a growth mindset. You have to be willing to throw things up in the air and say, 'OK, fine, we'll do it this way'. I haven't stayed in one school all the time. That's helped me work with different colleagues, under different people, and look at different points of view.' This adaptability, shaped significantly by different teaching experiences, has strengthened his willingness to work across schools, curricula and cultures and enriched his practice, preventing stagnation.

Another teacher simply said: 'Tomorrow's another day... nothing's ever impossible.' This teacher attributes much of her endurance to values instilled by her mother: optimism, perseverance and a belief in possibility. She draws strength from this mindset when facing stress, setbacks or difficult parents, and views challenges as part of the landscape rather than deal-breakers.

93 Skaalvik, E.M. and Skaalvik, S. (2017) 'Teacher Stress and Teacher Self-Efficacy: Relations and Consequences' in McIntyre, T.M., McIntyre, S.E. and Francis, D.J. (eds.) *Educator Stress: An Occupational Health Perspective* (pp.101–125). Cham: Springer.

Flexible human-centred leadership and culture

For over 20 years, Mei has remained in the classroom, not because the work is easy, but because the leadership around her is human. Across different phases of her career, she has experienced leaders who understood that teaching is relational work, not just a performance measure. She recalls the contrast vividly: schools where rigid accountability created fear and silence, and others where flexibility, trust and compassion shaped daily practice. In the latter, she was given autonomy, listened to when life became complex and supported to grow rather than pushed to prove herself. That culture sustained her. As Mei puts it, 'I stayed because I was treated like a person, not a problem.'

Human-centred leadership

Positive school cultures led by flexible, relational leaders were described as crucial for retention. Participants distinguished between toxic, rigid accountability cultures and human-centred environments where autonomy and compassion coexist. Leithwood et al.[94] found that human-centred leadership directly impacts teacher satisfaction and retention. Mary Myatt has often spoken about the aim of leaders treating staff as humans first, professionals second,[95] and this was a strong theme that was highlighted throughout all our teacher interviews.

One teacher spoke warmly about the leadership at a school she had spent most of her career in: 'There was a great head at the time. He valued his staff. He paid me full time, but let me have period 1 free so I could drop off my daughter at school.' This supportive, empathetic leader, who offered flexibility and valued staff wellbeing, was crucial in her decision to stay. She highlighted how such human-centred policies help sustain teachers during demanding life phases.

94 Leithwood, K., Harris, A. and Hopkins, D. (2008) 'Seven strong claims about successful school leadership' in *School Leadership & Management*, 28(1), pp.27–42.

95 Myatt, M. 'Humans first, professionals second' [online] Available at: www.marymyatt.com/blog/humans-first-professionals-second (Accessed: 30 April 2026).

Another teacher recalled how a colleague's partner had died and the colleague had been given time off. 'Why would you turn that into a formal HR thing? You can't regulate not being a ****.' They felt this style of leadership is emotionally intelligent and flexible – qualities that make people feel safe and appreciated, especially during personal challenges. Another remembered how surprised they were that a new leader had said: '"Of course you can take your child to their first day of school." Staff have stayed because they were given working patterns that suit their lives.'

This empathy and responsiveness in leadership build long-term loyalty because there is the recognition that teachers need personal lives that function alongside professional roles. Furthermore, teachers spoke about how they appreciated a can-do, flexible approach by leaders: 'All of our meetings are on the same day so staff can plan around childcare. PPA is also timetabled at the end of the day, and staff can take it at home.' They explained how this engineering of the timetable and school calendar to support staff wellbeing removes unpredictability and creates a sustainable work–life balance.

In the same school, there is a model of examining work–life balance through the lens of the most disadvantaged member of staff: 'If leaders can cover and support, they will. They don't want you to miss those moments with your kids. Our most vulnerable member of staff might be a single parent as well.' The key strategy here is personalised, humane leadership, and staff trust is built by honouring family commitments and offering flexibility without guilt or penalty. Ultimately, this teacher summed it up beautifully: 'Your family comes first. Your health comes first. If you're not happy, you can't do the job we want.' This school culture, which prioritises staff welfare and family commitments, can be rare in many schools. Yet, it has helped sustain this teacher's career.

Flexibility

On flexibility, many of the teachers we interviewed work for schools who have reduced contact time and offered flexible starts to support teacher wellbeing: 'The average non-contact time for a teacher is 35%. Plus, every teacher has one morning a week where they can come in by 10:40.' These practical interventions signal respect for teachers' time, energy and life outside school, helping to keep them in the profession long-term. In another school, 56% of the staff work parttime and teachers are routinely allowed time off for personal milestones, with two annual 'child ill days' offered also. The teacher from this school highlighted this had not been the norm in other schools they had worked in, so this school did stand out for its exceptional flexibility, particularly with regard to family life and individual circumstances. They felt this level of flexibility reflects a deep commitment to staff wellbeing and autonomy, both of which are cited as critical to retention by the National Foundation for Educational Research (NFER); in particular, autonomy over decisions, suggesting that when teachers feel trusted and empowered they are more likely to stay in teaching rather than leave.[96]

Another teacher highlighted that a crucial factor in her retention was the school's willingness to accommodate parttime working, especially after maternity leave. She later acknowledged that her reluctance to move schools was partly driven by concern that she wouldn't find this flexibility elsewhere, highlighting how work–life compatibility is central to long-term retention. However, teachers we interviewed did admit that this had taken a big mindset shift from leaders: 'If you need it, you get it… If that's going to really help you out, then do that thing. But leadership can still be different. There is this attitude that you can be a teacher on four days, but you can't be a manager on four days.' She described a powerful shift in the school's leadership model here, from rigid policy enforcement to case-by-case equity. This individualised approach is vital in supporting staff wellbeing, especially around family and caregiving. However, she does highlight that there are still ongoing issues with access to parttime roles, especially for women in leadership.

Even in schools where leaders were not able to offer the level of flexibility to enable all the staff who wanted it to work parttime, colleagues we interviewed appreciated leaders' efforts in helping work–life balance: 'We are expected to do one meeting a week and there is not a stupid workload.' Another added: 'No emails after a certain time and no emails on weekends. That just made such a difference.' This teacher commends his previous school for implementing a staff email curfew, a small but meaningful policy. He contrasts this tangible act of care with tokenistic wellbeing gestures, advocating for practical workload policies that respect teachers' personal time and psychological headspace.

Another teacher admired leaders who acted as gatekeepers, protecting staff from unnecessary initiatives and making brave decisions based

96 NFER (2020) 'Teacher autonomy: how does it relate to job satisfaction and retention?', Slough: NFER [online] Available at: www.nfer.ac.uk/media/r1ubcb4s/teacher_autonomy_how_does_it_relate_to_job_satisfaction_and_retention.pdf (Accessed: 30 April 2026).

on what is right for children. She laments that current accountability systems have eroded this courageous leadership, replacing it with fear and compliance. On this topic, a different teacher added: 'I'm not one for non-negotiables... it's not how I run my department, and not how the heads I've worked for have run their schools.' She values leadership that fosters trust and flexibility, rather than compliance, contrasting this with performative systems and criticising the over-regulation of frameworks like the Early Career Framework (ECF) when applied rigidly.

Recognition and culture

Furthermore, teachers admired leaders who 'model what they want staff to do... who are visible on the playground, teach lessons, do break and lunch duties. They roll up their sleeves.' This teacher explained that leaders like this cultivate trust by being actively present, emotionally honest and supportive in a crisis. This relational approach addresses a major retention challenge: staff feeling devalued or unseen. A recent peer-reviewed study examining teacher retention in rural schools found that teachers' decisions to stay are strongly linked to feeling valued and recognised by their school community – including by school leaders. The research showed that interpersonal practices that support teachers' sense of worth; being seen by colleagues and the broader community; and positive recognition of their professional identity are central to their job satisfaction and retention decisions.[97]

The study cited above uses a theory-of-recognition lens to show that teachers' decisions to stay are shaped by whether their professional identity is recognised by the community they work in. Recognition here does not mean praise alone; it includes:

- being listened to
- having expertise acknowledged
- feeling trusted and respected
- having one's work made visible and meaningful.

These are not isolated acts. They are patterns of behaviour that accumulate over time. That accumulation is what we call *school culture*. A school culture that consistently values dialogue over directives, treats

97 Cuervo, H. (2025) 'Teacher job satisfaction and retention in small rural schools: A theory of recognition approach' in *International Journal of Educational Research*, 134, pp.1–10.

teachers as professionals rather than operatives and notices effort, growth and contribution creates the conditions in which teachers feel seen. Whether that is 'freshly squeezed orange juice every Friday' or 'SLT who cook breakfast for staff on Monday mornings', small, consistent acts of care help staff feel respected. The culture very much signals whether a workplace values its people.

Yet, it doesn't have to be acts like this that build a positive, human-centred culture. Other teachers spoke about the way leaders treat them: 'One leader I worked with built a culture of nudging, of empowering people and saying "you'd be great at this". They respected institutional wisdom but also encouraged opportunity.' They actively fostered development cultures where experienced staff are both respected and nudged to evolve. They also publicly acknowledged the contribution of experienced teachers: 'We have service badges every five years to honour the giants. Then new staff thrive because they stand on their shoulders.' This makes institutional memory and long service visible and meaningful, which fosters pride and retains experienced staff who feel respected for their legacy.

Simple praise was also cited as being extremely powerful: 'There's a culture of saying: "that's amazing, please keep doing this", which really makes a huge difference.' This teacher juxtaposed this experience with working at a school where there was a lack of praise or recognition for experienced teachers, describing how effective practitioners were often taken for granted. He felt this under-recognition eroded morale and retention for mid- and late-career staff who contributed vast institutional knowledge and pastoral expertise. Another teacher summed it up: 'The school makes so much difference... culture means everything. You can feel it within minutes.' This teacher provided a stark comparison between positive and toxic school cultures. In one challenging school, he felt devalued and unsupported. Conversely, in his current school, decisions are explicitly made with staff and student welfare in mind. This makes a real difference to his morale.

A positive culture and trust from leaders in schools seemed to have a strong connection during our interviews. One interviewee spoke about how lucky he has been with the leaders he has worked with: 'every headteacher I've had has given me trust, belief and time. I've never had a leader make me do a job I didn't want to do.' He stays in teaching because his leaders have always seen him as competent and capable. This trust builds psychological safety, which supports his creativity and satisfaction. This experience means that he feels supported and not micromanaged, which has helped him to weather difficult years and stay committed. Another teacher built on this by emphasising the importance of working with leaders who trust their staff's professional expertise – especially across subject boundaries.

The alternative can be tiring: 'If you don't feel trusted, that's exhausting... you're always looking over your back.' This underscores the importance of working in institutions with strong collegial cultures, where staff are trusted and supported: 'They encourage you to try things out. There's no blame attached if something doesn't work.' The value of leadership that listens, follows up and creates systems that help teachers thrive was a recurring theme throughout many interviews. This teacher's current school culture contrasted strongly with a past experience of toxic leadership that nearly drove her out of the profession. She added: 'the culture here is that the SLT actually care and the Trust's mantra is "advantaging the disadvantaged" and that comes through in everything.' The alignment between this teacher's values and her school's mission helps her feel purposeful and appreciated. As research states, leaders cannot just 'tell' teachers they are valued and expect retention to improve. Teachers infer value from culture through:

- consistency between words and actions
- how leaders behave under pressure
- whose wellbeing is protected when trade-offs are made.[98]

This explains why two schools with similar workload and pay can have very different retention outcomes: culture determines how demands are experienced.

98 Cuervo, H. (2025) 'Teacher job satisfaction and retention in small rural schools: A theory of recognition approach' in *International Journal of Educational Research*, 134, pp.1–10.

Professional identity and self-efficacy

When Maya talks about why she is still teaching after more than two decades, she rarely mentions stamina or sacrifice. Instead, she talks about confidence – hard-won and quietly sustained. Over the years, she has learned to trust her professional judgement: to know when a lesson has landed, when it hasn't and what to do next. That growing sense of competence matters. It means that challenges feel surmountable rather than defeating.

As her practice developed, so did her professional identity. Teaching became something she owned, not something done to her. Even when policy shifted or expectations changed, she held onto a clear sense of purpose: helping young people think, grow and succeed. Feedback and reflection sharpened her craft rather than eroding her confidence. She stayed because she felt effective, credible and anchored in her role. 'I didn't just survive teaching,' she says. 'I became myself through it.'

Self-efficacy

Long-serving teachers who were interviewed for this book described an evolving professional identity grounded in competence, confidence and the satisfaction of mastery. This, in turn, led to feelings of self-efficacy. *Self-efficacy* is defined by three core elements, drawn from the work of Albert Bandura.[99] Together, they explain why people believe they can succeed in a task and persist when it is difficult:

- Beliefs about competence: It reflects a person's judgement about their current skills and capability to perform a specific task successfully.
- Beliefs about effort and persistence: The belief that 'if I keep trying, I can improve or succeed'; high self-efficacy leads people to persist in the face of difficulty rather than withdrawing or avoiding challenge.
- Beliefs about impact: The belief that 'my actions make a difference'; people with strong self-efficacy believe their effort can influence outcomes, rather than seeing success or failure as outside their control.

99 Bandura, A. (1997) *Self-efficacy: The exercise of control*. New York: W.H. Freeman.

Professional identity

Tschannen-Moran and Hoy[100] define self-efficacy as a strong predictor of teacher perseverance. Our participants suggested that strong professional identity buffers against external pressures: 'I don't feel the pressure the same in the classroom because I know what's good and what isn't. I know what I'm doing. I'm on very solid ground.' This teacher feels a strong sense of professional competence and autonomy and is confident in her practice. She explained that this means she feels she is less affected by external validation, such as Ofsted. Other teachers added that their professional identity as a teacher has now become intertwined with who they are as a person: 'It's part of who I am.' She does not frame teaching as a phase or stepping stone, but rather as a lifelong pursuit.

This theme of teaching as an integral part of personal identity suggests that, for some, retention is less about staying in a role and more about staying true to oneself. Another teacher also highlighted this, noting her love of being in the classroom, especially following her return from illness: 'Standing in front of children, that's what I'm good at. I thought, this is where I should be.'

Others spoke of teaching as being like a calling, with one teacher describing how they entered teaching after discovering that they enjoyed explaining complex ideas to their peers during her chemistry degree. From the very first classroom experience, they felt a powerful vocational pull: 'From the moment I stepped inside a classroom I knew I was going to be a teacher. I am absolutely fascinated by how people learn.' They characterise teaching as intellectually stimulating, varied and energising, which has kept them engaged for nearly 30 years.

Others spoke of family being a motivator to enter the profession, through parents who were educators. Some recalled early childhood play mimicking classroom scenarios, and these teachers felt their lifelong identity as a teacher was solidified by this early socialisation and family tradition.

Professional growth

The connection between self-efficacy and professional growth is reciprocal and reinforcing: self-efficacy enables growth, and growth

100 Tschannen-Moran, M. and Hoy, A.W. (2001) 'Teacher efficacy: Capturing an elusive construct' in *Teaching and Teacher Education*, 17(7), pp.783–805.

strengthens self-efficacy. According to Albert Bandura, self-efficacy shapes whether individuals:

- take on challenge
- persist through difficulty
- recover from setbacks.[101]

In contrast, low self-efficacy leads to risk avoidance and surface compliance, even when professional development is available. This is because professional growth requires vulnerability, and self-efficacy makes vulnerability tolerable. Many of the teachers we interviewed cited professional-growth opportunities as a key lever for crafting a strong professional identity, which led to them feeling competent. 'PhD, coaching, research, leadership development. The best schools I have worked in have always allowed me to target CPD to help me get to the next career step.' By continuously evolving and diversifying his professional life, without leaving the classroom, this teacher maintained energy and relevance. This flexible-growth model has contributed significantly to his longevity.

Another spoke about the transformational power of mentoring colleagues: 'I've mentored since my second or third year of teaching and I pass on what those older teachers taught me.' They viewed mentorship as both a moral duty and a source of renewal. Teaching is sustainable when it's not only about delivery but also about stewardship of the profession. Another added: 'Our most experienced staff lead coaching groups. They're role models – strategically placed to guide others.' This helps veteran teachers feel valued, as they strengthen their professional identity by shaping others' practice. This recognition of their expertise, rather than marginalisation, keeps them engaged and anchored in the school.

Others have been offered promotions, which have both challenged and sustained them: 'I was offered a new role, "whole school lead practitioner", and went parttime to allow space for external work. It's kind of a halfway house, still authentic because I'm in the classroom.' Another said: 'My job now is to whisper in people's ears; quality assure CPD and connect people.' Their schools adapted to their strengths and ambitions, allowing them to evolve their roles. The flexibility to shape their workload and contributions has helped retain them.

101 Bandura, A. (1997) *Self-efficacy: The exercise of control*. New York: W.H. Freeman.

Some teachers had looked to both internal and external opportunities to develop and shape their professional identities. 'I look after ITT, EVC, trips. I'm also research lead at school. It's about not doing the same thing forever – variety keeps you engaged.' Another described the opportunities they have had more widely: 'We worked with the British Council, went to Svalbard, Egypt. You can't just be stuck in a classroom; you lose connection to the real world.' These evolving roles have given them autonomy, influence and fresh motivation. It's not just teaching students; it's shaping the profession that sustains them.

But teachers we interviewed did acknowledge that pressure on leaders for outcomes sometimes mean these opportunities are not available, and so their commitments don't always allow time to pursue interests: 'Experienced teachers need space to reflect. Their problems are persistent and complex. Some end up having to go parttime for wellbeing. Not because they want to but they need to in order to remain in the profession.' This teacher went even further by arguing for more tailored CPD, coaching and workload considerations for veteran staff. He cautioned that blanket approaches miss the rich, tacit knowledge that experienced teachers bring.

Unfortunately, many teachers we interviewed felt they had been overlooked for opportunities and promotions, due to their length of service. Some teachers felt this sometimes bordered on discrimination and implicit bias: 'You end up kind of putting up with an awful lot of nonsense and have to sometimes be bloody-minded, with an attitude of "you will not push me out of here..."' This teacher was grappling with the intersection of identity and promotion barriers, acknowledging covert discrimination and lack of diversity in leadership. Despite minimal overt racism, she notes how systemic biases may have impeded her career advancement.

Others criticised inexperienced teachers being promoted too quickly: 'I didn't feel like a good teacher until year 7 or 8, yet we're giving NPQLTDs to people in their second year.' He was critical of systems that fast-track early career teachers into leadership without the depth of practice needed to translate theory into context. He felt this creates disillusionment, weakens implementation and devalues veteran staff, many of whom leave due to lack of recognition.

Autonomy

Almost all the teachers we interviewed spoke at length about the way agency, or the lack of it, in schools can make or break a strong professional identity and feelings of self-efficacy. Professional agency and identity are interdependent. This is because teachers develop professional identity through active engagement in their work, making decisions, taking initiative, adapting practice and shaping their professional environment. From a socio-cultural perspective, identity and agency are understood not as fixed traits but as co-constructed through practice and reflection. Agency is part of teachers' ongoing identity negotiation, where they act in ways that affirm their values, beliefs and professional commitments. This iterative process contributes to identity formation over time.[102]

Professional identity includes teachers' beliefs about themselves as professionals and is developed in relation to their agency: the capacity to make meaningful choices in their work rather than just follow prescriptions.[103] Teachers in our interviews reported that they had felt most expert in their fields when there was a feeling that leaders created the conditions just to 'let us do what we're here to do; to recognise the fact that we do actually know what we're doing'.

Another stressed the importance of leaders holding respect for teacher expertise. This teacher felt like professional trust, including limited micromanagement and emphasis on teacher judgement, cultivates job satisfaction and reduces the attrition associated with excessive scrutiny or performativity. They added: 'You just get the best people you can and let them crack on. There isn't a set checklist; some subjects use bought-in schemes, some don't – it's their decision.' This was reinforced by another interviewee: 'You hire the best people and let them do their job. My current team is led by someone who trusts us, and that's why I probably love where I work.'

102 Vähäsantanen, K., Paloniemi, S., Hökkä, P.K. and Eteläpelto, A. (2017) 'An agency-promoting learning arena for developing shared work practices' in Goller, M. and Paloniemi, S. (eds.) *Agency at work: An agentic perspective on professional learning and development* (pp.351–371). Springer International Publishing / Springer Nature.

103 Vähäsantanen, K., Paloniemi, S., Hökkä, P.K. and Eteläpelto, A. (2017) 'An agency-promoting learning arena for developing shared work practices' in Goller, M. and Paloniemi, S. (eds.) *Agency at work: An agentic perspective on professional learning and development* (pp.351–371). Springer International Publishing / Springer Nature.

This professional trust and agency can really help staff to flourish, with one teacher stating: 'I was given this huge space to be the sort of teacher I wanted to be.' She felt that she had really benefited from high levels of autonomy and professional trust, which allowed her creativity and agency to flourish. She critiques modern systems that constrain teachers through excessive standardisation, advocating for the return of autonomy as a key to retention.

Many teachers criticised the overly-prescriptive view that leaders sometimes have of managing teachers, claiming that managerialism and unnecessary processes erode trust and add fatigue. Many said they see reducing pointless workload as central to keeping experienced teachers in the job: 'Unfortunately, we still ask teachers to do really stupid things. We haven't removed the heavy administrative lifting.' Another critique a teacher added is the loss of teacher agency due to over-prescriptive curricula and performative accountability. He cites being forced to follow the 'Michaela method' using booklets that he felt undermined his professional judgement: 'We were told to use the booklets, then later told not to rely on them… all that time and energy wasted.'

Yet, this feeling about aligned curricula was not universally seen as a negative in the teacher interviews. Indeed, research on curriculum coherence shows that when curricula are aligned (that is, concepts, materials, assessments and pedagogy are systematically organised), teachers are better able to exercise professional judgement and agency because they understand the *why* and *how* of classroom content rather than reacting to incoherent expectations.

Curriculum coherence provides a shared structure that supports decision-making rather than constraining it. For example, a longitudinal study of curriculum-design frameworks found that when teachers engage with coherent curricular structures, they develop deeper subject expertise and greater confidence in their professional judgements, effectively positioning them as epistemic agents rather than passive implementers of externally imposed materials.[104] This suggests that coherent, aligned curriculum materials can empower teachers to make meaningful decisions about teaching and learning.

104 Pountney, R., Rata, E. and Swift, D. (2025) 'Exploring curriculum coherence and professional knowledge' in Wyse, D., Baumfield, V., Mockler, N. and Rearden, M., (eds.) *The BERA-SAGE Handbook of Research-Informed Education Practice and Policy*. London: BERA / Sage, pp.791–814.

However, many teachers we interviewed did share the teacher's concerns about this. They felt that there was an erosion of professional autonomy due to overly scripted curricula in large academy chains. Many worried about a homogenisation of teaching, where the characters and pedagogical personalities of educators are being squeezed out of the profession by uniformity. One added: 'I like to have control over the material I'm teaching... otherwise I don't feel confident in it.' Another went further than this and stated: 'We're creating robotic staff... tick-box teaching. Where's the creativity and flair?'

This worry about the rise of standardisation and loss of individuality in schools was felt to be a symptom of the corporatisation of teaching, which has contributed to experienced teachers leaving the profession. But, they had all found ways to navigate it: 'I'll have that up [on the board], but that doesn't mean I have to deliver it that way.' So, despite external pressures towards standardisation, teachers find ways to preserve their autonomy and adapt expectations to suit the subject and their students. This theme of gentle renegade professionalism, meeting expectations while remaining true to pedagogical values, shows how experienced teachers navigate policy shifts while maintaining authenticity.

Others pointed to a forced alignment on teaching strategies and techniques, often based on what they felt was poorly understood and implemented cognitive-science research: 'There needs to be more flexibility and common sense in the training system. All lessons having to look the same removes creativity and pushes staff out.' Another added: 'You've got to have a range of tools in your toolbox. I don't think people who stay a long time think in binary ways.' They went on to challenge educational polarisation such as 'traditional' versus 'progressive', instead emphasising the need for flexibility, adaptability and openness. This theme of effortless nuance recurs throughout many of the reflections in these interviews, presenting adaptability, not dogma, as the foundation of longevity in the profession.

As one teacher so succinctly stated, teachers need to have a curiosity about learning and comfort with admitting what they don't know. This openness to learning has helped sustain her interest and prevent stagnation over a long career. She views teaching as a constant opportunity to discover more, both about her subject and her students.

Accountability and toxic leadership

After many years in the classroom, Lena is clear about what almost drove her out of teaching – and what kept her in it. It wasn't the students or the workload alone, but the weight of constant accountability. There were stretches of her career when every lesson felt judged before it began, when spreadsheets and targets seemed to matter more than professional judgement. Teaching narrowed into something defensive, and her confidence wavered. What enabled Lena to stay was a gradual shift in how she related to those pressures. She learned to distinguish between accountability that supported improvement and accountability that simply demanded compliance. By grounding her decisions in her subject knowledge and in what she could see working with her students, she began to push back quietly against performative demands. Reflection and evidence became tools for clarity rather than fear.

Over time, she rebuilt a sense of agency. Teaching stopped feeling like something done to her and returned to something she actively shaped. 'I didn't ignore accountability,' she reflects. 'I learned not to let it hollow out my practice.'

Autonomy

Research from Worth and Van den Brande connects limited teacher autonomy to poorer job satisfaction, perceptions of unmanageable workload and lower intentions to stay in the profession. They highlighted that teachers with lower autonomy are more likely to report unmanageable workload and lower job satisfaction – both of which are strongly associated with intentions to leave teaching – whereas those with autonomy (the ability to influence professional-development goals and aspects of daily work) is positively correlated with job satisfaction and retention.[105] This suggests that systems characterised by tight accountability, low autonomy and heavy performance demands can

105 Worth, J. and Van den Brande, J. (2020) 'Teacher autonomy: how does it relate to job satisfaction and retention?', Slough: NFER [online] Available at: www.nfer.ac.uk/publications/teacher-autonomy-how-does-it-relate-to-job-satisfaction-and-retention (Accessed: 30 April 2026).

worsen teacher wellbeing and contribute to attrition because limited autonomy is tightly linked to these negative workplace experiences.

The drain on wellbeing through accountability was one of the most prevalent threads in almost all the interviews we conducted. None of the teachers we spoke to believed that teachers should have no accountability. As public servants, who are paid by the taxpayer, they were clear that there needs to be some level of accountability to ensure that students are making as much progress as possible; yet all of them recalled the sometimes excessive pressure they felt, which can be explained somewhat by neoliberalism and the marketisation of education.

Neoliberalism and the marketisation of education

Neoliberalism and the marketisation of education in England refer to a set of ideas and policies that apply market-like logics to schools, such as competition, choice, efficiency and consumerism.[106] Originating during Margaret Thatcher's tenure as prime minister, they reshaped how schools and universities are organised, governed and judged.

Neoliberalism emphasises the efficiency of markets, individual choice and competition, and assumes that market mechanisms deliver better outcomes than centrally planned or state-led provision. It often holds that competitiveness and consumer behaviour can improve quality and innovation.[107] This led to the introduction of market principles into the organisation and governance of schools, including:

- school autonomy and competition: where schools are encouraged to compete for students and funding, often through performance measures
- parental choice as a driving force: positioning parents as consumers and schools as providers
- diversity of provision: such as the expansion of academies and free schools that operate with greater independence from local authorities.

These reforms reflect a move away from collective provision and standardised state management towards a market-oriented system where competition and choice are seen as mechanisms for raising

106 Ingleby, E. (2021) *Neoliberalism Across Education: Policy And Practice From Early Childhood Through Adult Learning*. London: Palgrave.

107 Hall, R. and Pulsford, M. (2019) 'Neoliberalism and primary education: Impacts of neoliberal policy on the lived experiences of primary school communities' in *Power and Education*, 11(3), pp.241–251.

standards. These neoliberal policy agendas inflect everyday school life and teacher relationships, of course, by forcing schools to compete with one another and leaders to reshape how success is defined and measured in education, prioritising accountability and outcomes tied to competition rather than collective educational equity. For an already stressed school leader, this level of competition could only lead to an increased sense of anxiety and fear.

Many of the teachers we interviewed were critical of the compliance-driven culture in schools, which they saw as deprofessionalising and counterproductive: 'Leaders are fearful and they've passed that fear on. You then begin to think you're going to be found lacking... that fear comes down through auditing.' Others agreed: 'That whole feeling that result days are something to be afraid of.' This teacher described the nightmares they had weeks before GCSE results day and how they felt demotivated by the punitive, target-driven accountability system. Another recalled the time their results went down one year and they felt that they were 'dragged over hot coals' for it, despite having a great prior track record. When they raised this with their senior leadership team link, they were told: 'The paradigm of being a teacher is different to what it was... and is that a problem for you?' This led to a bigger frustration with the all-encompassing role of being a teacher: 'We're doing everything and now we're even blamed for students not learning. That's not sustainable.'

Accountability

External accountability was a major theme – including public perception and parent–school disconnect. Teachers noted rising hostility on social media and declining parental engagement. Research shows that when teachers perceive positive societal appreciation, it relates to their sense of professional worth, job satisfaction and motivation – all of which are linked in the broader literature to decisions about whether to remain in teaching. A recent study found that societal attitudes towards the teaching profession influence teachers' sense of pride and motivation and can predict job-satisfaction outcomes.[108] Feeling valued by society helps sustain teachers' commitment and can buffer against attrition, particularly in challenging environments where professional respect and status are important for morale.

108 Dreer-Göthe, B. (2025) 'How appreciation predicts teachers' job satisfaction, emotional exhaustion, and quitting intentions' in *Educational Studies*, 51(6), pp.1279–1299.

Another external accountability pressure is Ofsted. At the time of this book being completed, a new framework was just beginning to be rolled out in schools. Already, several leaders have spoken out about their experiences and the rise in the level of scrutiny the inspection brings.[109] There are a lot of anxieties in the sector around the new language of 'needs attention', as it may act as a badge of shame. This new framework follows the tragic death of headteacher Ruth Perry, who took her own life on 8 January 2023, only 54 days after an Ofsted inspection she described as 'rude' and 'intimidating.'[110] The subsequent national fallout understandably caused a lot of resentment between school leaders and the inspectorate, and when Sir Martyn Oliver replaced Amanda Spielman as His Majesty's Chief Inspector, he promised change, pledging that Ofsted must 'help' not 'hinder' leaders.[111]

Despite the pressure many teachers felt during Ofsted inspections, some were defiant: 'We don't gear up for Ofsted. We lead how we want to lead all year. As part of this, our leaders have needed to change the mood music and celebrate teachers – not blame them.' This teacher was grateful that the leaders in her school shielded her staff from performative pressures. By focusing on substance over show, she creates a stable, trusting culture where teachers can do their best work.

Academisation and central teams in academies were sometimes viewed with suspicion, as an unnecessary extra layer of accountability. 'I am worried about autonomy and future changes under our new MAT governance. We joined because it was getting untenable to do the things we had to do as a small, one-form entry primary. But we seem to be overrun by MAT central staff, pulling us in different directions.' Another added: 'We were just completely shut down... our opinions didn't really hold any sway.' This teacher very much felt this was a turning point in their career, where they had experienced the imposition of rigid top-down decisions. She recalls a specific moment when the leadership disregarded the English team's professional input. This episode crystallised a loss of agency and voice, prompting her to consider leaving the profession

109 Rigby, A. (2026) 'What we learned from four Ofsted report card inspections' on *SchoolsWeek* [online] Available at: https://schoolsweek.co.uk/what-we-learned-from-four-ofsted-report-card-inspections (Accessed: 30 April 2026).

110 www.inquest.org.uk/blog/my-sister-ruth-perry

111 The Hoot (2026) '"Ofsted must help, not hinder" – Sir Martyn Oliver on the new framework' [online] Available at: https://thehoot.news/topics/ofsted-must-help-not-hinder-sir-martyn-oliver-on-the-new-framework (Accessed: 30 April 2026).

altogether. This is a key example of how structural disempowerment can corrode commitment.

Toxic leadership

We heard examples of teachers facing bullying behaviour from leaders. Research identifies workplace bullying as repeated, prolonged hostile behaviour with a power imbalance.[112] Workplace bullying in schools can involve school managers and principals as perpetrators against staff, contributing to stress and burnout. Workplace-bullying prevalence among education staff has been documented and linked to job stress and organisational climate.[113] Studies analysing educators' descriptions find that principals or senior leadership are often cited as the main perpetrators of workplace bullying towards teachers, including behaviours such as shouting, humiliation and threats. Victims reported emotional withdrawal, stress and professional disengagement as consequences.[114]

This research shows that bullying emerges from organisational contexts with chaotic leadership, lack of accountability and power imbalances, where leaders can occupy dominant roles in bullying dynamics.[115] One of the teachers we interviewed said: 'I was coached out of my job and made to feel incompetent. I think older teachers are pushed out, not just because they cost more, but because we challenge.' Yet, despite career setbacks, she has remained because she is confident in her professional identity and committed to pushing back against dehumanising trends in education.

Not all teachers are this strong. Another experienced toxic leadership and bullying that ultimately drove him to leave his long-term school: 'It was made quite clear. Doors were going to close in my face and I needed to go.' Despite adversity, his resilience, moral clarity and ability to rebuild in a new context sustained his professional identity.

112 Ariza-Montes, A., Muniz R.N.M., Leal-Rodríguez, A.L. and Leal-Millán, A.G. (2016) 'Workplace Bullying Among Teachers' in *Journal of Occupational and Environmental Medicine*, 58(8), pp.818–827.

113 Ariza-Montes, A., Muniz R.N.M., Leal-Rodríguez, A.L. and Leal-Millán, A.G. (2016) 'Workplace Bullying Among Teachers' in *Journal of Occupational and Environmental Medicine*, 58(8), pp.818–827.

114 De Wet, C. (2014) 'Educators' understanding of workplace bullying' in *South African Journal of Education*, 34(1) [online] Available at: https://files.eric.ed.gov/fulltext/EJ1136350.pdf

115 De Wet, C. (2014) 'Educators' understanding of workplace bullying' in *South African Journal of Education*, 34(1) [online] Available at: https://files.eric.ed.gov/fulltext/EJ1136350.pdf

Abrupt leadership changes often destroy morale, many teachers told us. This often triggered staff departures and reshaped culture negatively. Many provided vivid examples of favouritism and nepotism during internal hiring processes, devaluation of experienced staff during restructures and loss of professional dignity in interview experiences. These episodes highlight how school leadership can make or break retention, particularly for experienced staff. One teacher remembered a harrowing incident that left a culture and legacy of fear for her: a 'leader walked into my room, stopped the lesson, asked everyone to put their pens down, then said "there's no learning going on". I spent most of my maternity leave trying to get a job outside of teaching due to this'. The dehumanising and punitive nature of this leader's accountability system nearly pushed this teacher out of the profession. Unfortunately, this seems to be a common story.

Women, motherhood and family life

After more than a decade in the profession, Aisha can trace the moments when staying in teaching felt most fragile – and the moments that made it possible. Becoming a mother reshaped everything. She remembers returning to work exhausted and uncertain, trying to reconcile the demands of the classroom with the realities of early parenthood. In some schools, flexibility was treated as a favour rather than a right; fulltime expectations returned overnight, and the message was clear: adapt or step aside. Those environments made her question whether teaching could stretch to fit a life beyond school.

What kept Aisha in the profession was encountering leaders who understood that careers unfold in stages. Parttime working, phased returns and open conversations signalled trust rather than doubt. With that support, her confidence grew rather than eroded. Teaching remained demanding, but it became sustainable. 'I didn't lose my ambition when I became a mother,' she says. 'I just needed a profession that recognised I was still a whole person.'

Maternity and paternity

Female teachers shared many experiences with us of how they had needed to negotiate motherhood and teaching. While some felt supported through parttime working and phased returns, others highlighted inflexible cultures that pushed women out. This was highlighted in the 'Missing Mothers' report, which stated that women in their 30s – the largest group leaving teaching annually – are disproportionately mothers, and that workload, lack of flexibility and poor support during and after maternity leave are primary drivers of attrition. It notes that many women leave because schools fail to offer flexibility that is standard in other professions, creating a cycle of attrition that undermines recruitment and retention efforts.[116]

Earlier research by The MaternityTeacher / PaternityTeacher (MTPT) Project documents that among female teachers aged 30–39 who left the profession, around half identified motherhood-related factors (such as juggling work and childcare, inflexible hours and work–family tensions) as contributing to their decision to leave.[117] The motherhood penalty in teaching is not just about individual choices. It reflects structural and cultural barriers in schools that make it hard for mothers to remain in or progress within the profession. Both of this book's authors, Haili and Sam, have experienced this firsthand – as had many of the teachers we interviewed.

A teacher commented: 'As a young mum, I was exhausted. The guilt was quite high. Some flexibility would have made a huge difference.' This phase of her life brought her closest to leaving, as she highlights the lack of structural support for carers and the need for policy changes that honour both professional and personal identities. Another spoke about all the things they had missed out on: 'All of those hours where I could have been in a ball pit, I wasted marking. I will never get that time back. I think younger teachers now aren't as ready to put in the hours as it used to be... and I don't know whether that's a good or bad thing.'

These reflections on workload culture reveal a tension between previous expectations of total commitment and the current generation's pursuit of balance. She seems to admire the boundaries newer teachers set, even as she wrestles with her own historical over-commitment and regrets. Another teacher shared these feelings: 'I've put school first and I regret that. I now tell my mentees, this is a job, not your life.' Another spoke about how she felt that she had been 'passed over for promotion after returning from maternity leave.' She highlights structural inflexibility

116 The New Britain Project (2024) 'Missing Mothers' [online] Available at: www.newbritain.org.uk/missing-mothers (Accessed: 30 April 2026).

117 The MTPT Project (2021) 'Doing the Washing Up Badly' [online] Available at: www.mtpt.org.uk/light-research (Accessed: 13 May 2026).

and gendered expectations as ongoing barriers she has constantly faced. Another detailed that she'd had to make the difficult decision to step away from leadership: 'It was fine to be teaching, but the extra responsibility was just physically too much.' This conscious decision to step back from leadership responsibilities when her children were young and health issues emerged reflects a broader critique of the system's limited respect for those who choose sustained classroom excellence over hierarchical advancement.

Female experiences

Navigating these periods that seem most to affect women, including menopause, meant that teachers had needed to create boundaries for themselves and have guilt-free time off: 'Sometimes you just have to prioritise your own life. Go home at 3:00 and don't feel guilty.' Another agreed: 'That's how I'm still here. I made my job doable by keeping boundaries; no more weekends, no more late nights.' This teacher feels they made a pivotal decision: no more taking work home. She arrives early, finishes tasks during school hours and protects her personal time fiercely. Her sustainability ethos illustrates how long-term teachers can survive and thrive without self-sacrifice.

Family life

Some male teachers we interviewed spoke of the pressures of balancing teaching with family life or caring responsibilities: 'Other than some planning, I don't do anything else outside of school anymore. I come in early and I'm done by 5:00.' In recent years, he has consciously reshaped his workload, focusing on efficiency and sustainability. He now uses whole-class feedback and efficient marking strategies, setting a model for how teachers can adapt over time to prevent burnout.

Professional development

After more than 15 years in the classroom, Mark is clear about what made the difference between staying in teaching and quietly planning an exit. It wasn't a lighter timetable or fewer challenges, but the quality of his professional learning. He recalls long stretches where CPD felt generic and disconnected from his subject, delivered to him rather than shaped with him. In those moments, teaching began to feel static, as though his expertise had plateaued.

What changed was encountering CPD that treated him as a practitioner, not a novice. Subject-specific sessions led by colleagues, time to collaborate on curriculum and space to refine his craft at a stage-appropriate level reignited his sense of purpose. Learning became collective and sustained, not episodic. His confidence deepened alongside his competence. 'I stayed,' Mark reflects, 'because I was still learning – and because that learning mattered to my classroom.'

High-quality, subject-specific CPD is a key retention factor cited in research on teacher retention.[118] A systematic review of research on CPD found that participation in well-designed CPD initiatives correlates with increased teacher job satisfaction and a greater likelihood of remaining within the profession, and that structures such as personalised pathways and collaborative-learning communities significantly contribute to retention.[119] Evidence given at the UK Education Committee's retention review explicitly noted that improving CPD and up-to-date pedagogical training relevant to different career stages is part of successful retention strategies.[120] Often, CPD in schools does not seem to take into account

118 Education Endowment Foundation (2023) 'Three takeaways from the evidence on improving teacher recruitment and retention' [online] Available at: https://educationendowmentfoundation.org.uk/news/eef-blog-three-takeaways-from-the-evidence-on-improving-teacher-recruitment-and-retention (Accessed: 30 April 2026).

119 Rajendran, J., Santhi, J. and Kumar Chauhan, R.K. (2023) 'The Impact of Continuous Professional Development on Teacher Retention and Performance' in *Journal of Harbin Engineering University*, 44(8), pp.1348–1356.

120 UK Parliament 'Continuing professional development' [online] Available at: https://publications.parliament.uk/pa/cm201617/cmselect/cmeduc/199/19909.htm (Accessed: 30 April 2026).

career stage and can be a bit 'one size fits all'. This can be frustrating for more experienced teachers, who told us they see training go and then come back round again with a different name.

One teacher of almost 30 years felt that CPD had not really kept him in the classroom: 'Sometimes no CPD is better than bad CPD. We still do what all schools do – chasing silver bullets.' He is critical of the profession's tendency to overreact to accountability pressure, and values meaningful CPD and strategic focus while being disillusioned by superficial or performative initiatives. Another was sceptical of initiatives lauded as the next big thing in teacher development, saying about instructional coaching: 'Up until recently, it's all generic... most of it is rubbish.' This teacher felt that sticking to certain pre-decided teaching moves and steps, with no contextualisation, was patronising and ineffective. This reveals a need for more bespoke, practitioner-driven approaches.

Another interviewee recalled a time when teachers had access to rich, sustained CPD, such as 10-day maths courses and week-long art residencies. She contrasts this with today's fragmented, performative training, calling for more meaningful, collaborative and enriching professional learning to help retain passionate teachers. This was echoed by other teachers, one of whom drew a clear distinction between 'sticking-plaster CPD' and the deep, sustained learning experiences that have re-engaged him. His positive experience with courses including the National Professional Qualification for Senior Leadership (NPQSL), Exemplary Leadership and operational business apprenticeships gave him both intellectual challenge and practical tools, contributing to his renewed professional energy: 'The one-day stuff with a nice lunch didn't do much. But year-long leadership and evidence-informed CPD changed everything for me.' There was lots of criticism of this 'one and done' or 'inspirational' teacher development, with teachers being critical of generic CPD, describing it as demotivating for experienced teachers.

Due to a lack of relevant and effective professional development in schools, teachers have needed to seek other ways of nourishing themselves professionally. For many, this comes down to a thirst for learning that they feel all long-serving teachers must possess. One teacher commented: 'I had no training... so I had to build my own induction. All my CPD has always been around my subject.' Starting without formal training forced him to become a self-directed learner. This autonomy fostered curiosity, ownership and agency – all key ingredients in a long, motivated teaching career.

Another's drive for continuous growth has protected her from stagnation. She seeks intellectually stimulating CPD and avoids passive compliance with educational fads. Yet another teacher travelled around the world and taught in different countries: 'I've made my work really interesting. I've never stayed stagnant.' And another teacher describes herself as a 'frustrated academic' and as 'eternally curious'. She crafts her own CPD journey through reading widely and deeply, using video tools such as IRIS for self-reflection and leading and participating in twilights. This intellectual autonomy has kept her teaching vibrant and relevant. Her ability to self-direct growth is a key factor in her sustained passion.

This theme of self-directed growth was also highlighted by another teacher we interviewed, who said: 'The Chartered College still teaches me something every time I open the website… that's crazy after so many years doing this job!' She critiques prior CPD as 'latest bandwagon'-driven, but describes the school's recent evidence-informed approach, especially their partnership with the Chartered College of Teaching, as transformational. This suggests that ongoing learning and subject-relevant CPD play a crucial role in motivating experienced teachers to stay intellectually engaged and professionally fulfilled.

Others cited social-media networks where they have been given the opportunity to connect with other teachers and schools as transformational: 'I honestly think my career was made from Twitter: the connections I made, research schools. It gave me the opportunity to be constantly outward-looking.' Another described these experiences as the 'professional oxygen' necessary to remain energised in the long-term: 'All of those things have filled my classroom work; they've not taken me away from it.'

Subject-specific professional-development opportunities came up time and time again in the interviews as powerful experiences for teachers: 'The opportunity to go back and focus on an area would just refire people in their subjects.' Indeed, this teacher suggested that there should be a state-funded sabbatical system to refresh teachers' disciplinary identity. She believes that access to university study, research or cultural immersion could profoundly support retention for mid- and late-career teachers.

Some teachers spoke about how their schools had got it right, with leaders advocating for a more personal, developmental approach rooted in coaching and subject-specific collaboration. In this system, they felt that experienced teachers were trusted to lead and influence others:

'We're a school that really believes in succession planning. Many of us arrived here inexperienced and grew into leadership.' Another teacher spoke about how leaders treated professional development with the same intentionality as a curriculum. They explained that professional development is delivered bi-weekly via shortened days and is based on classroom observations and staff needs. Topics are adapted to suit departmental and career-stage priorities, and staff are given agency in choosing themes.

Another teacher highlighted the importance of dialogue-based, in-situ learning. She values networking and collaboration through formal programmes such as NPQSL, which she described as particularly stimulating before the pandemic, although the loss of face-to-face CPD has, in her view, diminished the profession's intellectual energy.

Another teacher highlighted the power of peer-led developmental models: 'We did peer observations using IRIS... and had a whole departmental day on how we did demonstrations.' This approach fostered a shared culture of continuous improvement, where feedback was collegial rather than punitive, while a different teacher spoke about how leaders in the school had worked hard to support developing internal capacity through a structured instructional-coaching programme based on Jim Knight's model, delivered by trained peer coaches. This was supported by subject-specific CPD cycles involving academics and resource development and creating 'pipeline roles' to provide developmental leadership opportunities for experienced staff without pulling them out of teaching.

Sadly, though, there were many teachers we questioned who felt they had not been given useful professional-development opportunities. 'I've skimmed the surface of a lot of PD and schools haven't actively invested in helping me do it. I really want to do a Master's but haven't found a school willing to support it yet.' Here, this teacher expresses frustration at the lack of targeted CPD investment. Most of his professional growth came from extracurricular activities such as scouting, language skills and self-directed learning. He notes systemic barriers that are put up against teachers if they decide that they do not want to go into a leadership role.

This was mirrored by another teacher we interviewed, who added: 'Once I hit about 15 years and it was clear I wasn't going to be head of department, I dropped down the list.' This lack of opportunity for professional growth is, in her view, a key risk factor for attrition, particularly for mid- and late-career teachers. The opportunity for professional development to be interest-driven and subject-specific was frequently acknowledged, and it is this respect for autonomy that they felt had kept them motivated and evolving. Another interviewee added: 'When someone believes in you and gives you a chance, it makes all the difference.'

Many teachers felt a frustration that there weren't more professional-development opportunities that catered to teachers who wanted to hone their craft and remain in the classroom, rather than climbing the ladder to leadership: 'There's a problem in schools with what we do as a system with people like me; how do we harness our years and years of experience?' She expresses frustration at being managed by less-experienced staff, and a lack of meaningful developmental pathways. Though she would enjoy mentoring or leading pedagogical development, this work is not incentivised or resourced.

Another added: 'There isn't a structure like in the NHS where you can be an expert teacher and feel rewarded and recognised for that.' Another teacher noted that, to keep experienced teachers, schools must create varied pathways for those who wish to develop without necessarily moving into formal leadership: 'Every three or four years, they've given me something new to do to push me out of my comfort zone. You can lead working groups, be a research lead, literacy lead... schools just need to be creative.'

Love of subject

For Tom, the decision to remain in teaching was never really a decision at all. Even when the pressures of the job mounted – new initiatives, heavier workloads, the steady churn of change – what drew him back each day was the subject itself. In quieter moments, he noticed that the parts of the job that exhausted him were rarely the lessons; it was everything that sat around them. The classroom, by contrast, remained a place of intellectual energy. Years into his career, that connection only deepened. Teaching allowed him to keep thinking, reading, questioning – never quite reaching the end of what his subject had to offer. Students' misconceptions sparked curiosity rather than frustration; their insights sent him back to his own understanding. 'I didn't stay because it was easy,' Tom reflects. 'I stayed because my subject still mattered to me and teaching meant I never had to stop learning it.'

Studies using teaching-motivation scales repeatedly identify subject interest and intrinsic passion for teaching as key motivational patterns – not only for entering teaching, but also for ongoing engagement and professional commitment. For example, research summarised in 'teachers' motivation to choose teaching and remain' shows that intrinsic motivations such as passion for teaching a subject are among the reasons some teachers remain engaged in the profession.[121] Also, work on teacher motivation consistently highlights that love of subject, enjoyment of teaching it and the fulfilment teachers derive both from content and student interaction are closely connected with job satisfaction and occupational commitment.[122] In the interviews we conducted, love of subject seemed to be a common and recurrent theme that teachers cited for helping them remain in the profession long-term.

Comments such as: 'I love my subject and I want everyone else to love English' and: 'It was really to do with passing on the passion for my subject – I know it's something where I can make a difference' show that these teachers feel that their intrinsic motivation, rooted in subject love and student impact, forms the bedrock of their professional longevity. Another teacher added: 'I don't think my subject is more important than anyone else's. But no subject is more important than mine either. When art is valued by the school, by the students and by the parents – that's what keeps me.' This teacher has stayed in a school where her subject has been seen as integral, not peripheral. When schools diminish the arts, she has moved on. Subject value equals professional worth.

Not only does love of subject help teachers to remain in the profession, it is also a main driver for them entering the profession in the first place. From the outset, one teacher described a strong intellectual passion for English literature as a driver for entering and staying in the profession. She framed teaching as an extension of her academic joy and sees the act of teaching itself as inherently rewarding, especially when students are intellectually engaged: 'I became a teacher because I wanted to talk

121 Onyefulu, C., Madalinska-Michalak, J. and Bavli, B. (2022) 'Teachers' motivation to choose teaching and remain in the profession: A comparative mixed methods study in Jamaica, Poland and Turkey' in *Power and Education*, 15(1), pp.37–65.

122 O'Reilly, P.E. (2014) 'Teachers at Work: Factors Influencing Satisfaction, Retention and the Professional Well-Being of Elementary and Secondary Educators', City University of New York [online] Available at: https://academicworks.cuny.edu/cgi/viewcontent.cgi?article=1087&context=gc_etds& (Accessed: 30 April 2026).

about books and get paid for it and inspire other people.' Another stated that his career in teaching is fundamentally grounded in his love for his subject (and the relationships that this helps him build with students). He highlighted the day-to-day joy of students thanking him after lessons and voluntarily spending time in his classroom during breaks. These affirmations of impact provide a powerful emotional anchor, especially during difficult times.

Many highlighted that classroom teaching enables them to stay connected to this passion, giving them purpose and emotional engagement that sustains them through challenges. One teacher in particular warned of what can happen when this connection is lost: 'Some of my ECTs end up teaching outside of their specialism. Their enthusiasm just dissipates.' This teacher strongly believes subject expertise is vital for retention. Teaching out of specialism has drained the enthusiasm of her mentees, and she feels fortunate to have remained an English specialist throughout her career, protecting her passion and confidence.

Professional agency

For nearly 28 years, Helen has taught through waves of reform, policy shifts and changing expectations. She remembers periods when teaching felt increasingly constrained, when scripts, targets and policies narrowed her professional judgement. Those moments were the hardest. What sustained her was not compliance, but agency. In schools where she was trusted to make decisions about pedagogy and assessment, teaching regained its meaning. She could adapt lessons to her students, exercise her subject expertise and respond thoughtfully rather than mechanically. That autonomy shaped how she saw herself: not as a deliverer of policy, but as a professional with responsibility and judgement. Even when external pressures intensified, the freedom to decide how learning happened made the work sustainable. 'I could still think,' she reflects. 'I could still choose.' That sense of ownership kept her invested, curious and committed – long after others had left.

The terms *teacher autonomy* and *teacher agency* are often used interchangeably, but in research they mean distinct (though related)

things. The difference matters, especially when thinking about teacher retention.

Autonomy

Teacher autonomy refers to the degree of freedom or discretion teachers are granted within a system. It is usually structural or formal, conferred by policy, leadership or organisation, and is about granting teachers permission. Examples include teachers being given freedom to choose teaching methods, control over assessment practices and flexibility in curriculum enactment. Essentially, autonomy answers the question 'What am I allowed to decide?' It is about formal freedom or discretion granted to teachers to make pedagogical choices in their work. Yet, a teacher can be given autonomy, but that alone does not guarantee meaningful professional action.[123] Indeed, structural features of the English system significantly constrain autonomy for teachers, so that perhaps it is not possible. These include:

- high-stakes accountability (Ofsted, performance data, league tables), which narrows acceptable practice
- centralised curriculum and assessment expectations (national curriculum, GCSEs, exam boards), which limit decision-making
- MAT structures, which often standardise pedagogy, curriculum and assessment to ensure consistency.

As a result, most teachers cannot freely decide what to teach, how success is measured and which pedagogies are legitimate. This means autonomy as complete professional discretion is largely incompatible with the English system, and some might debate whether teachers, as professionals who are public servants, should be granted full autonomy anyway.

Agency

However, *teacher agency* may be compatible with the system. It refers to a teacher's capacity to act purposefully and make meaningful professional choices within (and sometimes despite) constraints. Drawing on Priestley, Biesta & Robinson,[124] agency is:

123 Lennert da Silva, A.L. and Mølstad, C.E. (2020) 'Teacher autonomy and teacher agency: a comparative study in Brazilian and Norwegian lower secondary education' in *The Curriculum Journal*, 31, pp.115–131.

124 Biesta, G., Priestley, M. and Robinson, S. (2015) 'The role of beliefs in teacher agency' in *Teachers and Teaching*, 21(6), pp.624–640.

- ecological (shaped by context, culture and conditions)
- temporal (influenced by past experience, present context and future goals)
- relational (enabled or constrained by leadership, trust and professional culture).

Agency answers the question 'Am I able to act professionally in ways that matter?' Teachers can exercise agency, even in low-autonomy environments, for example by interpreting policy thoughtfully; conversely, teachers can lack agency even when autonomy exists, due to fear, lack of confidence or punitive cultures. The key distinction is that *autonomy = freedom* and *agency = purposeful action*. Interestingly, policies often focus on increasing autonomy, assuming agency will follow. Research shows this is not automatic.[125] Agency depends on trust, professional identity, competence and supportive conditions, not just permission. Therefore, you can give a teacher autonomy, but the culture and conditions in a school must be purposefully created to enable agency.

Lack of agency

Many of the teachers we interviewed spoke about the lack of agency they felt during certain times of their career. One interviewee described the implementation across their school of teaching strategies from a book, where retrieval activities labelled as 'Do Now' were mandated at the start of every single lesson, with senior leaders prowling the halls checking that teachers were all complying: 'I often felt that decisions were already made for me before I entered the room; my role was reduced to implementing them rather than exercising any professional judgement.'

Another spoke about when they joined a Multi-Academy Trust and an off-the-shelf curriculum was enforced across English in the Trust: 'There was no space to adapt lessons to the pupils in front of me – I was expected to follow the script, even when it clearly wasn't working.' They recalled teachers being checked up on throughout lessons by the curriculum leader, who would walk down the corridor and check what slide everybody was on at what time. They added: 'Over time, I stopped thinking professionally and focused on compliance, because thinking critically didn't seem to be valued or welcomed. It became exhausting

125 Biesta, G., Priestley, M. and Robinson, S. (2015) 'The role of beliefs in teacher agency' in *Teachers and Teaching*, 21(6), pp.624–640.

having to justify every small decision, even when the outcomes were positive and students were learning well.'

Professional agency

In schools where teachers had stayed, they spoke about how they had been given decision-making powers on what went on in their classrooms, even if they had an aligned curriculum: 'Being trusted to make pedagogical decisions made me feel like a professional again, rather than someone simply delivering someone else's ideas.' Despite sharing planning with the rest of the department, it was expected that this teacher would adapt the resources for her class context and be able to conduct the learning at their own pace.

Another spoke about using the WalkThrus strategies and how they had been told that they'd be expected to adapt the techniques for their own class and phase: 'Having autonomy over how I teach restored my confidence and motivation, and reminded me why I entered the profession in the first place. I stayed because I was allowed to use my judgement and adapt my practice, not just follow instructions handed down from above.'

Systems and routines

For 19 years, Ben has taught in the same school, a rarity even he sometimes reflects on with surprise. What keeps him there is not a lack of challenge, but the presence of reliable systems. From the start, expectations were clear: routines were consistent, policies stable and changes introduced thoughtfully rather than reactively. This predictability created space for him to focus on teaching rather than constantly recalibrating to new demands. Over time, those systems became a source of professional security. Behaviour routines worked, assessment processes were understood and support structures were dependable. Because the foundations held steady, Ben could refine his practice year on year instead of reinventing it. The school felt calm, purposeful and coherent. 'I knew where I stood,' he says. 'That consistency meant I could concentrate on getting better at my job, not surviving it.'

Research on school climate – the overall quality of school life, including safety, norms and organisational routines, consistently finds associations with teacher retention. Positive school climate, characterised by clear expectations and routines, is associated with higher teacher engagement and satisfaction that, in turn, predict retention.[126] Research by the Learning Policy Institute, which analyses teacher working conditions, explicitly finds that leadership, climate and clear organisational routines are significant predictors of retention,[127] while Tom Bennett's independent review of behaviour in schools (commissioned by the UK government) argues that consistent behaviour policies and routines optimise staff wellbeing and retention by reducing stress and saving time – factors teachers report as central to decisions to stay or leave.[128] This research was very much echoed by the lived experience of the teachers we interviewed.

One teacher described his school's recent journey from instability and underperformance to a much more cohesive, mission-driven institution. He stated that there were times when 'you couldn't tell the difference between lesson time and lunchtime', signalling the absence of clear structure and expectations. A cultural transformation has given him the emotional and instructional bandwidth to focus on teaching – reducing feelings of burnout and reinforcing his professional identity. He described how leadership implemented behavioural clarity, with shared scripting, common language and consistent application of rules. There is also strong pastoral and leadership backing for all staff during behaviour incidents. Another teacher agreed, saying that 'predictability supports our most vulnerable learners and staff'. This environment has empowered staff to focus on teaching, not firefighting.

Another teacher has recently considered leaving because systems are not clear and consistent. They add: 'Improved behaviour systems and

126 Cohen, J., McCabe,E., Michelli, N.M. and Pickeral, T. (2009) 'School Climate: Research, Policy, Teacher Education and Practice' in *Teachers College Record*, 111, pp.180–213.

127 Berry, B., Bastian, K.C., Darling-Hammond, L. and Kini, T. (2019) 'How Teaching and Learning Conditions Affect Teacher Retention and School Performance in North Carolina' [online] Available at: https://learningpolicyinstitute.org/sites/default/files/product-files/Leandro_Working_Conditions_REPORT.pdf (Accessed: 30 April 2026).

128 Bennett, T. (2017) 'Creating a Culture: How school leaders can optimise behaviour' [online] Available at: https://assets.publishing.service.gov.uk/media/5a7506e4ed915d3c7d529cec/Tom_Bennett_Independent_Review_of_Behaviour_in_Schools.pdf (Accessed: 30 April 2026).

a more balanced accountability model would make the profession more attractive and sustainable. We need to enshrine the right to disruption-free learning. If you don't, teachers are held accountable for outcomes they can't fully control.'

This conscious crafting of culture may become even more vital in the fight to retain our most expert teachers. Evidence from various sources suggests that poor behaviour in schools has risen. The NASUWT Teachers' Union has reported a rise in violence and abuse,[129] and Ofsted has also highlighted an increase in disruptive behaviour within schools.[130] They found that this is especially true of persistent low-level disruption in class, such as students refusing to do what they are told or talking back to teachers.[131]

Throughout all this thematic analysis, it has been clear that what leaders do really matters. This includes deliberate recruitment and retention strategies they may have created – which is our final theme.

---

129 NASUWT 'Violence and Abuse of Teachers on the Rise' [online] Available at: www.nasuwt.org.uk/article-listing/violence-and-abuse-of-teachers-on-the-rise.html

130 Ofsted (2023) 'The Annual Report of His Majesty's Chief Inspector of Education, Children's Services and Skills 2022/23' [online] Available at: https://assets.publishing.service.gov.uk/media/655f2551c39e5a001392e4ca/31587_Ofsted_Annual_Report_2022-23_WEB.pdf (Accessed: 30 April 2026).

131 Maisey, R. (2024) 'A deep dive into behaviour in schools' on Nuffield Foundation [online] Available at: www.nuffieldfoundation.org/news/a-deep-dive-into-behaviour-in-schools (Accessed: 30 April 2026).

Deliberate recruitment and retention strategies

For Claire, staying in teaching was never about sheer endurance. There were points in her career when the demands felt heavy – new initiatives, personal responsibilities, the quiet fatigue that can build over time. What made the difference was how her school responded. Leaders noticed when pressure was rising and acted early: flexible timetables during difficult periods, protected time for professional learning and open conversations about workload rather than silent expectation.

Those strategies signalled something important – that her presence mattered. Support was practical rather than performative, and retention was treated as an ongoing commitment, not a crisis response. As a result, Claire felt able to grow rather than simply cope. Her confidence deepened, her practice sharpened and her sense of belonging strengthened. 'They didn't just ask me to stay,' she reflects. 'They made it possible.'

It is no secret that, in the last decade, many schools have found it difficult to recruit and retain high-quality teachers. One of the leaders we interviewed said: 'I've never known anything like it… zero applicants for English posts, where there used to be 30.' But they added that they have spent time 'crafting a compelling, values-driven school culture that attracts and retains through authenticity, not perks'. One of these strategies was adopting a stance of early transparency to build buy-in. By showing the school's real culture during recruitment, this Head ensures new staff are already aligned with expectations and ethos: 'All interview candidates observe the day and walk the building. It's got to be right for them, and right for us.'

Another teacher told how their leaders try to support their workload through employing 'academic support assistants' who 'create differentiated resources for teachers'. Long-term, 'they also serve as a recruitment pipeline into teaching'. This means that support staff aren't just a stopgap; they are embedded into the teaching process, helping to reduce planning load while also offering a growth route into teaching. It's both efficient and developmental. Another teacher told us about his school's robust package of structural supports they've implemented to retain teachers, which include:

- enhanced pay through Trust-wide scales
- doubling of planning, preparation and assessment (PPA / non-contact) time
- flexible scheduling (for example guaranteed late starts or early finishes)
- additional planning days beyond INSET
- introduction of two personal days annually for life admin or wellbeing needs.

These innovations signal that retention is a leadership priority in this school, not an afterthought. Teachers seemed very happy with these changes, and the teacher claimed that 'we break every government statistic in the book for retention. Eight or nine people have even returned after leaving'.

Conclusion

The findings suggest that teacher retention is multidimensional. It depends on a complex interplay of personal purpose, relational cultures, leadership behaviours, structural conditions and professional agency. It also depends on some of the wider barriers in society – particularly when it comes to the retention of people of colour. In our focus groups, we interviewed teachers who spoke passionately about this. We believe understanding this issue is vital. Therefore, we have included the following chapter exploring this theme in more depth, which starts with an exploration of some recent research on this issue.

CHAPTER SIX:

Retention of teachers from marginalised ethnic groups

Research review

Research by the National Foundation for Educational Research (NFER) says retention of teachers from marginalised ethnic groups is shaped by general pressures that affect everyone, as well as additional race-related pressures that schools often underestimate. Indeed, retention is lower for people of colour compared with white teachers. The review notes this is partly because teachers from marginalised ethnic groups are more concentrated in London, where retention is lower for all teachers, but some gaps remain even after accounting for region, age and experience.[132]

Workload is a major driver of leaving for all groups, but people of colour also report three additional 'push' factors:

- overt and covert racial discrimination from staff, students and parents
- disillusionment about being able to make a difference (particularly for students from marginalised backgrounds)
- lack of progression opportunities.

All these experiences were also described to us by teachers in our interviews.

The NFER review highlights a 'hidden workload' for teachers from marginalised ethnic groups: managing microaggressions, stereotyping, exclusion and the risk of being labelled 'aggressive' if they challenge racism. This obviously has a huge effect on wellbeing, satisfaction and progression. Indeed, the review implies retention is also undermined by blocked progression – including racialised role expectations that limit advancement. Colleagues say that this can make staying feel like 'treading water'.

132 Sharp, C. and Aston, K. (2024) 'Ethnic diversity in the teaching workforce: evidence review', Slough: NFER [online] Available at: www.nfer.ac.uk/publications/ethnic-diversity-in-the-teaching-workforce-evidence-review (Accessed: 30 April 2026).

This is why school culture and leadership composition matter. The review highlights that schools with more diverse senior leadership teams are associated with higher retention rates for people of colour, likely because diversity both signals and supports a more equitable culture, as well as providing much-needed navigation and support.

Another recent paper examined patterns of marginalised ethnic groups' underrepresentation and where teachers are deployed across England (2015–2021).[133] It used aggregated datasets to map disproportionality by region, local authority, phase and role. It notes that, although applications to teacher-training from marginalised ethnic groups have increased, they have lower acceptance rates, worse employment outcomes after training and higher dropout from the profession. It also highlights that people of colour are reported elsewhere as more likely to move schools and less likely to be promoted into leadership. Both these dynamics can damage retention by disrupting stability and limiting long-term career prospects. This again highlights that retention problems sit within a wider pipeline and progression picture, where inequities in entry, early-career outcomes and advancement combine with higher mobility and dropout patterns to sustain under-representation, especially in leadership.

It is due to these systemic barriers and issues that retaining teachers from marginalised ethnic groups in England depends less on generic retention levers alone and more on addressing racism, leadership culture and progression barriers. This is also highlighted in a report by the Institute of Education at University College London.[134] Like the other research summarised here, this report reveals that retention is lower for people of colour than for white British teachers nationally; the report cautions that recruitment on its own won't fix shortages if people continue to leave, claiming that this is a revolving-door dynamic.

In interviews for the report, racism and associated inequalities sit at the forefront of retention decisions, more than workload. Teachers describe both overt racism and covert microaggressions as damaging wellbeing, satisfaction and progression. Again, like other research, the

133 Gorard, S., Chen, W., Tan, Y., Huat See, B., Gazmuri, C., Tereshchenko, A., Demie, F. and Siddiqui, N. (2023) 'The disproportionality of ethnic minority teachers in England: trends, patterns, and problems', *Routledge Open Res*, 2(13), pp.1–31.

134 Tereshchenko, A., Mills, M. and Bradbury, A. (2020) 'Making progress? Employment and retention of BAME teachers in England', London: UCL Institute of Education [online] Available at: https://discovery.ucl.ac.uk/id/eprint/10117331/1/IOE_Report_BAME_Teachers.pdf (Accessed: 13 May 2026).

report introduces the idea of a hidden workload, where teachers from marginalised ethnic groups carry the same high workload as everyone else, plus the cumulative effort of navigating racism, leading to a racial battle fatigue, which also contributes to burnout, turnover and attrition. Racial literacy and explicit equity leadership matter. The report suggests leaders who rely on 'colour-blind' approaches can worsen climate and make schools feel hostile or unsafe for people of colour. For experienced teachers from marginalised ethnic groups, the single barrier to retention is stalled career progression – a 'glass ceiling' that becomes more visible over time, with senior promotions perceived as less accessible.

In July 2025, the Teaching Commission published a report based on 18 months of hearing expert testimonies about the retention crisis in England's schools. The commission was led by Baroness Mary Bousted, and was made up of a range of teachers, leaders and wider sector representation from higher education, policy and teaching unions. The report highlighted that a clear representation gap sits behind retention concerns.[135] It notes that, while around 37% of primary and 36% of secondary students are from marginalised ethnic backgrounds, only 10% of teachers identify as black, Asian or mixed heritage; therefore, the workforce does not reflect the student population.

It states that discrimination is a significant retention pressure, citing evidence that 28% of teachers from marginalised ethnic groups reported workplace discrimination as a major source of stress – around three times the rate for white teachers – positioning this as a driver of attrition and reduced wellbeing. It also states that policy silence on race undermines retention, as key national policies and frameworks such as the Teachers' Standards, the Initial Teacher Training and Early Career Framework (ITTECF) and the Ofsted inspection framework often don't explicitly name race, racism or antiracism, which signals that racism is not a priority and allows structural barriers to persist. Not only does this affect recruitment and retention, but it also impacts on racial literacy across the system.

Like the other research, the commission's report highlights that problems begin at entry and continue across careers. It describes trainees experiencing racism and microaggressions on placements and sometimes being told it's 'part of the experience'; this links to later patterns of blocked progression and continued discrimination, arguing

135 Teaching Commission (2025) 'Shaping the future of teaching' [online] Available at: https://teachingcommission.co.uk/report (Accessed: 30 April 2026).

the issue is not a lack of applicants but a system that fails to support and retain them.

Leadership representation and culture are also key levers. The report argues that diversity in leadership is powerful for recruitment and retention, but warns against tokenism and describes the added emotional labour of being 'the only one', plus microaggressions and repeated legitimacy-testing, calling this a structural, not a pipeline, issue.

The report also gives some suggestions to improve retention, recommending that a comprehensive antiracism framework in ITT and schools should be introduced and that training on antiracism should be embedded in partnerships. It also suggests that schools should ensure clear reporting routes and specialist handling of complaints, and should train mentors and tutors in antiracist, culturally competent, trauma-informed support.

As this book went to press, Mission 44 had funded a four-year-long project with Being Luminary, the Chartered College of Teaching and Chiltern Learning Trust: 'The Increasing Diversity in ITT' project. The project is focused on dismantling the systemic barriers that trainee teachers from marginalised ethnic groups face throughout the ITT journey, from application to leadership. The project aims to provide support, training and resources to strengthen the practice of School-Centred ITT providers (SCITTs) and placement schools – a move that is much needed and will no doubt contribute to a fairer education system for all.

Teachers' stories

Testimony about the retention of teachers from marginalised ethnic groups carries particular weight when it comes from those with lived experience, because it names realities that are often invisible to colleagues who don't live them. Retention isn't about only workload or pay; it's also about belonging, credibility, safety and the daily accumulation of small signals that say 'you're welcome here' or 'you're on probation'. People who have navigated these conditions can describe the texture of them: the extra scrutiny on behaviour management, the pressure to represent a whole community, the emotional labour of challenging bias, the isolation of being 'the only one' and the way promotion pathways can narrow when you're not read as leadership material.

When white teachers speak *for* these experiences, even with good intentions, the message can become softened, misframed or filtered through what feels comfortable to hear. It risks turning structural harm into individual misunderstanding. Prioritising lived-experience testimony corrects an imbalance of epistemic authority: it recognises that those closest to the problem hold the clearest knowledge of how it operates and what would meaningfully change it. This is why, as well as including the interviews we did with teachers from marginalised ethnic groups in our thematic review, we also reproduce three key transcript interviews without editing here. It is key that we read their experiences in their own words.

This doesn't mean white teachers have no role. They do: to listen without defensiveness; to amplify without appropriating; to challenge patterns in hiring, mentoring, timetabling, discipline and progression; and to take accountability for changing culture. There are some schools out there who are doing this work, and we have included a case study from a Trust in the North East to share their good practice at the end of Chapter 12.

But the compass should be set by those who can say, with specificity, what retention feels like from the inside and what conditions would make staying a realistic, healthy choice. Centring that testimony is not an act of exclusion; it's a commitment to accuracy and justice that matches the lived truth of the people schools most need to keep.

We want to thank Allana, Yamina and Amjad personally for giving up their time and energy to share their thoughts and experiences with us, as they are so often called upon to educate others – an act that can be exhausting in itself.

Allana Gay: former secondary senior leader, primary headteacher, education consultant and cofounder of BAMEed

I think a big part of the reason we have such terrible retention rates of black and global majority teachers is structural. So the profession tries to diversify without ensuring that they've created an inclusive environment for diversification; they see diversity as the outcome, as opposed to inclusion happening as the main action that they need to take. I think, because of that, people are walking into environments that are not prepared to host them, and they're expected to get on and just be like everyone else when, in reality, your experiences are not like everyone else's. Your individuality is pulled away.

I think it's also high risk for people from global majority heritage to be in some education spaces across the UK – especially now in the current political climate that we have – and that means that, if you're not somewhere where you're going to have a community, that's willing to surround you, you also don't feel that psychological safety. Then you hear of the experiences of others who have gone into those environments: been targeted, been harassed, faced lots of microaggressions, been blamed for things, been pigeonholed into doing behaviour, and specific classes – the low-achieving classes, and dragging them through and getting no real credit and valuation of their work – it disheartens others.

That's at the teacher level, at the leadership level; I just think that the expectations to perform and be continually on high performance is higher for those from global majority heritage simply because the level of scrutiny is higher. The things you can get away with, or the things that you receive some bits of empathy towards are much, much fewer and you are judged very much on performance. You are also blamed very easily for most of the things that can be taken for granted by some of my white colleagues. So, that then leads to a lot of frustration for those leaders and they also exit the profession.

This is both systemic and societal. There is a public perception when you have someone who looks different, or is from a different culture or a different ethnicity, coming into a space that has been traditionally white. So, we do need to recognise that, across a profession where the headteachers have traditionally been white, that is what people expect. If they imagine a headteacher, they're going to imagine a white, in most cases male, coming up to sort the school out and put it in order and then have lots of females around him who are scurrying about doing the work that they do.

When you are from a global majority heritage, you have the usual responsibility of leadership, but you have that added responsibility of representing your race, because how you are perceived is going to create assumptions about leaders who look like you, or who come from your background. So, you feel like you're that representation and therefore you have that pressure from both sides to represent in a system that is very standardised and inflexible in what a leader should look like and how a leader should behave. That's evidenced by our National Professional Qualifications, where there isn't any attention paid to individuality or personality or inclusion. The fact that there is not any attention paid to cultural contribution in leadership and in ECT level at any point across government training is an indicator of how much that's valued within the school. So, therefore you don't have that valuation and you're expected to fit into the framework as opposed to the framework being flexible and accommodating and accessible so that you can grow within the framework.

Despite this, most teachers will stay for the students. If the students and the student population are very open, accommodating, friendly and they get on really well with them, then the teachers are more likely to remain to try to make change happen.

I think there's an underlying difficulty when it comes to relationships with staff in some places, simply because it depends on that member of staff's experience and how they perceive the world around them. If you go into an environment that's always been predominantly white, then that may operate as a clique. Being able to enter into that clique means conforming and changing your own patterns of behaviour, in order to blend with what they're doing. I think one of the common examples is when we decide what we're doing for the staff parties and it's something where we're going to a pub. So, if you're a Muslim, then you're not invited. If you are from a strongly Christian background, as some global majority are, then you're also not invited.

It becomes a thing when you think of what constitutes the culture. It's not a culture of contribution, it's not a culture that takes into account multiculturalism. The culture that pervades is one that looks at domination over everything else, and because that seeps into our schools and exists within our schools, unless leaders are actively doing something to create an inclusive environment, they will instead end up putting forward whatever is the dominant culture and expect everyone to conform to it. That's really hard sometimes, because having to explain your presence and explain your difference continually is a tiring task. It's emotionally draining. Having to do that with people who are unwilling to educate themselves within an education environment means that you're always on call.

In some schools that I've worked at in London, I was the only black senior leader that had ever walked the halls of that school – which then also meant that parents who are a global majority heritage had expectations of me. The students who were there expected me to understand. But let's be real. I am a Caribbean born, educated, raised female who came here and was racialised as black. So therefore, as much as I can empathise with some of the issues that they were facing in the education system itself, I didn't understand it. So I then have to go and represent them the best I can, because I feel the pressure of the expectation of the diaspora itself upon me and what I'm doing. In order for me to facilitate that, I went and educated myself.

I understand a larger, much wider range of cultures now, but that's not common within schools. You don't have headteachers or teachers necessarily who are going to walk into spaces and say, 'oh, these are the cultures I'm going to face. These are the people I'm going to need and these are the people I'm going to have experiences with. Let me go and really educate myself so that I can really emphasise how much I'm supporting them'. They don't have that level of allyship. It is more of a benign level of allyship where they say, 'but I came to work here, so therefore you should appreciate my presence', as opposed to, 'I came to work here. I want you to appreciate my presence, but I also recognise the additional workload that I've chosen to take on in being here to educate all of these groups. And I'm down for it. I'm going to do it.'

To do this well, you have to be an excellent listener, and not listen to solve; listen to understand. That's incredibly difficult for leaders to do because we are trained to solve the problem. But listening to understand the history and understand the story takes time. Then to think about the frameworks that you're putting in your school and whether those frameworks and policies that you have in place are going to constrict that story or whether they're going to allow that story to bloom even further.

I'd also say that leaders need to prepare the school environment. So, all of the members of staff at all levels should be well aware of inclusion practice. And I mean actual practice, not 'we are an inclusive school' on a poster or plaque. But we practise these measures of inclusion. We have this level of flexibility. This is where we show our accessibility. This is where we show our understanding. And when we don't understand, this is where we show our continual learning and make sure that every member of staff is incredibly aware of that. Because then when things like microaggressions occur, there is a response.

One of the most disheartening things within education is when a teacher reports an issue and there's no response, because that tells them they're not important enough and they're being fussy and that their needs aren't significant enough. Who wants to stay in that environment for the longer term? It is hostile, it's aggressive, it's exclusionary. You cannot stay in this profession with the workload itself and the responsibilities and the accountabilities to then find yourself excluded and on the fringe of your own peer group. You're not going to stay because you break down way too fast. So therefore, you then say, 'we have a recruitment and retention crisis' or 'there's not enough teachers coming through the pipeline'. It's not the pipeline that's burst. The pipeline is doing exactly what it's intending to do in diverting people away from the profession. Until we change the underlying culture that comes with it and understand that successful schools work as teams and, within those teams, there is understanding and there is appreciation and value – everyone and their inherent value is taken and they're given the dignity of response.

I think a lot of the problem is also that leaders wait until there is diversity to then try to learn and respond: they're not proactive about it. We need to get some level of proactivity across the sector if we're actually genuinely going to welcome differences into our schools. They don't prioritise it. Therefore, you end up with incidents where the leadership were probably scrambling, thinking, 'what should we do?' I've heard from teachers, for example, who'd say, 'some child walked up to me and called me a racist slur'. The response of the school was 'you need to educate them'. Why is the responsibility on the person who just faced a racist slur to educate them on why that's inappropriate to say? Why does the school system not kick in there and have clear sanctions the child is going to face and, during the point of sanction, this is the education they're going to get? This is how they're going to learn, and then they're going to apologise, because we need to go back to reconciling the relationship between the child and that member of staff. So, if you're from a global majority heritage, you're going into that environment and you need to educate them to do better. 'We don't have a lot of difference around here.' And you get all of the excuses, but none of the accountability, but you face all the responsibility.

If all you get throughout your career is this level of discrimination, when it comes to career progression, you're going to face another level of discrimination; when it comes to stereotyping in the school and which classes you're going to get, you're going to face another level of discrimination. You're going to face microaggressions and feel the responsibility – from parents, from families – that you are going to be the person that will understand and be there for that child. You have to be that safe place for all of those people, for them to come and have their experiences and learn from you. But where are you safe?

When you come together as a collective with your friends, and when you get a group of any age or stage teachers from global majority heritage together, you hear the stories. You hear it from others and you think, 'I thought it was just me'. As a collective, there's only so much support you can give each other until you go back to the silo and you face it alone again. That's what we found at BAMEed. We'd have people who'd come and we'd support them and we'd give them the coaching and get their heads corrected and say, 'right, we're going to go forward with this'. But you're sending them back out into the trenches, knowing very well they'll be back to get some more support.

As much as we try to say it is about finding the right environment, I think more of the right environments need to stand up and say, we are the right environment. This is what we do. It's not about just saying that we are an inclusive school and we want to hire diversely; it needs to actually genuinely be a part of the culture, and you have to be able to evidence it. There are the right environments out there. If you have a positive environment, you will attract other people into that positive environment.

When it comes to promotions and career progression, traditionally, people from black and global majority heritage are going to wait for someone to tap on their shoulder and say, 'you'll be really good. You should go and apply for this'. That's partly because, in their own heads, they're thinking, 'I need to finish XYZ on my list before I'll go for head of department' or 'I need to do this level of study before I go for an assistant head role'. And there's not enough provision and coaching to grow them to understand what those different roles mean and how sometimes you can step into a role and still continue to grow and fulfil that role.

I don't know how much grace people give themselves to allow themselves to enter into that role because this can be part of their cultural upbringing. Our parents will tell us that we have to be twice as good, work twice as hard, to get half the reward. So, we should be making sure that, when we go in there, we're representing really well. So we don't put ourselves forward. Yes, there are opportunities and there are places where you can do incredibly well and make that progression. But there are also other schools who will hire people from global majority heritage as instructors rather than teachers, because then you get to pay them less and you're making a saving, but you're going to get teaching quality. So you have to look out for when those things happen, and we need to know how they're resolved, because there need to be laws in place and rules that are applied – and applied publicly – so that we know that there's a resolution and people are being treated fairly and safeguarded as well.

It comes down to the simplest things. When you get to a certain level within schools, the governing boards are the people who are involved in the recruitment and they come in with their own biases and their own lack of training around it. So a simple thing like your accent and how you pronounce specific words can be to your detriment and you won't be hired. While you have that happening externally, internally you're also thinking, 'oh my goodness, is my accent formal enough for this post?' You end up having your own inward conversation that brings you down and, at the same time, there's an outward situation that's occurring, that's also going to bring your confidence down.

Even national frameworks like the Early Career Framework are minimally effective because they depend on the deficit model. They pick up people at their lowest, dust them off and send them back in. So whether it's coaching or ECT mentoring, it's all looking at how we show someone the job – but without showing them how to exist within the existing structures and framework. We are simply teaching people how to code-switch and get into the box, so that if you fit in the box, then you can progress and you can go further.

Of course, you can make change from the inside sometimes, and sometimes that does work. Sometimes people find their stride and they're able to go and do that. But if we really want to be effective, we have to start with where the problem lies, and that starts with the training programmes that we do. The National Professional Qualifications need reform, but they need reform with people who genuinely understand inclusion at the core of making those reforms happen. We need to change the way we do governance so that, if governors are going to be a part of recruitment, they should have to go through some stringent HR training and processes, so that they understand their own biases and don't bring them into that education environment; hiring on your gut feeling about someone, due to unconscious bias or even conscious bias, is not the way forward.

If we really want to solve the issues of inclusivity that we have, we have to create an environment where inclusivity is the norm and we have to be bold about it, no matter what's happening in political or social spheres. It needs to be really focused on education itself, and then we need to draw the leaders out. Part of the problem that we have is there are so many negative stories around what global majority heritage teachers and leaders have experienced in education. That includes the vast number of non-disclosure agreements that are signed and people being forced out of their positions. We need to be able to change the narrative within the communities themselves.

In the first place, it took a huge amount of work to even get most people to respect the fact that if you're from a global majority heritage, you are going to go and be a teacher. We've been able to do that and get people into teaching and leadership. Yet, if we want to go further, we now have to go back into the communities and say: and we are able to keep them safe – that they're safe in their careers and they're able to be themselves; we don't take them in and break them. If we can do that, that is going to open up and allow a lot more people to enter the profession.

But, to do that, we need to do a lot more work with the people who are recruiting our teachers so that they don't push their own ideas and agendas, because the NFER data showed that they are atrocious at converting people from global majority heritage backgrounds into entry-level teaching roles. If you think of the power that an ITT provider has, they can turn around to schools who don't make trainee teachers feel safe and say, actually, we're going to blacklist you because you're not providing an appropriate experience and you're not ready for inclusion and diversity. So, you need to go fix that as a part of your core culture and a part of your processes.

But they won't do it. Until they do, we can't meaningfully fix anything.

Yamina Bibi: Trust leader, consultant and CPD trainer

As somebody who's literally left teaching and, as a British Bangladeshi Muslim, I think both the systemic and the systematic racism that people from the black, Asian and minority ethnic community suffer, plus the burden of responsibility they face, is almost impossible to shoulder. It is really challenging to represent your whole community.

I was the first deputy headteacher in my school who was a person of colour – and my school was based in East London, where one of the largest British Bangladeshi communities lives. I thought that was really interesting. But then what came with that, as somebody in that senior position, and what Samina Chowdhury calls in her book *Drilling Through Concrete Ceilings*, having done that, I still felt a real sense of responsibility to represent my community. When you're visibly Muslim as well, you are always really trying to model the kind of ethics and standards that everybody everywhere wants of you; the burden of that led to burnout for me. This is what a lot of people feel, regardless of what stage they are in their career. Of course, everyone talks about representation and how we want more role models. Yes, we do, but what care is taken and where's the due diligence in supporting those colleagues when they do get to those positions and have to represent, because there's a real additional layer of responsibility?

With systemic racism, there are ways in which systems seem to play against BAME teachers quite actively. And that's not just only my experience; in all the networks I am in, I hear it pretty much all the time. Often, it is the constant microaggressions. Yet, it doesn't feel micro when it's happening to you. For example, teachers who say, 'I've been a middle leader for 20 years and it doesn't matter what I do, I can go and get an NPQSL, NPQH – I can have all the qualifications possible – yet, for some reason, I can't seem to get through'.

Some people have said they've been told that 'your face just doesn't fit here' or 'you just don't fit'. Even that language is so coded, and people from the global majority backgrounds know that's code for basically you're not white enough. So, it doesn't matter how competent you become, how much you've accomplished, when you're there, whether it's at senior leadership level, even in middle leadership or teaching, you still feel like you're not good enough. For me personally, it wasn't something that I was going to deal with any longer. I realised that the only way I could make change, even though I was so proud to work in that school and I love that school, is by being out of the system. Being in the system, I just felt like I was facing systemic racism. That kind of systemic racism comes from every angle, not just within school leadership. It comes from parents; it comes sometimes from young people.

So, there's both implicit racism and explicit racism. I think when you talk to white colleagues about the explicit racism, everybody reacts in a horrified way: 'oh my God, that's really shocking'. But, it's when we start talking about the implicit racism, the microaggressions, that people don't quite believe it. They'll say things like, 'are you sure that's the way it was meant to be interpreted?' or 'I'm sure it wasn't meant that way'. Like Stephen Covey says, it's not about the intention; it's about the action. We judge others by their actions and we judge ourselves by our intentions. So you've got people at the top who therefore eradicate your experiences or negate your experiences – why would I then speak up? Also, colleagues who have spoken up in the past, or reported any kind of bullying or harassment or discrimination, have felt like they've then been isolated and mistreated, which has forced them to leave.

Masking is also a big thing. I've masked for pretty much most of my career. There are events that I go to where I tend to be the only one. My husband and I will go to some events and we'll be trying to spot the brown person. I know that sounds really ridiculous but, in a way, I've used it to my advantage because I know that I'll be remembered. Even if they don't remember my name, they'll be, 'you know, the Hijabi girl'. And I'm like, yes! In actual fact, though, it should not be that way. When we look at teaching, for example, it's not great in terms of diversity, but there is diversity there at teaching level. But as you move up the leadership scale, we know from the National Foundation of Educational Research, what that looks like for middle leaders and senior leaders. Many from the global majority will say they face systemic racism. They face microaggressions. They don't feel like they belong. They don't have psychological safety. They cannot be their authentic self.

Now, doing this work, I think I agree that we can't be our authentic selves because I'm not accepted. And so, instead of just trying to fight and mask and be inauthentic and what some may think is fake, I decided to leave the system. I feel such a sense of belonging now within my Trust, but also within the community, that I've curated myself, such as BAMEed or the Belonging Effect. It is in those spaces that I can be my most authentic, without judgement.

Interestingly, a lot of people have said to me since I left teaching that I've become braver, like they've never heard me speak like this. I spoke at the Racial Equity Network Dinner, and everyone said I was so passionate. 'I think I was just angry, guys!' But, by that point, you do then become the angry brown person. Lots of my black female friends will say that they specifically don't say anything in SLT meetings or in teacher meetings because they don't want to be identified as the angry black woman. They feel that they cannot speak up and share their ideas because they are so scared that people would think they're too angry. Within a year and a bit, they had left that school and they eventually left UK teaching. That, in itself, tells you the severe problem that we have.

One of the key problems is that people think retention is a funding issue; we can't deny that perhaps that is the case. But what happens on the day-to-day basis in schools, and the lived experiences of teachers and middle leaders and senior leaders, is just as big an issue. A teacher's daily interactions with senior leadership and with other colleagues has a huge impact on retention. Even when people do manage to break that 'concrete ceiling', getting on with the job can seem impossible because people are still seen as a threat.

There was an article in the *Harvard Business Review*, which was called 'Going from Pet to Threat'. It spoke about this idea that when somebody from the global majority is hired, they tend to be really nurtured at the beginning, almost treated as a pet. Then the minute they start to speak up and really advocate for themselves, they then begin to experience microaggressions, or explicit racism or neglect in some way, because they're seen as a threat. There is this feeling that they don't fit into our culture. What does that even mean? That's code as well about fitting in. So, you feel like you have to assimilate. Even down to the way we speak, the accent, the way we dress. Those in-school microaggressions are so subtle, they're so hard to quantify. It almost feels like you're being over the top if you even speak about it.

For example, I spoke about this at one of our events, about how I always dress in a smart-casual way. I don't even know what casual is, to be fair! But whenever I turn up to events, even on weekends, everybody else might be in casual wear and I'm there suited and booted. The reason I do that is because I know that I represent. For me, representation means even the way I dress, because people might expect me to dress casually, but actually, it's not the way I want to present myself. I know that I've had to work 10 times harder to even get to that position.

I speak to so many of my friends who are syphoned off and put into the box of 'pastoral'. Leaders will say, 'you're great with the community of kids. You are such a great role model'. Again, this is code for, 'you're better at behaviour than me because I don't know how to deal with kids like that' or 'I don't understand their culture' or 'I don't understand how to create belonging, but you do because you're part of that community'. That is exactly why I've been so deliberate throughout my whole career to make sure I become a teaching and learning expert, that I'm not just a diversity hire, I'm not just speaking about diversity and inclusion, although that's what I often do now. But actually, I do that alongside teaching and learning.

The thing I want people I meet to know me most for is my pedagogy, my practice, my sharing of teaching and learning ideas. But, actually, that's taken me a long, long time. Even now, people will say, 'do you want to come and speak about diversity?' I've got 16 years in the classroom of well-above-average outcomes, leading departments, working in one of the best schools in the country. And yet you just want to talk about diversity. And you know what the truth is? I don't actually think I'm an inclusion expert at all. It's just that I share my lived experiences and people happen to share their lived experiences. But that day-to-day experience of microaggressions, of feeling like you have to mask all the time, of being told that you should be something, even though your passion might be something else, is one of the reasons why our Mission 44 project, with Being Luminary, the Chartered College of Teaching and Chiltern Learning Trust, specifically has this kind of strand. The reason we've done that is because we've realised that, actually, we don't have enough global majority teacher educators, which is probably also leading to a low retention rate.

Then, the lack of progression or even an advocacy or championing of people to then become a teaching and learning expert is also a problem. That is a predominantly white male space and they're worried about having diversity because what will that mean? Is it a club that they just don't want us to be part of because they're worried that, when we go to it, we'll see that there is quite systemic racism and then they're worried we'll call it out? What is it that stops headteachers and CEOs from advocating for teachers and middle leaders from the global majority? That lack of advocacy is yet another reason why teachers leave; they don't feel like they've got anyone who's going to celebrate them.

Plus, the current policies and the NPQs don't go far enough when they're thinking about the systemic racism that global majority teachers inevitably face. Even when I wrote the *Schools Week* article last year about the Teaching Commission, I had lots of interesting comments like, 'Yeah, but that's not the case for everyone'. This was mostly from white leaders, I have to say, who said, 'but we're doing so much great work: even though we don't have a lot of black or Asian people in our community, we still do a lot of great work'. Tell me more, and they'll say, 'we celebrate culture day'. I have to just be straight up and tell them that is just really performative.

I completely understand that the intention is there and people want to celebrate other cultures. There's a space for culture days; I love dressing up in my salwar kemiz, I like turning up and feeding people. I love it. But, ultimately, that's quite informative, isn't it? It's not actually getting to the deeper work. They would say that they're creating belonging by showboating different people's cultures. But, again, that's an additional burden or responsibility that people have. I'll cook some rice and curry for you and then I'm looking at some of my white colleagues, going 'what did you bring?' 'I just went to Morrisons.' All of those things just become performative and then add an additional layer of responsibility for people from black and Asian and global majority communities.

I think, when we're thinking about diversity, we're thinking about the global society, right? So the first thing leaders can do is acknowledge that. Secondly, I would say colleagues need to have racial literacy training that's ongoing, that's specifically part of a strategic action plan. If you put it on an action plan, something you're accounting and reporting, you're more likely to do it. If you look at the antiracism work by Leeds Beckett University, even though it's aimed at ITT providers, there are some really specific actions leaders could take. However, mostly it's about actually building your own antiracism knowledge and acknowledging the fact that we all have unconscious bias and doing that work yourself, not relying on the intellectual work of the BAME teachers themselves.

For example, yesterday I was delivering ECT training and I was saying to my trainees, when I grew up, sexual orientation just wasn't something that I knew about. I didn't have friends who were gay or from the LGBTQ community. I grew up in a very specific kind of traditional conservative household. I had to go and do that work. I had to do a lot of unlearning to then learn and ensure that my social circle and my professional circle is wide so that those identities that I haven't experienced is something that I'm experiencing. I'm learning about myself and also engaging. My friends do the same thing for me, and I think that's so powerful. It's not performative. It's actually genuinely lived, not laminated, as Mary Myatt says. People from the global majority know when you're being performative in your words.

The third thing I would recommend is coaching. I think coaching for all is inclusive, not just for global majority teachers and middle leaders or leaders, but it's also just inclusive for everyone. I think coaching should be embedded and systemwide. It should just be something that's provided for all schools and all people in schools, because I just think it's another way of being able to have a safe space for you to share those things. Things like affinity-group coaching, where you have people with different protected characteristics who are trained up as coaches, and then they group-coach people from similar communities, like affinity groups. You know, just because sometimes it's safer to be able to say things with people who have the same experience. That's not to say that people who don't share those experiences can't be part of that. It's just to say that there's also this kind of additional space because there will be things that I will say: I had my hijab pulled off and I was spat at and called a terrorist. Sometimes it is safer to talk through things with people who understand your world. People outside of it can sympathise but may find it difficult to relate.

The Mission 44 project I am working on will also really help with practical tools for leaders, that they can use to do the work themselves. This means the burden and responsibility is not on the person of colour. We need to just acknowledge the fact that the system won't change until white leaders start to lead this work and don't just rely on global majority teachers and leaders to share their experiences. They're the people who have the most power in that situation, not me and not the other person from the global majority. It is about using our power and privilege to change the system, challenge the system and advocate for people from a minority group, whatever their protected characteristic.

Amjad Ali: Trust Training and Inclusion Lead at Chiltern Learning Trust, author and consultant

I've learned that being a BAME teacher in England often means carrying two realities at once: the everyday work of teaching, and the quiet labour of navigating how you are perceived. For a while, the profession can feel like a fairly open field. You can teach well, take on responsibility, become a Head of Year or a middle leader – roles that schools are comfortable offering. But I've seen, again and again, that the bottleneck appears after that. Progression beyond middle leadership seems to depend less on merit and more on familiarity. People often hire in the mirror of themselves; they promote what looks like the leadership they already recognise. When you don't fit that image, you're treated as a risk.

Alongside that are the 'deaths by a thousand cuts': the constant microaggressions that some dismiss as insignificant. I can walk into a formal meeting in a three-piece suit and still get greeted with 'alright, bro', as if professionalism doesn't quite belong to me. People drop slang into conversations with me that they wouldn't use with others, or tell me, surprised, 'I didn't realise you spoke so well'. I'm British. I teach English. Yet the assumption sits there anyway, wearing me down through repetition, like an axe tapping at a tree until it falls.

What makes it harder is how little of the official 'support' seems to touch the problem. Programmes get launched, reports get written, initiatives get announced – and then nothing meaningful changes. I've watched organisations publish recommendations, gather data, hold discussions and still fail to build lasting structures that actually retain global majority heritage teachers or help us progress. At one point, it felt so stark that I ended up starting my own charity: a network that offers free coaching, leadership pipeline webinars, CV workshops, volunteer-led work filling gaps that shouldn't exist.

Even during Covid, when the stakes were literally life and death, the absence of guidance was telling. I remember writing a health risk assessment for schools because the government hadn't produced one. As a Pakistani man, I was at significantly higher risk – not because a virus is 'racist', but because inequality is built into the systems around us.

And the pattern repeats in professional development. The content of leadership qualifications might be fine, but where is the antiracism training? Where is the recognition that culture shapes experience in schools? Meanwhile, it has started to feel easier for organisations to quietly 'cancel' EDI roles and initiatives, as if inclusion is optional when it becomes politically inconvenient.

Over time, I've become less interested in hearing that another report is on the way. We already know what the issues are. What we need is change – sometimes systemic, yes, but also individual and organisational, because it often isn't coming from the top. People have to use their own intellect: read, listen, watch, learn. Don't rely on the exhaustion of those experiencing the harm to educate everyone else.

I also wish more leaders understood this: when someone raises inequality, don't respond with 'what about me?' Solidarity isn't a competition. We're not free until we're all free. And if schools want true inclusion, they need to think seriously about belonging, about whether their culture rewards sameness (*homophily*) or values difference (*heterophily*). Too often, the talent is there, but leaders' lenses are trained only on the people who feel familiar. The first step is to look around and admit that the problem isn't a lack of good candidates. It's the narrowness of what leadership is allowed to look like.

Conclusion

This chapter shows that the retention of teachers from marginalised ethnic groups cannot be addressed through generic workforce strategies alone. The research evidence is consistent: while workload, accountability pressure and cost of living shape decisions for everyone, people of colour often face additional, race-related pressures that schools underestimate. Discrimination (both overt and covert), disillusionment about being able to make change and restricted progression opportunities are not peripheral issues; they are decisive forces that reduce wellbeing, confidence and long-term commitment. Retention, therefore, becomes less a question of individual resilience and more a reflection of whether the system is safe, fair and genuinely inclusive.

This chapter also locates retention within a wider pipeline and progression picture. Underrepresentation is reproduced not only through leaving, but through barriers at entry (training acceptance and placements), early career experiences and the 'glass' or 'concrete' ceilings encountered over time. When teachers cannot see credible routes into senior leadership, because leadership is still imagined in a narrow, familiar image, staying can feel like treading water. This contributes to higher mobility between schools, stalled careers and continued underrepresentation in leadership, which then feeds back into weaker retention.

Teacher testimony gives language to what the data signals. It describes the isolation of being the only one, the pressure to represent whole communities. It also shows how easily inclusion becomes performative: posters and culture days cannot compensate for biased recruitment and weak complaint responses.

Taken together, the message is clear. Retention will not improve through recruitment drives that funnel more teachers into unchanged environments. It requires racial literacy and leadership cultures that value difference rather than reward sameness. If schools want teachers from marginalised ethnic groups to stay, thrive and lead, the conditions for staying must be real: safety, dignity, belonging and genuine opportunity.

Part 3
Covid-19

CHAPTER SEVEN:
Impact of the Covid-19 pandemic

The Covid-19 pandemic represented the most significant disruption to schooling in England in living memory. Schools closed, reopened and adapted repeatedly under extraordinary conditions, while teachers were asked to redesign pedagogy, assessment and pastoral support almost overnight. Understandably, concerns quickly emerged about the impact of the pandemic on teacher wellbeing and retention. Would the crisis accelerate attrition from a profession already experiencing long-standing recruitment and retention challenges? Or might the economic uncertainty and moral purpose of teaching lead more teachers to stay?

The answer, as the evidence shows, is complex. National workforce data initially suggested improved retention during the early stages of the pandemic, yet this apparent stability masked deeper structural and emotional pressures.[136] As England has moved into the post-pandemic period, retention challenges have resurfaced with renewed intensity.

Teacher retention in England before the pandemic

Prior to Covid-19, teacher retention in England was already a significant concern. Long-term data from the Department for Education showed that only around two-thirds of teachers remained in the profession five years after qualification, with attrition particularly pronounced among early career teachers.[137] Research consistently identified workload, accountability pressure and limited professional autonomy as key drivers of teacher exit.[138, 139]

136 Department for Education (2021) *School workforce in England: November 2020*. London: DfE.

137 Long, R. and Bridges, E. (2026) 'Teacher recruitment and retention in England' [online] Available at: https://commonslibrary.parliament.uk/research-briefings/cbp-7222/#:~:text=Postgraduate%20teacher%20training%20recruitment,(64%25%20below%20target) (Accessed: 30 April 2026).

138 Allen, R. and Sims, S. (2018) *The Teacher Gap*. London: Routledge.

139 Worth, J. and Van den Brande, J. (2020) *Teacher workload and retention*. London: NFER.

Importantly, these pressures were unevenly distributed. Teachers working in schools serving disadvantaged communities were more likely to leave, contributing to systemic inequity.[140] Retention challenges, therefore, were not merely individual choices but reflections of wider structural conditions in English schooling.

The early pandemic: a temporary retention effect

During the first year of the pandemic, national workforce data showed a temporary reduction in teacher attrition. Department for Education (DfE) figures for 2019–20 indicated that the proportion of teachers leaving the state-funded sector fell to historically low levels: around 7%.[141] Analysis by the National Foundation for Educational Research (NFER) suggested that this was due not to improved working conditions, but rather to constrained labour-market opportunities during lockdowns.[142] In other words, teachers stayed because leaving felt risky, not because teaching had become easier. Similar patterns were observed in other professions during the same period, where economic uncertainty reduced job mobility.[143] For some teachers, the moral significance of supporting students during a national crisis may also have reinforced commitment to the profession, at least temporarily. However, researchers cautioned against interpreting these figures as evidence of a genuine improvement in retention. NFER explicitly described this period as one of delayed attrition, where decisions to leave were postponed rather than resolved.[144]

140 Allen, R. and Sims, S. (2018) *The Teacher Gap*. London: Routledge.

141 Department for Education (2021) *School workforce in England: November 2020*. London: DfE.

142 Worth, J. and Faulkner-Ellis, H. (2022) 'Teacher Labour Market in England – Annual Report 2022', Slough: NFER [online] Available at: www.nfer.ac.uk/publications/teacher-labour-market-in-england-annual-report-2022 (Accessed: 30 April 2026).

143 Henehan, K. (2021) 'Uneven steps: Changes in youth unemployment and study since the onset of Covid-19' on Resolution Foundation [online] Available at: www.resolutionfoundation.org/publications/uneven-steps (Accessed: 30 April 2026).

144 Worth, J. and Faulkner-Ellis, H. (2022) 'Teacher Labour Market in England – Annual Report 2022', Slough: NFER [online] Available at: www.nfer.ac.uk/publications/teacher-labour-market-in-england-annual-report-2022 (Accessed: 30 April 2026).

Workload, stress and emotional labour during Covid-19

While fewer teachers left during the early pandemic, working conditions deteriorated significantly. Studies document sharp increases in workload, emotional labour and stress during periods of school closure and reopening. A study by Kim and Asbury identified that teachers were required to design remote learning, maintain engagement with vulnerable students, manage safeguarding concerns and adapt to constantly changing guidance.[145] This study found that there were widespread reports of exhaustion, anxiety and moral distress during the pandemic. Teachers described feeling responsible not only for learning loss, but also for students' mental health and wellbeing, often without adequate support.

Similar findings are reported in international systematic reviews, which identify teaching during Covid-19 as a period of heightened burnout risk.[146, 147] Crucially, these pressures are strongly associated in the literature with intentions to leave the profession. Teacher wellbeing is not a soft outcome; it is a robust predictor of retention.[148] The pandemic intensified many of the factors already linked to attrition, even if their effects were temporarily hidden in workforce data.

Post-pandemic rebound: attrition after restrictions lifted

As restrictions eased and the labour market reopened, teacher attrition rates began to rise again. NFER analysis of post-pandemic workforce trends suggests that leaving rates returned to, or exceeded, pre-pandemic levels, particularly among early career teachers.[149] This supports the argument that Covid-19 delayed rather than prevented exits.

---

145 Kim, L.E. and Asbury, K. (2020) 'Like a rug had been pulled from under you: The impact of COVID-19 on teachers in England' in *British Journal of Educational Psychology*, 90(4), pp.1062–1083.

146 Sokal, L., Trudel, L.E. and Babb, J. (2020) 'Canadian Teachers' Attitudes toward Change, Efficacy, and Burnout during the COVID-19 Pandemic' in *International Journal of Educational Research* Open, 1, Article 100016.

147 Pressley, T. (2021) 'Factors contributing to teacher burnout during COVID-19' in *Educational Researcher*, 50(5), pp.325–327.

148 Borman, G.D. and Dowling, N.M. (2008) 'Teacher attrition and retention: A meta-analytic and narrative review' in *Review of Educational Research*, 78(3), pp.367–409.

149 McLean, D., Worth, J. and Smith, A. (2024) 'Teacher Labour Market in England Annual Report 2024', Slough: NFER [online] Available at: www.nfer.ac.uk/publications/teacher-labour-market-in-england-annual-report-2024 (Accessed: 30 April 2026).

National surveys indicate that workload and stress remain central concerns. In NFER's 'Teacher Labour Market in England Annual Report',[150] over 90% of teachers considering leaving cited workload as a key reason, with student behaviour emerging as an increasingly prominent issue. Behaviour challenges, widely reported by school leaders, were often linked to the disruption of routines and social norms during lockdowns, placing additional strain on teachers.[151] The cumulative effect is significant. Teachers who remained through the pandemic now reported feeling depleted, with less emotional and cognitive capacity to absorb further demands. In this sense, Covid-19 has had a long-tail effect on retention, shaping conditions long after the immediate crisis ended.

As we have previously stated, teacher professional identities build upon events and interactions shaped in the context of life experiences.[152] There are multiple histories that shape the way teachers understand their roles,[153] and the experience of teaching in unfamiliar circumstances during the Covid-19 pandemic could be one lived experience that may have shaped teacher identity constructs.

Researchers have used a variety of different terms to identify these identity-changing events, including *critical incidents*[154] and *nuclear episodes*.[155] Although these critical incidents may occur infrequently, they have the potential to signal a significant turning point or change in teachers' identity development. Critical incidents tend to be significant and important high or low points – what makes these events critical are

150 McLean, D., Worth, J. and Smith, A. (2024) 'Teacher Labour Market in England Annual Report 2024', Slough: NFER [online] Available at: www.nfer.ac.uk/publications/teacher-labour-market-in-england-annual-report-2024 (Accessed: 30 April 2026).

151 Ofsted (2022) 'Education recovery in schools: summer 2022' on Gov.uk [online] Available at: www.gov.uk/government/publications/education-recovery-in-schools-summer-2022/education-recovery-in-schools-summer-2022 (Accessed: 30 April 2026).

152 Day, C. (2002) *Developing Teachers: The Challenges of Lifelong Learning*. London: Routledge.

153 Cannata, M. (2010) 'Understanding the Teacher Job Search Process: Espoused Preferences and Preferences in Use' in *Teachers College Record*, 112(12), pp.2889–2934.

154 Tripp, D. (1994) 'Teachers' lives, critical incidents, and professional practice' in *International Journal of Qualitative Studies in Education*, 7(1), pp.65–76.

155 McAdams, D.P. (1985) *Power, intimacy, and the life story: Personological inquiries into identity*. Homewood: Dorsey Press.

the meanings assigned to those experiences by the individual.[156] These critical events, such as the closure of schools and switch to online learning in 2020, may have the potential to challenge teachers' goals, values and beliefs and may result in adjustments of their professional identity.

However, Alsup expresses that a tension about professional identities is not always negative, as tensions between subjectivities can actually provide the site or impetus for important identity development – a type of transcendence – to take place.[157] Yet if the tensions are too great for teachers and there is little support for negotiating the dissonance, teachers may not be able to translate these contradictions into identity growth.

As well as critical incidents, shifts towards collaborative professional communities have also forced teacher professional identities to adjust to institutionalised collaboration structures.[158] Internal expectations of what a teacher role consists of are developed and fostered through interactions with colleagues and observations of teaching and learning. Therefore, many teachers' ideas about what is considered acceptable behaviour has been constructed by their observations and involvement in their current work settings. Once this internal scaffold of the school environment was taken away during the pandemic, this may have resulted in teachers experiencing a misrecognition of their professional identities and a feeling of low confidence.

Bandura defined feelings of professional confidence as 'judgements about how well one can organise and execute courses of action required to deal with prospective situations that contain many ambiguous, unpredictable, and often stress, elements'.[159] He also claimed that sustained effort and perseverance in the face of difficulty is likely to strengthen teachers' sense of confidence and result in a stronger sense of agency and positive professional identity. However, he also emphasised the power of collective efficacy, claiming that 'the strength of schools lies in teachers' sense of collective efficacy that they can solve their problems and improve their lives through collective effort.'[160]

156 Schutz, P.A., Hong, J. and Cross Francis, D. (eds.) (2018) *Research on Teacher Identity: Mapping Challenges and Innovations*. New York: Springer.

157 Alsup, J. (2006) *Teacher Identity Discourses: Negotiating Personal and Professional Spaces*. New York: Routledge.

158 Hargreaves, A. and Fullan, M. (2012) *Professional Capital: Transforming Teaching in Every School*. New York: Teachers College Press.

159 Bandura, A. (1982) 'Self-efficacy mechanism in human agency' in *American Psychologist*, 37(2), pp.122–147.

160 Bandura, A. (1982) 'Self-efficacy mechanism in human agency' in *American Psychologist*, 37(2), pp.143–144.

A strong sense of self-belief, as part of a professional teacher identity, helps teachers to feel positive about their value in society and, if taken away, may result in teachers finding it difficult to be motivated to achieve organisational goals.[161] A sense of collective self-efficacy is inextricably entwined with the emotional concept of belonging, and these emotions play a key part in shaping professional identity.[162] Some teachers may have found that this feeling was shaken due to the negative portrayal of teachers in the media and the sometimes dismissive attitude of the public due to school closures. This may have been worsened by the isolation felt by some teachers from their colleagues, as the usual interactions in the workplace were replaced by the occasional email or message on an online platform.

Differential impact: who was most affected?

The impact of Covid-19 on retention has not been evenly distributed. Research suggests that certain groups of teachers have been particularly vulnerable:

- **Early career teachers**, whose induction and mentoring were disrupted by remote teaching, reducing professional confidence and support[163]
- **Teacher-mothers**, who experienced intensified work–family conflict during school closures, exacerbating pre-existing gendered retention patterns[164]
- **Teachers in high-deprivation schools**, where the pastoral and academic consequences of the pandemic were most acute, increasing emotional labour and stress.[165]

These patterns reinforce the argument that retention is deeply connected to working conditions and organisational support, not simply to individual resilience.

161 Goddard, R., Hoy, W. and Hoy, A. (2000) 'Collective Teacher Efficacy: Its Meaning, Measure, and Impact on Student Achievement' in *American Educational Research Journal*, 37(2), pp.479–507.

162 Schutz, P.A. and Zembylas, M. (2009) *Advances in Teacher Emotion Research: The Impact on Teachers' Lives*. New York: Springer.

163 Worth, J. (2022) *Early career teacher retention after COVID-19*. London: NFER.

164 The New Britain Project (2024) 'Missing Mothers' [online] Available at: www.newbritain.org.uk/missing-mothers (Accessed: 30 April 2026).

165 Allen, R., Jerrim, J. and Sims, S. (2022) 'How did the COVID-19 pandemic affect educational inequality?' in *Oxford Review of Education*, 48(3), pp.323–341.

Accountability, trust and the post-pandemic climate

One striking finding from post-pandemic research is the tension between heightened accountability expectations and diminished capacity among teachers. Ofsted inspections resumed rapidly after periods of closure, and many teachers reported anxiety about being judged against standards that did not account for pandemic disruption. Indeed, research on performativity suggests that such accountability pressures can undermine professional agency and contribute to burnout.[166] In the post-pandemic context, where teachers were already emotionally stretched, the return of high-stakes accountability may have further weakened retention.

While the pandemic may not have completely changed teacher-retention patterns, it has sharpened existing lessons about teacher retention in England. Retention cannot be separated from working conditions, as temporary improvements in retention during Covid-19 were driven by external constraints, not by healthier professional environments. The pandemic also highlighted that wellbeing is central, not peripheral. Emotional labour, stress and burnout are directly linked to attrition and must be addressed systemically. Similarly, the DfE's own retention initiatives now acknowledge the importance of flexible working and wellbeing, although implementation remains uneven.

If the pandemic offered one enduring lesson, it is this: Teachers stayed not because the work was easy, but because they felt needed. Whether they continue to stay will depend on whether the system now learns how to need them well.

166 Ball, S.J. (2003) 'The teacher's soul and the terrors of performativity' in *Journal of Education Policy*, 18(2), pp.215–228.

CHAPTER EIGHT: Portrayal of teachers in the media during the pandemic

Introduction

Despite teaching sometimes having the reputation of a noble profession, teachers have consistently, over the last 200 years, been 'maligned and unappreciated', according to Cohen and Scheer in *The Work of Teachers in America*. They attribute the low status of teachers to being stereotypically aligned with women's work and with those who lack the skills for success in the business sector. Interestingly, they make the connection between teachers' 'ongoing role as transmitters of one generation's values to the next' with teachers' identity, and they suggest that being a teacher is not only about what teachers do in the classroom, as they are expected to embody their roles and behave in ways that reflect the values they transmit to their students.[167]

For England, Part Two of the Teachers' Standards states: 'A teacher is expected to demonstrate consistently high standards of personal and professional conduct... uphold public trust in the profession and maintain high standards of ethics and behaviour, within and outside school.'[168] This could be considered a difficult position: to be constantly expected to be 'on duty' and under public scrutiny in every element of teachers' lives. It could also be harmful, as teachers themselves come to represent the 'tensions and values associated with their jobs',[169] and they can become a scapegoat for both the positive and negative actions of schools and education systems more widely. This was highlighted during the school closures of Covid-19, when some parents were frustrated at

167 Cohen, R.M. and Scheer, S. (eds.) (1997) *The Work of Teachers in America: A Social History Through Stories*. London: Routledge, p.4.

168 Department for Education (2023) 'Teachers' Standards: An Overview' [online] Available at: https://assets.publishing.service.gov.uk/government/uploads/system/uploads/attachment_data/file/665522/Teachers_standard_information.pdf

169 Cohen, R.M. and Scheer, S. (eds.) (1997) *The Work of Teachers in America: A Social History Through Stories*. London: Routledge, p.4.

needing to work themselves while also educating their children, and a minority of parents took to social media to criticise teachers.

Print media

The way teachers' work is described in the national print media can act as a vehicle for teachers to construct and reconstruct their professional identity, pedagogy and practice.[170] An important aspect of identity formation is understanding how others see them, and the media can serve as a useful lens to view this. Newspaper coverage, then, has a relevance for teachers' professional lives and their constructs of professional identity because it can enhance their understanding of who they are as educators. Images and depictions of teachers in national newspaper reports could add to existing stereotypes of teachers or construct new ideas in the perception of the public about what teachers' working lives and attributes are, which could, in turn, impact on how teachers see themselves.

As identity formation can be constructed by the understanding of society, negative stories about teachers could become embedded in the values and structures of society, making it difficult for teachers to manage their own image or identity in a public sphere. If teachers' experiences in a social structure, such as the national print media, are positive, the stronger their agency and reflexivity might become. If the media are portraying teachers in a negative light and perpetuating dismissive stereotypes of teachers, perhaps teachers may find themselves feeling less positive about their roles and their professional identity.

A column by journalist Rod Liddle, in *The Sun* on 9 December 2020, stated 'Covid has made heroes of many of our frontline workers... but not teachers'. In the column, Liddle juxtaposed the behaviour of teachers and schools against NHS staff, criticising school closures and intimating that cancelling exams let our children down – a decision, of course, that had nothing to do with the nation's teachers. He prompted readers to consider 'is there any profession in the country which has had an easier, stress-free nine months than the teaching profession?'[171]

170 Kirby, D. (2016) 'The Influence of Teacher Media Images on Professional Teacher Identities' [online] Available at: https://discovery.ucl.ac.uk/id/eprint/1519713/1/Kirby_The%20Influence%20of% 20Teacher%20Media%20Images%20on%20 Professional%20Teacher%20Identities_Fin al_Davina_Kirby_2016.pdf

171 Liddle, R. (2020) 'Covid has made heroes of many of our frontline workers... but not teachers' on *The Sun* [online] Available at: www.thesun.co.uk/news/13432637/covid-frontline-heroes-not-teachers-rod-liddle (Accessed: 12 May 2026).

While this would undoubtedly have been upsetting for teachers to read, there may be more implications for how this might shift teachers' perceptions of their own professional identity. The role of the press has often reflected the concerns of society, but has also often shaped them. This means that negative coverage in the press about teachers' work during the pandemic may have led to a decline in public opinion about teachers, possibly resulting in teachers feeling like they are not valued, thus affecting their identity. Teachers who feel underappreciated and disrespected may lose the motivation to work, especially in times of difficulty, which leads to lower occupational commitment and job performance, and potentially to attrition.[172]

The effect of media comments on teachers was explored in a study by Kim and Asbury, who questioned teachers on how the portrayal of their profession in the media during the pandemic had altered their perception of how their profession is valued by society. Teachers in the study felt that the newspaper coverage had caused reputational damage and did not accurately represent teachers' views, with one participant stating 'teachers are coming across as this whinging, work-shy group, who don't want to go back to work'.[173] Teachers in the study objected to the way in which concerns about learning loss and a potentially growing gap between more and less advantaged students were presented in the media, and how the 'crisis' narrative implied teachers were at fault for not stepping up to be heroes. This made teachers feel that the press were purposefully being hateful or spiteful to teachers, to point the finger of blame at somebody.

Online and social media

Due to the changing attitude of the national press towards teachers, some may have experienced changes to their professional identity throughout different stages of their career, and some of these changes may be due

172 Carlo, A., Michel, A., Jean, C.C., Bucheton, D., Demougin, P., Gordon, J., Sellier, M., Udave, J.P. and Valette, S. (2013) 'Study on Policy Measures to Improve the Attractiveness of the Teaching Profession in Europe' on International Task Force on Teachers for Education 2030 [online] Available at: https://teachertaskforce.org/knowledge-hub/study-policy-measures-improve-attractiveness-teaching-profession-europe-final-0 (Accessed: 30 April 2026).

173 Kim, L.E., Oxley, L. and Asbury, K. (2022) '"My brain feels like a browser with 100 tabs open": A longitudinal study of teachers' mental health and well-being during the COVID-19 pandemic' in *British Journal of Educational Psychology*, 92(1), pp.299–318: p312.

to media influences. The impact on individual teachers due to these influences can have negative consequences that lead to additional stress. These might include the digital bullying or harassment of teachers, such as challenging teachers' authority on YouTube videos[174] or the abuse of teachers on TikTok videos.[175] The negative media stories shared on Twitter (now X) during school closures, often by tabloid newspapers such as the *Daily Mail*, were accompanied by rude and negative comments about teachers, as we discuss earlier in Chapter 1.

This was, ironically, a time when many teachers felt that they had never worked harder, planning both online lessons and face-to-face lessons for vulnerable students. It is easy to see why reading such negative comments, when teachers were already feeling under a great amount of stress, may have had an impact on the way they felt about their professional identities. For experienced teachers, who had been teaching for a longer period, this may have represented a change in the way that society viewed their profession. There can sometimes be a discord between the teacher identity expected by the public and the identity that is experienced by the teacher,[176] and this can be a difficult tension to manage.

As a backdrop to some of the challenges teachers faced during the pandemic, the profession was subjected to ongoing public critiques, particularly around teachers' response to national decisions about school reopenings, which schools and teachers had no responsibility for. This led to the profession being widely denigrated as 'lazy' and 'scaremongers'.[177] Before the negative depiction of teachers in the national press during the pandemic, many teachers already believed that society did not value their profession,[178] and the pandemic, and the way in which teachers

174 Kyriacou, C. and Zuin, A. (2014) 'It's the permanence of online abuse that makes cyberbullying so damaging for children' on The Conversation [online] Available at: http://theconversation.com/its-the-permanence-of-online-abuse-that-makescyberbullying-so-damaging-for-children-29874 (Accessed: 30 April 2026).

175 Dunkley, E. and Shearing, H. (2021) 'TikTok abuse "is pushing teachers over the edge" on BBC [online] Available at: www.bbc.co.uk/news/education-59264238 (Accessed: 30 April 2026).

176 Provenzo, E.F., McCloskey, G.N., Kottkamp, R.B. and Cohn, M.M. (1989) 'Metaphor and meaning in the language of teachers' in *Teachers College Record*, 90(4), pp.551–573.

177 Dabrowski, A. (2020) 'Teacher Wellbeing During a Pandemic: Surviving or Thriving?' in *Social Education Research*, 2(1), pp.35–40.

178 OECD (2020) 'Teachers & educators' [online] Available at: https://gpseducation.oecd.org/revieweducationpolicies/#!node=41728&filter=Secondary (Accessed: 30 April 2026).

were portrayed during it, may have exacerbated these pre-existing negative beliefs.

Historic coverage

For more experienced teachers, this negative media coverage may have contrasted with some of the more positive stories in the press over the last decade. A search of national newspaper articles in 2010 reveals mostly positive stories about the impact of individual teachers on students, or obituaries of prolific educators, where their work is discussed positively. There was even the launch of a new national award for teachers in 2008: 'Today's lesson: brilliant teachers: Awards celebrate the humble talent of those who dedicate themselves to Britain's pupils' from *The Guardian*.[179] An analysis of public feeling from the national newspaper letter pages suggests that teachers were enjoying a period of support and validation for their work. The publicity surrounding this may have highlighted the altruistic nature of teaching as a social enterprise and the potential of teachers to change lives.

Other articles in the *Daily Mail* stressed how hard teachers work: '900,000 toil for ten hours a week unpaid'[180] and 'Teachers and lawyers put in the most overtime',[181] and demanded that teachers are given respect: 'By the way... Why teachers deserve more respect than doctors'.[182] This demonstrates that, 13 years ago, the tabloid media seemed to have more respect for teachers and their work and recognised the incredible contribution they made to society, even equating their contribution to that of doctors who save lives. While the *Daily Mail* also covered several salacious stories about teachers seducing their students in 2010, an analysis of headlines does seem to highlight a more positive portrayal of teaching as a profession.

Previous studies on changing press representations of teachers, such as Peter Cunningham's exploration of teacher headlines in 1950, 1970 and 1990, illuminated the fluctuation of public opinion. Cunningham

179 *The Guardian* (2008) 'Today's lesson: brilliant teachers: Awards celebrate the humble talent of those who dedicate themselves to Britain's pupils' [online] Available at: www.theguardian.com/theguardian/teaching-awards-2008 (Accessed: 12 May 2026).
180 *Daily Mail* (2012) '900,000 toil for ten hours a week unpaid'
181 *Daily Mail* (2012) 'Teachers and lawyers put in the most overtime'
182 *Daily Mail* (2012) 'By the way... Why teachers deserve more respect than doctors'

revealed that the press greatly influence the attitudes of the public and, as sometimes stories about teachers are not documented in a balanced manner, this may illicit extreme reactions in the public towards the teaching profession.[183] This complex relationship between the public's opinions and what the press document, suggests that there is no simple cause-and-effect relationship. But the negative stories in newspapers about teachers, during the pandemic and since, could provide a foundation for negative public opinion about teachers' work.

Veteran teachers

More experienced teachers may already be battling against stereotypes and embedded tropes about the veteran teacher, in addition to the negative comments about work rate. McCulloch and Ben-Peretz explored the portrayal of veteran teachers in British literature and found that experienced teachers are often associated with individualistic features and seen as nonconformists, who are out of touch and outmoded in their approach to teaching.[184] With the reliance on new forms of technology for remote learning, this stereotype of experienced teachers being incapable of change and struggling with innovative teaching strategies may have worsened the negative messages in the press about teachers being unwilling to adapt and provide an education for students against the odds.

Positive media portrayals

Perhaps the media is one of the cultural factors that has contributed to the construction of a low social status for teachers. This finding appears to be confirmed by Hansen's research on the portrayal of teachers in the British press[185] and by Alhamdan et al.'s comparative study of the representation of teachers in newspapers in five countries.[186] Hansen

183 Cunningham, P. (1992) 'Teachers' professional image and the Press 1950–1990' in *History of Education*, 21(1), pp.37–56.

184 Mcculloch, G. and Ben-Peretz, M. (2009) 'International perspectives on veteran teachers: Introduction' in *Teachers and Teaching*, 15(4), pp.403–408.

185 Hansen, A. (2009) 'Researching "teachers in the news": the portrayal of teachers in the British national and regional press' in *Education 3–13: International Journal of Primary, Elementary and Early Years Education*, 7(4), pp.335–347.

186 Alhamdan, B., Al-Saadi, K., Baroutsis, A., Du Plessis, A., Hamid, O.M. and Honan, E. (2014) 'Media representation of teachers across five countries' in *Comparative Education*, 50(4), pp.490–505.

investigated the image of teachers in British newspaper headlines between 1991 and 2005, and his analysis revealed a considerable change from a mostly negative to a mostly positive portrayal of teachers. Specifically, it showed that, while newspaper headlines in the early 1990s focused on problems in education and teachers' conflicts with teacher unions and the government, newspaper headlines in the early 2000s carried a much more sympathetic and supportive tone towards teachers. This mostly positive coverage seems to have continued until the Covid-19 pandemic, when public support for teachers began to shift, around the same period as the negative stories were printed in the national press.

Conclusion

On the other hand, Alhamdan et al.'s comparative analysis revealed four different categories of teacher identity constructed across the newspapers they studied:

- The caring practitioner
- The transparent (un)professional
- The moral and social role model
- The transformative intellectual.[187]

The transparent (un)professional seems to echo some of the headlines in the English press during the pandemic that accused teachers of being paid their full salaries to sit at home and do nothing, often comparing them to workers who had been made redundant or continued to work throughout. These workers were hailed as heroes, making a great sacrifice for their countries, while teachers were painted as shirkers who didn't want to do their duty. There was a vilification of teaching unions in tabloid newspapers, with headlines claiming the unions were 'callous'[188] for fighting for schools to close to keep teachers safe, and that unions were wrong to encourage teachers to 'skip' the queue for the vaccine, as it would mean the more vulnerable were harmed further.

187 Alhamdan, B., Al-Saadi, K., Baroutsis, A., Du Plessis, A., Hamid, O.M. and Honan, E. (2014) 'Media representation of teachers across five countries' in *Comparative Education*, 50(4), pp.490–505.

188 *Daily Mail* (2020) 'Teaching unions put pressure on Government to delay school reopenings' [online] Available at: www.dailymail.co.uk/wires/pa/article9094261/Teaching-unions-pressure-Government-delay-school-reopenings.html

The newspaper articles already referenced also accused the teaching unions of having a 'Pitiful "can't do" attitude that puts teachers firmly before pupils',[189] implying that schools and teachers were to blame for lost learning and that teachers should risk their own health for their students. Other headlines denigrated teachers' setting of work, claiming that some teachers gave parents 'only two hours of work'[190] for home-learning and that teachers were responsible for the deterioration of students' mental health due to being 'kept away from class'.[191] A recent study questioned both teaching staff and senior leaders in primary and secondary schools and found that teachers were affected by the media portrayal during the pandemic.[192] The deterioration of teachers' mental health linked to the changing depiction of teachers in England's national newspapers could signal a change in the public image and representation of teachers, from a position of respect to one of less status and value.

Newspapers all over the world seem to publish articles about teachers that are frequently unfair and partially substantiated. These often blame teachers for poor student performance and poor educational outcomes, and this, in turn, presents a negative image of teachers, creating a crisis mentality towards education and teachers, which teachers themselves cannot help but feel affected by. With these negative images surrounding teachers, this might only add to retention woes in England. Yet, teaching isn't the only tough job that has recently struggled to retain staff. How have other professions turned the tide?

---

189 Lawson, D. (2020) 'Pitiful "can't do" attitude of union that puts teachers firmly before pupils' on *Daily Mail* [online] Available at: https://www.dailymail.com/debate/article-8610315/DOMINIC-LAWSON-Pitiful-attitude-union-puts-teachers-firmly-pupils.html (Accessed: 13 May 2026).

190 Henry, J. (2020) 'Missing out on school is disaster that lasts forever – as the huge damage inflicted on youngsters by a long break from the classroom is laid bare by several new studies' on *Daily Mail* [online] Available at: www.dailymail.com/news/article-8607983/Missing-school-disaster-lasts-forever.html (Accessed: 13 May 2026).

191 Henry, J. (2020) 'Missing out on school is disaster that lasts forever – as the huge damage inflicted on youngsters by a long break from the classroom is laid bare by several new studies' on *Daily Mail* [online] Available at: www.dailymail.com/news/article-8607983/Missing-school-disaster-lasts-forever.html (Accessed: 13 May 2026).

192 Kim, L.E., Oxley, L. and Asbury, K. (2022) '"My brain feels like a browser with 100 tabs open": A longitudinal study of teachers' mental health and well-being during the COVID-19 pandemic' in *British Journal of Educational Psychology*, 92(1), pp.299–318.

Part 4
What can we learn from elsewhere?

CHAPTER NINE: What can we learn from other fields?

Comparisons with other professions

Teaching in England is sometimes described as a 'semi-profession' due to a combination of factors that distinguish it from what have been traditionally considered 'full' professions, such as careers in medicine or law, for instance. There is a myriad of different reasons for this. To start, so-called 'full' professions typically allow practitioners working within the field a significant amount of autonomy in decision-making, based on specialised expertise. Of course, teachers in England have often worked within structured curricula and government-mandated policies that have limited their professional autonomy.

Medicine

While teaching requires QTS in England, the length and rigour of training are often seen as less extensive than those for such professions as law or medicine. Medical training can take up to a decade, whereas teacher-training is typically completed in one or two years, following a degree, or included as part of a four-year undergraduate course for primary practitioners.

Teaching has historically struggled with lower societal status compared to more established professions. This perception stems partly from its association with being a caring vocation rather than a technical or scientific one. Professions with higher perceived prestige often have stricter entry barriers and require more specialised knowledge. To continue the example of medicine, doctors undergo extensive training that includes a medical degree (typically lasting five to six years), followed by years of postgraduate specialisation and practical experience. This lengthy process highlights the complexity and exclusivity of their knowledge base. The process to become a doctor is extremely competitive, with stringent academic requirements for admission to medical school. The need for ongoing professional development, examinations and licensing maintains high standards within the profession and creates a sense of exclusivity, which enhances the perception of prestige.

Furthermore, the medical profession in England is self-regulated by bodies including the General Medical Council. This independence allows doctors to set and enforce their own ethical and professional standards, distinguishing them from professions where oversight is external or government-driven, such as teaching. While there are professional bodies, including the Chartered College of Teaching, much oversight in education in England comes from such organisations as Ofsted and the Department for Education, which influence standards, practices and policies.

Historically, medicine has been associated with social status, intellect and altruism. While teachers shape future generations, the immediate impact of their work is less visible compared to doctors' life-saving actions. So, while both require extensive knowledge, the technical and scientific nature of medical knowledge is more readily associated with expertise than the pedagogical and relational skills that are more central to teaching.

Essentially, this debate about 'semi-professions' may largely come down to the dichotomy between knowledge and skills. Teaching as a profession involves a blend of tacit knowledge, which is experience based and often unarticulated, and explicit knowledge, which is more formal and theoretical. In recent years, with the emergence of a move towards cognitive science and the codification of teaching strategies, teaching knowledge is becoming more scientific and explicit. Having a reliance on just tacit knowledge can make it harder for the profession to be seen as grounded in a defined body of specialised expertise, which tends to be a hallmark of 'full' professions.

Obviously, categorising teaching as a 'semi-profession' has been much debated and seems a little unfair. Teaching requires just as much expertise and dedication as other professions, and many would argue that teachers have a greater impact on society than most. After all, it is the profession that creates all other professions. Yet, both structural and cultural factors have continued to undermine its professional standing throughout the last 30 years and more – some of which we have already discussed in this book. Efforts to professionalise teaching often focus on improving training, granting greater autonomy and enhancing its societal prestige – all common themes that have threaded through our interviews with serving, veteran teachers and leaders. In essence, the term 'semi-profession' reflects a perception rooted in historical, structural and societal factors, which have sought to undermine teachers and their importance, rather than the actual complexity or importance of the role.

Nursing, social work and policing

Yet, it is not just teachers who have been categorised as 'semi-professionals'; nurses, social workers and police officers are all often grouped in this category. While very different careers, they share several defining traits, such as their training. While requiring specialised training and qualifications, these fields have historically relied on experiential learning and on-the-job training before transitioning to degree-level qualifications. In addition, each of these professions emphasises evidence-based practices, which have aligned them closer to 'full' professions.

All four are governed by regulatory bodies (the Nursing and Midwifery Council [NMC] for nurses, Social Work England for social workers, the College of Policing for police and, of course, Ofsted for teachers). These bodies ensure adherence to ethical standards and provide mechanisms for public accountability. However, unlike 'full' professions, these roles historically lack the same level of autonomy. This could be because of their public-service orientation. All four fields are fundamentally service-oriented, dedicated to improving public welfare. The people who work in these fields often work in emotionally demanding and high-pressure environments, engaging directly with vulnerable populations. But they can also be very gendered, with teaching, nursing and social work being seen as extensions of caring or domestic work and policing being associated with more masculine ideals.

Traditionally, a degree was not required to work in any of these professions. Indeed, when both authors of this book, Haili and Sam, started teaching, we worked with many colleagues who didn't have one and, instead, had done a year at teacher-training college. It is only since the 1970s that teacher-training in England has required higher-education qualifications. By 1970, a three-year teacher-training course leading to a Bachelor of Education (BEd) had been introduced then, by the 1980s, the Postgraduate Certificate in Education (PGCE) had become a more common route. Having spoken to older colleagues from this time period, there was little regulation and, anecdotally, it seems that teachers were just left to their own devices, teaching what they were passionate about, with little compulsory professional development.

For nurses, degree-level education became mandatory in England in 2013, as part of the Nursing and Midwifery Council's (NMC) shift from diploma-based qualifications to a Bachelor of Science in Nursing. In the same year, it also became mandatory for social workers in England to hold a degree-level qualification, replacing diploma-level courses. Similarly, police-officer training traditionally never required a degree but, in 2020, the Policing Education Qualifications Framework (PEQF) mandated that all new officers must either have a degree or earn one through the Degree Apprenticeship Programme. This may be another reason why these roles have been frequently undervalued, despite their societal importance – they have often been seen as vocational professions rather than academic. This is actually bizarre when you think about it as, more than perhaps any other fields, these jobs involve navigating complex ethical dilemmas, where practitioners are often balancing the needs of individuals against broader societal or organisational expectations – a highly stressful situation to be in! Perhaps most important, though, is that what these four fields all face are significant retention challenges.

Benefits of teaching

Haili and Sam have both worked as teachers in the state secondary sector for almost 20 years, but have also worked in other fields. Both have sometimes been frustrated by the view that some teachers espouse that no job in the world is as difficult as teaching. There is no doubt that teaching is a tricky job, filled with pressure, complexities and challenges. It can be physically and emotionally demanding; in the toughest schools, teachers can be routinely verbally abused by students and parents alike. However, it is a profession that has many benefits. It is an incredibly stable job, with a decent pension, long holiday periods (also bookended by intense periods of teaching) and regular, structured pay increases. But it is the relationships and connections that make teaching more rewarding and morally satisfying than perhaps any other job. Haili had been out of the classroom in recent years, and it was this sense of community and belonging she missed the most, alongside the sense of satisfaction that teachers get from making a difference to young people's lives. She missed this so much it drew her back – despite the well-documented difficulties in schools.

Retention efforts in other professions

Lots of jobs are immensely hard, with long hours, stressful working conditions and low job security. In the eyes of many members of the general public, teachers moan far too much. It only takes a Google search to uncover vast swathes of posts on chat boards such as Mumsnet, or a glance at the *Daily Mail* comments section, to see the reputation teachers have for being martyrs. Indeed, in a recent Westminster Education Policy Forum conference, Sir Andrew Carter stated that 'those working in teaching need to "put up some banners about how great it is" to help tackle recruitment problems' and 'not air all their dirty linen in public'.[193]

This isn't an effort to gaslight teachers, or tell them to put up and shut up. It is also not a race to the bottom, with a Blue Peter badge given for the most difficult working conditions. It's an acknowledgement of the toughness of the job, injected with a big dose of reality. The grass is not always greener on the other side, and the retention problems in the other 'semi-professions' demonstrate this. It is perhaps useful then to explore the retention problems in each of these sectors, and also examine what initiatives have been put in place to mitigate these factors, including how successful they have been. Is there anything we can learn from these efforts for our sector?

Nursing

Background

Over the last decade, England's National Health Service (NHS) has faced significant challenges in recruiting and retaining nurses, leading to persistent workforce shortages. The high rate of nursing vacancies has been a persistent problem and, in December 2022, NHS trusts reported approximately 43,600 fulltime equivalent nursing vacancies, accounting for over a third of all NHS vacancies.[194]

From 2012 to 2022, the majority of those who left NHS-registered nursing (but stayed in work) took up other jobs within health and social care. Nearly two in five moved on to nursing jobs outside the NHS and adult social care, including in private hospitals, agencies and charities, with a further 5% moving to adult social-care nurse roles. Other common

193 Martin, M. (2024) 'We need a teacher "propaganda parade", says Carter' on *Tes magazine* [online] Available at: www.tes.com/magazine/news/general/we-need-teacher-propaganda-to-tackle-recruitment-crisis-says-andrew-carter (Accessed: 30 April 2026).

194 Bazeer, N., Rocks, S., Rachet-Jacquet, L., Shembavnekar, N., Kelly, E. and Charlesworth, A. (2022) 'How many NHS workers will we need over the coming decade?' on The Health Foundation [online] Available at: www.health.org.uk/reports-and-analysis/working-papers/how-many-nhs-workers-will-we-need-over-the-coming-decade (Accessed: 30 April 2026).

moves were to alternative health and care occupations, such as nursing auxiliaries and assistants (11%) and midwives (10%), most of which were within the NHS.[195]

Comparisons with teaching

This high turnover rate among NHS nurses increased from 9% to 11.5% over the same time period, with the absolute number of leavers reaching nearly 40,900 – the highest on record.[196] This has parallels with teaching where, according to the Department for Education's 'School workforce in England' report for the 2022–23 academic year, approximately 43,500 teachers left the state-funded sector. Of these, 92% departed for reasons other than retirement, such as changing careers or joining other UK education sectors.[197] This suggests that a portion of these teachers may have remained within the broader education field, albeit in non-teaching capacities.

Like teaching, the attrition rate among nursing students remains a concern. In teaching, the figures show that, in 2021–22, a quarter of teachers had quit after three years at the chalkface. After five years, almost a third had walked away.[198] In a similar way, across the UK, nearly a quarter (24%) of nursing students either did not graduate or failed to do so within the expected timeframe, indicating challenges in training sufficient numbers of new nurses.[199]

195 Bazeer, N., Rocks, S., Rachet-Jacquet, L., Shembavnekar, N., Kelly, E. and Charlesworth, A. (2022) 'How many NHS workers will we need over the coming decade?' on The Health Foundation [online] Available at: www.health.org.uk/reports-and-analysis/working-papers/how-many-nhs-workers-will-we-need-over-the-coming-decade (Accessed: 30 April 2026).

196 Bazeer, N., Rocks, S., Rachet-Jacquet, L., Shembavnekar, N., Kelly, E. and Charlesworth, A. (2022) 'How many NHS workers will we need over the coming decade?' on The Health Foundation [online] Available at: www.health.org.uk/reports-and-analysis/working-papers/how-many-nhs-workers-will-we-need-over-the-coming-decade (Accessed: 30 April 2026).

197 Department for Education (2024) 'School workforce in England' on Gov.uk [online] Available at: https://explore-education-statistics.service.gov.uk/find-statistics/school-workforce-in-england/2023 (Accessed: 30 April 2026).

198 UK Parliament (2024) 'Teacher recruitment, training and retention' [online] Available at: https://publications.parliament.uk/pa/cm5804/cmselect/cmeduc/119/report.html (Accessed: 30 April 2026).

199 Buchan, Prof J., Charlesworth, A., Gerschlick, B. and Seccombe, I. (2019) 'A critical moment: NHS staffing trends, retention and attrition' on The Health Foundation [online] Available at: www.health.org.uk/sites/default/files/upload/publications/2019/A%20Critical%20Moment_1.pdf (Accessed: 30 April 2026).

Filling the gaps

To address shortages, the NHS has increasingly relied on internationally educated nurses. In the six months leading up to September 2023, nearly half (49.9%) of new joiners were internationally educated, with significant numbers from India and the Philippines.[200] Of course, this raises ethical concerns about recruiting from nations with their own healthcare staffing challenges.

There have also been several initiatives to attract international teachers to come to teach in England to address domestic teacher shortages. These have included the International Teacher Recruitment Programme (ITRP), which aimed to recruit qualified teachers from overseas to fill vacancies in subjects experiencing shortages, such as science, technology, engineering and mathematics (STEM subjects). However, the ITRP has since closed to new applications and will not reopen.

The Department for Education has offered international relocation payments to assist with relocation expenses. Eligible teachers can receive two payments of £5000 each, which do not need to be repaid. Then there was the introduction of International Qualified Teacher Status (iQTS), which was partly designed to attract international teachers and provide a pathway for them to engage with the UK education system. This qualification allows teachers outside the UK to train and qualify under English standards, and makes it easier for international educators looking to teach within the UK, as it enables them to teach in UK schools legally. The dream was to create a pipeline of highly trained teachers who are familiar with the UK education system, which could help address subject shortages.

Retention initiatives

Like teaching, the retention issues in nursing are complex and multifaceted. Just like in our interviews, where the power of leaders in schools to make or break a career emerged as a theme, a systematic review by the British Journal of Nursing identified several factors that affect nurse retention, including leadership and management styles,

200 Nursing & Midwifery Council (2025) 'Sharp drop in international recruitment slows overall growth of UK Register' [online] Available at: www.nmc.org.uk/news/news-and-updates/sharp-drop-in-international-recruitment-slows-overall-growth-of-uk-register (Accessed: 30 April 2026).

opportunities for education and career advancement, work environment, staffing levels and financial remuneration.[201] Sound familiar?!

National Retention Programme

Over the last decade, however, several initiatives have been implemented to address the recruitment and retention challenges within the nursing workforce, not least the launch of the National Retention Programme. The programme was launched by NHS England in April 2020 as part of the NHS People Plan; it aims to improve staff experience and retain NHS personnel, while supporting their development. The key areas of focus are a drive to improve the overall work environment and job satisfaction for NHS employees, while developing strategies to decrease the number of staff leaving the NHS, thereby maintaining a stable and experienced workforce.

An important facet of this is a focus on supporting the career development of nurses by providing opportunities and resources for professional growth to encourage staff to continue their careers within the NHS. In December 2023, it was reported that the programme had led to approximately 14,000 fewer staff leaving the NHS in the 12 months up to August 2023, compared to the previous year.[202]

One of the trusts that benefited from this, United Lincolnshire Hospitals, implemented a weekly in-house menopause clinic led by the trust's wellbeing team and staff network; they have saved £9 million on agency staff, including nurses, so far. As part of the scheme, any staff member who thinks they are showing symptoms of menopause can self-refer themselves to the clinic, where they are initially triaged by a nurse and given advice on how to manage the condition, as well as being offered a range of wellbeing support available at the trust. If clinical support is required, the staff member is offered a 45-minute appointment with a specialist menopause doctor, with suggestions for treatment, prescription or onward referral shared with the staff member's GP. Staff may be offered cognitive behavioural therapy, where they are given advice and

201 Marufu, T.C., Collins, A., Vargas, L., Gillespie, L. and Almghairbi, D. (2021) 'Factors influencing retention among hospital nurses: systematic review' in *British Journal of Nursing*, 30(5), pp.302–308.

202 NHS England (2023) 'NHS retention drive expanded across the country with thousands fewer staff leaving frontline roles' [online] Available at: www.england.nhs.uk/2023/12/nhs-retention-drive-expanded-across-the-country-with-thousands-fewer-staff-leaving-frontline-roles (Accessed 1 May 2026).

tips to manage the effects of the menopause. The 'menopause support squads' were introduced by the trust as 3500 of their staff were women over 45 – more than a third of their workforce.

In teaching, too, women are at greater risk of leaving the profession, especially those aged 30–39, who constitute the largest demographic leaving the teaching profession annually.[203] This exodus is primarily attributed to challenges associated with motherhood rather than menopause, but it primarily affects women, just as the trends noticed in menopausal women leaving nursing, identified above.

This identification of key pinch points or the identification of particular groups of people at greater flight risk – then the implementation of targeted intervention that makes a real difference – is definitely something teaching could learn from. In a way, the Early Career Framework (ECF) is an example of this; it was identified that early career teachers were not lasting the distance, so longer mentor support and a consistent approach to professional development were rolled out. However, early analysis of the impact of the ECF has not indicated that it's made a huge difference to teacher retention. The feedback about it from teachers and mentors has not been wholly positive, with some early career teachers expressing concerns about increased workload associated with the learning part of the ECF, particularly regarding the time commitment required for training.

Although the intent was pure, perhaps the focus on yet more CPD for new teachers was wrong-headed, as it adds to one of the biggest challenges for new teachers: balancing workload. The focus instead of the NHS trust detailed above was more about a genuine cause of poor wellbeing for nurses, tackling it head-on, rather than just taking a deficit mindset of 'nurses need more training'.

Nursing and Midwifery Retention Self-Assessment Tool

Another initiative was the launch of the Nursing and Midwifery Retention Self-Assessment Tool, which is an evidence-based resource developed by NHS England to help healthcare organisations evaluate and enhance their strategies for retaining nursing and midwifery staff. It enables organisations to assess themselves against the seven elements of the NHS People Promise, focusing on factors that support staff in delivering high-quality care, thereby enhancing job satisfaction and retention.

203 The New Britain Project (2024) 'Missing Mothers' [online] Available at: www.newbritain.org.uk/missing-mothers (Accessed: 30 April 2026).

The tool was launched in 2022 and was designed to help develop trust and implement local, evidence-based retention-improvement plans, which are linked to the problems staff face in their contexts, rather than a generic national approach. It includes a dashboard for summarising results and a template retention-improvement plan to support line managers and employers.[204]

Again, there is lots to learn here. Often, national initiatives to retain teachers do not take regional contexts and the unique challenges they bring into account. An example of this was seen recently when one of this book's authors spoke to senior leaders in Cumbria, whose unique challenge was that they were losing teachers in their droves to the local nuclear power plant, Sellafield, as they could earn just as much and have more flexibility.

Another example is the retention issues in Cornwall, where its remote location and salaries that do not reflect the cost of living mean that teachers often move out of the area. Instead of treating teacher retention as a simple problem, where barriers and challenges are just one homogenous issue, it seems more prudent and effective to work in partnership with local education authorities and trusts in regional areas to co-construct initiatives and incentives that make a real difference to local teachers.

Flexible working

Like in many public-service roles, efforts have been made to promote flexible-working arrangements in nursing, including self-rostering and flexible retirement options. Some schools and Trusts are really embracing this approach in teaching too, with some brilliant case studies covered later on in this book in Chapter 12.

Midlands Partnership University NHS Foundation Trust introduced 9½-hour shifts, allowing nurses to work from 7am to 5pm or 8am to 6pm (with a half-hour break). Participation was voluntary, enabling staff to choose schedules that best suited their personal needs. This initiative led to improved continuity of care for patients, increased staff willingness to take on additional shifts during high-demand periods and positive feedback from nurses regarding the new shift patterns.[205]

204 NHS England 'Our NHS People Promise' [online] Available at: www.england.nhs.uk/our-nhs-people/online-version/lfaop/our-nhs-people-promise (Accessed: 1 May 2026).

205 University of Southampton (2024) 'Choice and consistent shift patterns could improve nurses' work-life balance' [online] Available at: www.southampton.ac.uk/news/2024/02/nurses-shifts.page (Accessed: 13 May 2026).

It is heartening to see schools and Trusts making moves to become more flexible. This can be really difficult to do in teaching, of course, as, primarily, teachers need to be in school in front of students, and leaders need to be visible. It is not as simple as just saying 'work from home' or 'come in later', as that is not the nature of the job. Yet promoting a culture where planning, preparation and assessment (PPA) can be taken from home and teachers are able to arrange internal swaps or cover to attend their children's sports days is not too difficult to make a reality.

If schools want to compete with industry for skilled graduates, something's got to give. It is a job-seeker's market, and both prospective and experienced teachers are voting with their feet. As this book went to press, the Chartered College of Teaching and Education Endowment Foundation were conducting research on the impact on teachers of being allowed to take their PPA at home.

Conclusion

So, what has been the impact of these initiatives? As of 2025, nursing vacancies in England fell to a record low of 7.5% – the lowest since records began in 2017, indicating the positive impact of recruitment and retention efforts.[206] The NHS achieved its target of expanding the nursing workforce by 50,000 over the parliamentary term.[207] While it's clear that these initiatives have led to notable improvements, challenges such as reliance on international recruitment and the need for sustainable, long-term retention strategies still remain, but they are definitely going in the right direction.

Social work

What about in social work? What can we learn from this field?

Background

After reading the previous section on nursing, readers will notice a pattern emerging. As of September 2021, English councils reported a 9.5% vacancy rate for fulltime equivalent adult social-worker positions, up

206 Nicholas, K. (2025) 'Evidence Brief: Nursing Attrition, Recruitment and Retention' from UK: Workforce, Training and Education Knowledge Management Team [online] Available at: www.ewin.nhs.uk/sites/default/files/Nursing%20Attrition%2C%20Recruitment%20and%20Retention_Evidence%20Brief.pdf (Accessed: 1 May 2026).

207 Department of Health and Social Care (2023) 'Over 50,000 extra nurses in NHS – hitting government target early' on Gov.uk [online] Available at: www.gov.uk/government/news/over-50000-extra-nurses-in-nhs-hitting-government-target-early (Accessed: 1 May 2026).

from 7.5% the previous year. In children's services, vacancies increased by 21% to 7900 positions.[208]

However, unfilled vacancies are not the only issue the social-work sector is facing. Just like in teaching, the turnover rate for social workers is also rising, with 17.1% leaving between 2021 and 2022.[209] This has led to an increased reliance on agency staff, with 6800 positions currently being covered by temporary workers.[210] When there is a high turnover and more transient workers, it can be hard to build a sense of community and purpose, and this is reflected in a 2021 survey, which indicated that 50% of social workers were unhappy in their roles, with over 60% planning to leave their current positions within the next 20 months.[211]

To some extent, there has been an attempt to backfill these vacancies with international candidates, through the introduction of the Health and Care Worker visa in February 2022, which has led to an increase in international recruitment. However, subsequent policy changes, including restrictions on care workers bringing dependents, resulted in a significant decline in visa applications, with an 82% drop reported in July 2024 compared to the same month in 2023.[212]

Retention initiatives

Workforce Recruitment and Retention Funds

The issues described above, which have remarkable similarities with both teaching and nursing, have resulted in several initiatives being implemented,

208 Samuel, M. (2026) 'Social work vacancies increased at Cafcass last year, amid drop in practitioner numbers' on CommunityCare [online] Available at: www.communitycare.co.uk/content/news/social-work-vacancies-increased-at-cafcass-last-year-amid-drop-in-practitioner-numbers (Accessed: 1 May 2026).

209 National Children's Bureau (2024) 'Outcomes of CSC Provision' [online] Available at: www.ncb.org.uk/sites/default/files/uploads/files/Outcomes%20of%20CSC%20provision_Full%20Report_Final%20January%202024.pdf

210 London Innovation and Improvement Alliance (2023) 'Big Listen Report' [online] Available at: www.liia.london/wp-content/uploads/2023/06/29.06.23-Big-Listen-Report.pdf

211 Social Work England (2026) 'Social worker survey results 2024' [online] Available at: www.socialworkengland.org.uk/about/publications/social-worker-survey-results-2024 (Accessed: 1 May 2026).

212 *Caring Times* (2024) 'As care worker visas drop 81%, Martin Green calls situation "untenable"' [online] Available at: https://caring-times.co.uk/as-care-worker-visas-drop-81-martin-green-calls-situation-untenable/#:~:text=As%20care%20worker%20visas%20drop,situation%20'untenable'%20%7C%20Caring%20Times (Accessed: 1 May 2026).

beginning with the Department of Health and Social Care allocating £462.5 million to local authorities through the Workforce Recruitment and Retention Funds (WRRF). These funds aimed to bolster workforce capacity by introducing financial incentives, training programmes and measures to improve working conditions. Financial incentives included:

- **enhanced pay rates** to make roles more competitive and appealing
- **retention bonuses** to encourage staff to remain in their positions by rewarding continued service within the sector
- **recruitment incentives** such as sign-on bonuses, provided to attract new entrants into the social-care workforce
- **overtime payments** to boost capacity and ensure the delivery of care services during periods of high demand
- **support for childcare costs** – some local authorities used WRRF funds to assist with childcare expenses.[213]

National Workforce Action Group

In addition, the National Workforce Action Group (NWAG) was established, to develop and test tools and resources that support recruitment and retention in children's social work. Their work focused on assisting local authorities in creating effective workforce strategies that foster positive working conditions and organisational culture. There have been great successes with this collaborative work, for example in Yorkshire and Humber, which was a region facing considerable workforce challenges due to rapid demographic, economic and technological changes, resulting in a rapid decline in workforce sustainability.

In response to this, the region and the NWAG adopted the national shared workforce priorities, adding a sixth priority on leadership to the list above. They structured monthly meetings to spotlight each priority, sharing national resources and local-authority practices. This approach fostered a collective agreement on regional priorities and a better understanding of each authority's contributions, and led to the creation of a repository of best practices and resources, promoting a unified strategic vision and facilitating action learning.[214]

---

213 Department for Health and Social Care (2024)

214 Macdonald, M.A. (2025) 'National Workload Action Group Final Report' on Department for Education [online] Available at: https://assets.publishing.service.gov.uk/media/68d51a8030734bac9ba0fcbc/National_Workload_Action_Group_Final_Report_September_2025.pdf (Accessed: 1 May 2026).

In the world of education, collaboration with external bodies and agencies has always been a central part of what schools do. Yet, due to tight budgets and capacity constraints, opportunities to do this seem to be decreasing.

Comparisons with teaching

Like in teaching (hence the need for this book!), retaining experienced social workers is a key priority. Cook et al. undertook research to learn more about what sustains experienced child and family social workers to remain in the profession. Social workers in the research study identified that they periodically encountered defining moments in their careers that they wrestled with.[215] Working through these dilemmas required them to re-examine what it means, personally and professionally, to be a social worker. This is essentially what we set out to do in this book for teaching, so we read this research with interest.

The researchers coined the term 'Critical Career Episodes' (CCEs) to describe these experiences, and highlighted that staying in the profession over the long-term entails successfully navigating a series of these. Cook et al. concluded that CCEs arise from a sense of misalignment between the demands of practice and the social worker's strongly held sense of identity. This is something that also regularly emerges as a theme in research about why teachers leave the profession, perhaps because both jobs often appeal to those with a strong sense of professional identity. These critical incidents therefore prompt identity work, where social workers attempt to bring their sense of identity and practice back into alignment.

Teachers are rarely afforded this opportunity as, in the hundreds of schools Haili and Sam visit, critical reflection has been replaced in school CPD schedules with other modalities, such as more directive instructional coaching, based solely on the codification of techniques. With the demise of the staffroom as well, when do teachers really get the chance to talk about their challenges and feelings with other colleagues? Due to the bureaucracy in teaching, there never seems to be enough time to do the things that really matter.

215 Cook, L., Carder, S. and Zschomler, D. (2025) '"Being a Social Worker… It's in My DNA": Retaining Experienced Child and Family Social Workers: The Role of Professional Identity' in *Child & Family Social Work*, 30, 4, pp.996–1005.

Policing

Another profession that struggles with the amount of red tape is the police. So, what do their recruitment and retention problems look like in comparison to the education sector?

Background

Over the last decade, police forces in England have faced significant challenges in recruitment and retention. Between 2010 and 2017, police-officer numbers declined by approximately 20,000 due to budget cuts.[216] In response to this, in 2019, the government initiated the Police Uplift Programme, aiming to recruit an additional 20,000 officers by March 2023.[217] This has had some positive impact; as of March 2024, there were 147,746 fulltime equivalent officers, marking a 0.2% increase from the previous year and the highest number since comparable records began.[218] This modest increase is certainly something teaching could learn from, so let's explore what the Uplift Programme involved.

Retention initiatives

Police Uplift Programme

The Police Uplift Programme aimed to bolster police presence, enhance public safety and improve outcomes for victims of crime. The Programme represented a collaborative effort among the Home Office, the National Police Chiefs' Council (NPCC) and the College of Policing, with personnel seconded from each organisation to ensure effective implementation.[219]

Nottinghamshire Police, for example, utilised 'Poliscope modelling' to identify areas most in need of additional capacity to address complex

216 Home Office (2025) 'Police workforce, England and Wales: 31 March 2024' on Gov.uk [online] Available at: www.gov.uk/government/statistics/police-workforce-england-and-wales-31-march-2024/police-workforce-england-and-wales-31-march-2024 (Accessed: 1 May 2026).

217 Home Office (2025) 'Police workforce, England and Wales: 31 March 2024' on Gov.uk [online] Available at: www.gov.uk/government/statistics/police-workforce-england-and-wales-31-march-2024/police-workforce-england-and-wales-31-march-2024 (Accessed: 1 May 2026).

218 Home Office (2025) 'Police workforce, England and Wales: 31 March 2024' on Gov.uk [online] Available at: www.gov.uk/government/statistics/police-workforce-england-and-wales-31-march-2024/police-workforce-england-and-wales-31-march-2024 (Accessed: 1 May 2026).

219 National Police Chiefs Council (2025) 'Police Uplift Programme' [online] Available at: www.npcc.police.uk/our-work/police-uplift-programme (Accessed: 1 May 2026).

demands.[220] This strategic approach optimised resource allocation and improved service delivery, so that officers felt a sense of competence, motivation and autonomy.

In teaching, a lack of resources often erodes a teacher's motivation, as we saw from the research conducted for this book. Teachers are often expected to be all things to all people and don't have the resources to do the job as well as they would like. Yet, nationally, in a time of budget cuts and a cost-of-living crisis, not everything can be funded, and there needs to be more of an understanding of the complex demands in schools – demands that have increased since Covid-19. Many MPs and, indeed, Secretaries of State have never worked in schools, let alone served as teachers and leaders – which is why it is so important for them to hear from those working in schools about the challenges they face. Haili and Sam have both been lucky enough to speak to those serving in Westminster recently about teacher retention, but it would be great to see more teachers being given this opportunity.

In a similar vein to teaching, the Uplift Programme aimed to prioritise innovative training methods, leading to the creation of a blended learning programme. This initiative transformed learning across police forces in England and Wales by improving blended-learning design expertise and providing ongoing support to staff across all 43 police forces.

School-based teacher-training providers have really led the field in providing blended learning like this for new teaching, where on-the-job training is supplemented by subject knowledge and theory sessions. The ECF has also aimed to provide additional support for teachers in those first vital years. While it is too early to analyse the impact of these initiatives on retention properly, an evaluation from the National Foundation for Educational Research (NFER)[221] found mentoring was highly valued by ECTs, who reported feeling more confident, especially in areas such as lesson planning and classroom management. The structured guidance offered by mentors was seen as a critical factor in helping them navigate the early years of their teaching career. However, mentors do struggle

220 Poliscope 'Helping Nottinghamshire Police make the most of the Police Uplift Programme' [online] Available at: www.poliscope.org.uk/case-study-nottinghamshire (Accessed: 1 May 2026).

221 Walker, M. (2024) 'The Early Career Framework: Key findings for policymakers and school leaders from the early roll-out evaluation', Slough: NFER [online] Available at: www.nfer.ac.uk/blogs/the-early-career-framework-key-findings-for-policymakers-and-school-leaders-from-the-early-roll-out-evaluation (Accessed: 1 May 2026).

with workloads, so policymakers need to make mentor time statutory and enforce this in schools. There are still too many mentors, particularly in primary settings, who are spending time after school preparing to support new teachers, as they have not been given any time to do this during the school day.

Direct-entry and fast-track schemes

The police have also introduced direct-entry and fast-track schemes to attract professionals from other sectors. These schemes allow direct entry into higher ranks and accelerate promotion for existing officers. However, while intended to infuse diverse skills into the force, uptake has been limited, and the long-term impact on retention remains uncertain.[222]

There have been similar schemes in teaching in recent years, such as support from organisations including Now Teach, who provide support for career-changers to come into teaching, as well as fast-track schemes such as Future Leaders, which was a structured programme to prepare teachers to be senior leaders within a (traditionally) shorter timeframe. These fast-track schemes can be controversial. Both Haili and Sam have worked with leaders who have flown up the ladder quickly and done a great job and those who have clearly lacked the mental models to do the job well, due to a lack of experience. Unfortunately, when the latter happens, it can completely destroy the culture in a school. Headteacher of Dunston School, Sam Strickland, has publicly spoken about the dangers of this, writing on social-media platform X: 'People becoming Heads 5/6 years into teaching. Genuinely what is happening within the sector? Once you're in the chair you only know what you know. Be careful what you wish for'.[223]

Fast tracks to leadership won't fix the retention crisis we have with classroom teachers. Teachers in our research talked about the pressure they feel to apply for promotions themselves. It is an unfortunate side-effect of the system in education that those who are effective teachers are often promoted out of the classroom, taken away from where they make the biggest difference. This is why there need to be more career trajectories that make classroom teaching central (this is revisited in Chapter 10, which covers what we can learn from countries with better attrition rates).

222 UK Parliament (2016) 'Police and Crime Commissioners: here to stay: Government response to the Committee's Seventh Report of Session 2015–16' [online] Available at: https://publications.parliament.uk/pa/cm201617/cmselect/cmhaff/822/82204.htm (Accessed: 1 May 2026).

223 Mr Teece (2024) on X [online] Available at: https://x.com/MrTeece_/status/1864426065457824197 (Accessed: 1 May 2026).

Training standards and leadership-development programmes

The College of Policing recognised that promotion can take effective officers away from where they make the biggest difference, and introduced new training standards and leadership-development programmes to support officer progression and job satisfaction.[224] The initiative recognised that leadership standards were needed, which delineated the knowledge, skills and behaviours expected of police officers at various stages of their careers. These standards are structured into five organisational stages:

1. **Leadership Foundations:** Applicable to constables and staff with equivalent responsibilities; focus on upholding the Code of Ethics, professional behaviour and effective teamwork
2. **First-Line Leaders:** Targeted at sergeants and equivalent staff; emphasise team leadership, resource allocation and performance management
3. **Mid-Level Leaders:** For inspectors, chief inspectors and equivalent staff; concentrate on leading multiple teams, strategic resource management and fostering inclusive workplace cultures
4. **Senior Leaders:** Designed for superintendents, chief superintendents and equivalent staff; focus on strategic leadership, policy implementation and organisational change management
5. **Executive Leaders:** Aimed at chief officers and equivalent staff; emphasise organisational leadership, public trust and ethical governance.

Not only does this aim to provide a parity of understanding and a consistency of skills and attributes nationally, but it also identifies a clear trajectory for police officers, highlighting the different career paths officers can take.

In teaching, the Teachers' Standards set out the minimum expectations teachers should adhere to, and there are Headteachers' Standards, but there isn't anything official in between. This may be an area that policy can focus on, particularly as those choosing to leave the profession have mentioned toxic leadership as a factor contributing to their decision. Supportive leadership, where teachers are given the agency to use their professionalism and afforded opportunities for professional growth, is also a major theme in the research in this book, from the teachers who

224 College of Policing (2026) 'Police leadership programme' [online] Available at: www.college.police.uk/career-learning/leadership (Accessed: 1 May 2026).

have served 20 plus years in the classroom and have no intention to leave. It clearly matters, yet we have no consistency nationally of the standards leaders in schools should adhere to.

There has also been an effort in teaching to provide other pathways for teachers to progress in recent years, with the reformed National Professional Qualifications (NPQs), which aim to give teachers alternative routes to progress, outside the traditional middle and senior leadership roles. However, as previously discussed, while the materials in the NPQs are high quality, both Haili and Sam facilitate a range of these qualifications, and the vast majority of participants are either in traditional leadership roles or looking to enter them. As they are based around the Education Endowment Foundation (EEF)'s Implementation cycle, much of the content of the qualifications is generic and overlaps, so does not really provide the bespoke CPD they may have promised.

In policing, to support the implementation of these standards, the National Centre for Police Leadership (NCPL) was established; whereas, in teaching, the qualifications are written and designed by a range of national providers, such as Teach First, UCL and Ambition Institute, and delivered by local Teaching School Hubs. Each of the Teaching School Hubs and providers delivers the qualifications in different ways – some in hybrid models both online and in person and some on weekends away. The hybrid nature makes the training more accessible for teachers, but some providers who rely on face-to-face delivery have struggled with teachers being able to attend, as many schools are struggling to find cover for lessons. As facilitators of multiple NPQs, anecdotally, we have noticed attendance of face-to-face sessions going down.

Diversity

Efforts to improve workforce diversity have been rolled out in the police force. These have included targeted recruitment campaigns and setting diversity targets. Despite these initiatives, progress has been slow, with underrepresentation of marginalised ethnic groups persisting.[225]

In teaching, this is also a problem. Research indicates that the ethnic diversity of the teaching workforce in England has been gradually increasing, yet it remains disproportionately low compared to the student population and the broader working-age demographic. As of the

225 UK Parliament 'The Macpherson Report: Twenty-two years on' [online] Available at: https://publications.parliament.uk/pa/cm5802/cmselect/cmhaff/139/13907.htm (Accessed: 1 May 2026).

2021–22 academic year, 14.9% of teachers identified as belonging to a marginalised ethnic group, up from 11.2% in 2010–11. However, this figure still falls short of the 21.5% of the working-age population who identified as people of colour in the 2011 Census.[226] The underrepresentation is even more pronounced in leadership roles. Data from 2022 shows that 92.5% of headteachers were white British, indicating a significant lack of ethnic diversity at senior levels within schools.[227] The Department for Education has acknowledged the underrepresentation of people of colour in teaching and leadership positions and committed to actions aimed at increasing diversity.[228]

In 2024, NFER, funded by Mission 44, explored the barriers and solutions to achieving a more ethnically diverse teaching workforce from entry to senior-leadership level. Teachers from marginalised ethnic groups are overrepresented at Initial Teaching Training (ITT) application level, but evidence suggests they have lower acceptance rates onto ITT compared to their white counterparts.[229] Those who do begin ITT courses report experiencing isolation. This particularly occurs when there are few people of colour on their course. They also reported receiving poor preparation and support from ITT tutors and school mentors on the challenges of diversity and racism, plus the microaggressions they may face in teaching. NFER suggests providers should have Equality, Diversity and Inclusion (EDI) policies and training for teacher educators and should consider EDI when selecting school placements.[230]

226 Department for Education (2024) 'School workforce in England' on Gov.uk [online] Available at: https://explore-education-statistics.service.gov.uk/find-statistics/school-workforce-in-england/2023 (Accessed: 1 May 2026).

227 Department for Education (2024) 'School workforce in England' on Gov.uk [online] Available at: https://explore-education-statistics.service.gov.uk/find-statistics/school-workforce-in-england/2023 (Accessed: 1 May 2026).

228 Department for Education (2018) 'Diversity of the teaching workforce: statement of intent' on Gov.uk [online] Available at: www.gov.uk/government/publications/diversity-of-the-teaching-workforce-statement-of-intent (Accessed: 1 May 2026).

229 Sharp, C. and Aston, K. (2024) 'Ethnic diversity in the teaching workforce: evidence review', Slough: NFER [online] Available at: https://mission44.org/wp-content/uploads/2024/10/ethnic_diversity_in_the_teaching_workforce-1.pdf (Accessed: 1 May 2026).

230 Sharp, C. and Aston, K. (2024) 'Ethnic diversity in the teaching workforce: evidence review', Slough: NFER [online] Available at: https://mission44.org/wp-content/uploads/2024/10/ethnic_diversity_in_the_teaching_workforce-1.pdf (Accessed: 1 May 2026).

Experienced teachers from marginalised ethnic groups say they are frustrated by a lack of opportunities for progression, due to an absence of support, unfair treatment and experiencing an 'invisible glass ceiling'. The review highlighted that another key barrier to career progression is that teachers from marginalised ethnic groups are encouraged or self-select into middle-leadership roles that have limited opportunities for further progression, such as pastoral or behavioural responsibilities. A recommended approach from the review is to improve leadership development among senior teachers from marginalised ethnic groups by having selection panels for senior posts to include leaders from marginalised ethnic groups.

The analysis also outlines the benefits of mentoring support being offered to senior leaders from marginalised ethnic groups by suggesting that it should be available from same-race teachers and leaders, with mentors being trained and paid. It also finds that a positive institutional culture for racial equality is identified as the key enabler to encourage progression to leadership for people of colour. There is much work still to do here, in both the police force and the teaching workforce.

Conclusion

While the introduction of these standards and programmes represents a commitment to reforming police leadership at all levels, like the similar measures put into teaching, the effectiveness of these programmes in improving retention is still being evaluated. Yet, despite recruitment efforts, retention remains a challenge. In the year ending March 2023, 9192 officers left the service, the highest number since records began.[231] These findings suggest that, while various initiatives have been undertaken to improve police recruitment and retention in England, challenges persist, necessitating ongoing efforts and evaluation to achieve sustainable improvements.

What lessons can we learn in teaching?

Policymakers in education can draw several valuable lessons from initiatives used to retain professionals in the police, social-work and nursing sectors. We could begin with enhancing workplace wellbeing and support, as both nurses and social workers have benefited from initiatives

231 Dyfed-Powys Police Federation (2024) 'Poor pay and treatment pushing officers towards resignation' [online] Available at: https://polfed.org/dyfedpowys/news/2024/pay-and-morale-2023-results (Accessed: 1 May 2026).

aimed at reducing burnout and promoting wellbeing. Wellbeing has been a focus in schools over at least the last decade already, with many leaders drafting up wellbeing policies and organising activities for staff.

One of the schools Haili worked in regularly had cakes in the staffroom and secret-friend initiatives, but behaviour was atrocious, so the wellbeing strategies were just a ruse. In many of the schools we visit, the wellbeing policies are proudly pinned on a noticeboard in the staffroom, and staff speak about the wellbeing days they have each term, filled with bike rides, yoga and afternoon teas. For many staff, however, this forced fun would rather be spent catching up on work so they can go home on time.

That's not to say that doing team-building activities and nice things in school aren't worth doing – they can be great. But if cakes are followed by three parents' / carers' evenings and two data drops in the same week, or teachers not being supported with behaviour of students and parents, then it doesn't really mean anything.

Nursing

In nursing, a much more practical approach to wellbeing has been taken, with a focus on flexible-working arrangements, mentoring and programmes to support emotional resilience. Flexibility is tricky in teaching as, obviously, teachers need to be present in classrooms. However, as we discuss in Chapter 12 on schools and Trusts getting it right, strides are being made in this area. For mentorship, formal mentoring arrangements in teaching end after the first couple of years of teaching. However, teachers, of course, have informal mentors throughout their careers who help us navigate challenging situations and act as advice-givers, sounding boards and, hopefully, cheerleaders.

Instructional coaching has also swept across England in the last 10 years as an evidence-informed, impactful form of professional development.[232] Both Haili and Sam have been huge advocates of instructional coaching as we believe that a focus on teaching is a great way of helping teachers feel competent and motivated – as well as improving outcomes for students. However, if there is a focus just on technique and improving strategies, perhaps something about the more psychosocial and emotional side of mentoring and coaching is lost. Like in nursing, there needs to be the

232 Kraft, M.A., Blazar, D. and Hogan, D. (2018) 'The effect of teacher coaching on instruction and achievement: A meta-analysis of the causal evidence' in *Review of Educational Research*, 88(4), pp.547–588.

opportunity for both these types of mentoring and coaching, particularly as recent research has demonstrated that belonging and shared vision contribute to positive school cultures, increasing staff retention.[233]

The National Retention Programme in nursing has emphasised psychological safety at work; teaching, with its focus on accountability, could certainly do with a dose of this. Of course, teachers need to be held to standards, but belonging to a community, as we have seen from our interviews, is so important. There are many ways nursing has tried to develop this that teachers can learn from, beginning with building trust between senior leaders and teachers. In some schools, there is a clear divide between senior leaders and other colleagues – a kind of 'them' and 'us' mentality. Schools are naturally hierarchical places, but 'do as I say' cultures, rather than 'do as I do', end up becoming top-down, leaving teachers sometimes feeling powerless. A classic example of this is expecting all teachers to tackle uniform issues with students, and then senior leaders walking by students with their shirts out. This may seem petty, but it can really erode a teacher's trust and respect. Senior leadership should always lead by example and be actively invested in school initiatives. As famously said in *Spiderman*, 'with great power comes great responsibility'. Leaders create the weather in a school.

In addition, schools are becoming increasingly fragmented – particularly in secondaries. Many departments have their own staffrooms and social areas, so there may be whole terms that go by where they don't get the opportunity to communicate with each other meaningfully. This is why activities that promote collaboration and shared experiences are so vital, as they can help employees feel connected and valued. These activities are different from social opportunities, so approaches such as professional learning communities based around a shared inquiry project or action research project can help bring colleagues together and feel their voice and expertise really matter. Making sure all employees feel valued and respected, regardless of their background or identity, needs to be central to any efforts in improving belonging.

Chiltern Learning Trust, led by the incredible efforts of Sufian Sadiq, are really doing incredible things in this space – as outlined at the end of Chapter 12 on where schools and Trusts are getting it right. Ensuring

233 Id-Deen, L. and Nalu, N. (2026) 'Belonging Matters: Amplifying Teachers' Voices in Schools' in *Mathematics Teacher Educator* Vol.12 Issue 3 pp.185–194 on National Council of Teachers of Mathematics [online] Available at: https://pubs.nctm.org/view/journals/mte/12/3/article-p185.xml (Accessed: 1 May 2026).

that teachers from marginalised ethnic groups are visible in leadership positions is a start.

Social work

In social work, additional support structures such as mentoring and counselling services have been put in place, as well as reduced caseloads in high-pressure areas. Recognising teachers and their contributions would go a long way in supporting teachers' work, not just nationally but within schools too. Teachers constantly go above and beyond; they don't do it for a Blue Peter badge, but a 'well done' would definitely go a long way to beginning to create a culture of appreciation. This means a very busy headteacher relying on their leaders to help keep them aware of the great things that are going on in the school, as they can't keep an eye on everything. Communication is key. But this should include listening, understanding and empathising with each other. For teachers who may be struggling, this communication may often be missing. As detailed in our own teaching stories (Chapter 3), we have both had periods where we have found the jobs challenging. On those occasions, it can sometimes feel dangerous to admit these vulnerabilities, through fears we will be seen as incapable or failing at the job. In schools, we need to work more to remove the stigma around mental health, as this has had promising results in the nursing and social-work fields in terms of retention.

Professional development is another theme that emerged from the interviews for this book. When teachers have opportunities for professional development that is bespoke and aligned to their interests and needs, they feel supported and are more likely to be loyal and committed. Perhaps more important, they won't get bored! Almost all the long-serving teachers we spoke to passionately articulated the ways in which they had been granted the freedom and support to pursue their passions in education.

At the same time, some teachers we speak to feel a bit 'CPD-ed out'. The relentless drive to improve can become exhausting for teachers who are already feeling stressed. Therefore, although professional development is important, it is just part of a more complex jigsaw puzzle, centred around belonging and psychological safety. In practical terms, this could look like reduced administrative workloads for teachers, rather than performative wellbeing activities, as well as increased access to peer-support networks, not necessarily just instructional coaching. Greater flexibility in timetabling and remote-working options for non-teaching responsibilities are also integral to teacher retention, as more experienced teachers are seeking out more flexible jobs.

Police

As detailed earlier, the police have developed clear and attainable career-progression opportunities, through fast-track and direct-entry schemes, which have provided officers with transparent career-advancement routes. This could be a real lesson for teaching and a practical way forwards. The traditional routes of promotion in teaching, where teachers are removed from the classroom, are just not attracting as many teachers. A different approach is needed at national level, with real alternative pathways that teachers can transition through. There could also be more varied leadership-development programmes that aren't all based around the same model, as these end up as very generic and become aimed at those still wanting a traditional senior-leadership position. Singapore has really been leading the field internationally with this, and the next chapter explores what other countries with more successful retention rates for teachers have been doing.

Financial incentives

In nursing and social work, financial incentives have been introduced to improve retention. These have included retention bonuses and re-entry programmes for retired nurses and bursaries in retention for social workers in underserved areas. There are already bursaries for teacher-training in shortage subjects and, while this may have had a small positive impact on applications, one in three teachers still leave the profession within five years, bursary or not. Although many of the teachers we spoke to didn't feel they were motivated by money, in a cost-of-living crisis it would be privileged indeed to suggest it doesn't matter.

Budgets aside, there are money-related retention incentives that have been successful in other public-service professions that may have a positive impact on teacher retention. These might include retention rather than just recruitment bonuses for teachers in high-need schools or subjects, and housing or transportation subsidies to ease financial pressures, especially for teachers in urban or remote areas.

Pay also needs to be aligned with responsibilities – not just for official Teaching and Learning Responsibility (TLR) holders. When both Haili and Sam started teaching, there were staff who held historic TLR payments for ridiculous things, such as being key holders, and we are certainly not advocating that! However, teachers often shoulder extra responsibilities outside their normal roles; in industry, they would not be expected to do this for free. It is about ensuring that teacher salaries are competitive with other professions requiring similar qualifications, otherwise the lure to leave can be strong. It perhaps used to be the case that teachers may have needed to take a pay cut to leave the classroom. This simply is no longer true. There are many, many job options now available that still have the moral purpose teaching brings but are outside the classroom and are well paid. Therefore, teaching has to keep up to retain great teachers.

The Department for Education should consider additional pay for teachers with mentoring roles. In ITT, mentors were offered a payment for their work with trainee teachers in academic year 2024–25, but there is currently no indication that this will continue. Appreciation like this goes some way towards demonstrating to teachers that their work is important and really matters.

We have explored how other professions might be attempting to tackle their retention problems... how about other countries?

CHAPTER TEN:
What can we learn from other countries?

Teacher retention is not just an England problem. The Organisation for Economic Co-operation and Development (OECD) has highlighted a significant increase in teacher shortages across its member countries. Between 2015 and 2022, the proportion of students whose principals reported staff shortages rose from 29% to 46.7% on average.[234] However, teacher-retention rates vary significantly across countries, and there are some countries with notably higher teacher retention rates than England. Teachers in England are resigning at almost double the 4.6% average of 15 other countries surveyed by the OECD.[235] Who are these countries and what can we learn from them? Let's start with our other home nations: Scotland, Northern Ireland and Wales.

Scotland

Background

The latest official statistics show that the number of school teachers in Scotland continues to change year to year. In 2025, there were 53,475 fulltime equivalent teachers, a small increase from the previous year, and student–teacher ratios remained around 13.2:1, reflecting overall workforce scale.[236]

Like in England, Scotland also has issues with retaining early career teachers. Figures reported from the General Teaching Council for Scotland indicate that more than 1300 teachers who gained provisional registration left the register within five years, with numbers increasing

234 OECD (2024) 'Education Policy Outlook 2024: Reshaping Teaching into a Thriving Profession from ABCs to AI' [online] Available at: www.oecd.org/en/publications/education-policy-outlook-2024_dd5140e4-en.html (Accessed: 1 May 2026).

235 OECD (2024) 'Education Policy Outlook 2024: Reshaping Teaching into a Thriving Profession from ABCs to AI' [online] Available at: www.oecd.org/en/publications/education-policy-outlook-2024_dd5140e4-en.html (Accessed: 1 May 2026).

236 Scottish Government (2025) 'Pupil and teacher characteristics 2025 published' [online] Available at: www.gov.scot/news/pupil-and-teacher-characteristics-2025-published (Accessed: 1 May 2026).

year on year.[237] Another report notes similar figures, with 1337 teachers leaving the profession within five years of starting since 2018.[238] While this is worrying, it is nowhere near the crisis levels we see in England; available General Teaching Council for Scotland (GTCS) data suggests that around 1 in 12 to 1 in 14 teachers (approximately 7–9%) leave the profession within their first five years, unlike 1 in 3 in England.

The GTCS Registration Snapshot reports that approximately 5% of experienced teachers choose to leave the Register each year. During the 19-month period from August 2022 to March 2024, roughly 4815 individuals left the Register (including retirements, moves abroad and other exits)[239] – again, nowhere near as high as England, where about 41,200 fulltime equivalent teachers left their jobs in 2023–24. This is down from 42,600 in 2022–23 and the lowest since 2020, but still not where we need to be.[240]

Reasons collected from those leaving teaching in Scotland are very similar to England, and include lack of support; workload and bureaucracy; student-behaviour challenges; and workplace stress or culture issues.[241] However, unlike England, Scotland seems to have too many teachers for vacant positions, as another reason cited for teachers leaving the register

237 Scottish Liberal Democrats (2024) '1,300 teachers have quit within five years of starting work' [online] Available at: www.scotlibdems.org.uk/news/article/1300-teachers-have-quit-within-five-years-of-starting-work (Accessed: 1 May 2026).

238 STV News (2024) 'Hundreds of new teachers quit profession within five years, figures show: The General Teaching Council for Scotland said 1,337 teachers had left the register within five years' [online] Available at: https://news.stv.tv/scotland/hundreds-of-new-teachers-quit-profession-within-five-years-figures-show (Accessed: 1 May 2026).

239 The General Teaching Council for Scotland (2024) 'The GTC Scotland Register – Registration Snapshot report: Leaving the Register' [online] Available at: www.gtcs.org.uk/documents/pages/registration-snapshot-report-2024-09-leaving-the-register (Accessed: 1 May 2026).

240 Dyson, J. (2025) 'Fewer teachers quit and more return: 10 key workforce findings: Data suggests recruitment and retention pressures may be easing' on *SchoolsWeek* [online] Available at: https://schoolsweek.co.uk/fewer-teachers-quit-and-more-return-10-key-workforce-findings (Accessed: 1 May 2026).

241 The General Teaching Council for Scotland (2024) 'The GTC Scotland Register – Registration Snapshot report: Leaving the Register' [online] Available at: www.gtcs.org.uk/documents/pages/registration-snapshot-report-2024-09-leaving-the-register (Accessed: 1 May 2026).

is difficulty in securing posts.[242] This is a challenge many leaders in England wish they had, with one leader recently joking to me that, if you have a physics or chemistry degree and can string a sentence together, you've got a job for life.

It is difficult to compare the picture in England to Scotland as detailed longitudinal retention rates are not routinely published as a single headline metric in the same way as in England's national workforce reports. However, analyses by third parties such as Measuring Quality in Initial Teacher Education (MQuITE) suggest that around 70% of teachers remain after five years, with some moving to teach elsewhere – including England.[243]

Retention

While Scotland does not have a single high-profile national teacher-retention strategy, there is important work by government bodies, professional regulators and unions aimed at understanding and addressing teacher-retention issues in Scotland. This includes workforce planning, official reports and recommendations that relate to retention, working conditions and teacher supply. As we've already mentioned, the GTCS routinely publishes 'Registration Snapshot' reports that include data on teachers leaving the Register and inform retention planning. In its 2025 report,[244] GTCS highlighted that teachers are leaving sooner than expected, and made recommendations to improve teacher supply, specifically noting the importance of focusing on retention as part of workforce planning. These recommendations are used by GTCS and shared with the Scottish Government and stakeholders to help shape policy conversations about why teachers leave and how supply might be improved.

The Scottish Government allocates targeted funding to support local authorities and protect teacher numbers, which is directly related to

242 The General Teaching Council for Scotland (2024) 'The GTC Scotland Register – Registration Snapshot report: Leaving the Register' [online] Available at: www.gtcs.org.uk/documents/pages/registration-snapshot-report-2024-09-leaving-the-register (Accessed: 1 May 2026).

243 Measuring Quality in Initial Teacher Education 'Teacher Retention' on General Teaching Council Scotland [online] Available at: www.mquite.scot/teacher-retention (Accessed: 1 May 2026).

244 The General Teaching Council for Scotland (2025) 'GTC Scotland publishes registration report 2025 and makes recommendations to improve teacher supply' [online] Available at: www.gtcs.org.uk/news/news-and-updates/gtc-scotland-publishes-registration-report-2025-and-makes-recommendations-to-improve-teacher-supply (Accessed: 1 May 2026).

retaining teachers within schools. For the 2023–24 period, approximately £145.5 million was made available to local authorities specifically to help safeguard teacher posts and address supply and retention challenges.[245] This money was spent on:

- **protecting existing teacher posts**, to prevent local authorities from reducing teacher numbers in response to falling student rolls or budget pressure
- **maintaining student–teacher ratios**, to help local authorities meet national student–teacher ratio expectations, particularly in primary (maintaining ratios reduces workload pressure, which is strongly linked to retention)
- **sustaining permanent and fulltime contracts**, to convert temporary contracts into permanent posts and avoid moving teachers onto fractional or insecure contracts
- **supporting workforce-planning** during demographic change to plan redeployment, retrain more strategically and retain experienced staff rather than lose them permanently.[246]

This seems like a very different approach from England, as Scottish Government papers make it clear that the money has not been spent on pay rises, national CPD or wellbeing programmes, and has not been targeted directly at individual teachers. Instead, it was a structural retention measure, operating at system level.

Teacher unions and research groups in Scotland, such as the Educational Institute of Scotland's Teacher Workload Research Report,[247] examined workload and professional sustainability, which we know are key drivers of retention. This research highlights ongoing challenges that can lead to attrition and underpins calls for policy action to improve working conditions – so no different from England here then.

245 Scottish Government (2025) 'Teacher numbers and the teacher workforce planning process: FOI release' [online] Available at: www.gov.scot/publications/foi-202400439555 (Accessed: 1 May 2026).

246 Scottish Government (2025) 'Teacher numbers and the teacher workforce planning process: FOI release' [online] Available at: www.gov.scot/publications/foi-202400439555 (Accessed: 1 May 2026).

247 The Educational Institute of Scotland 'Workload Research' [online] Available at: www.eis.org.uk/Content/images/Campaigns/QualityEducation/WorkloadResearch.pdf

Northern Ireland

Background

Teacher retention is a growing concern across the UK, though – as we have begun to explore – it manifests differently in each jurisdiction. England's retention challenges are well documented through detailed national workforce statistics, while Northern Ireland's picture is less transparent but no less concerning.

Northern Ireland does not routinely publish longitudinal retention statistics in the same way as England, such as five-year post-qualification survival rates. However, a range of workforce indicators, union evidence and independent reviews strongly suggest that retention pressures are significant. Official workforce data from the Northern Ireland Statistics and Research Agency shows that the number of teachers has remained relatively stable in recent years. In 2024–25, there were approximately 21,800 teachers by headcount: around 20,100 fulltime equivalents.[248] On the surface, this stability might suggest a healthy workforce; however, headline numbers can mask underlying churn and dissatisfaction.

Evidence from teacher unions and independent reviews points to workload as a central issue. Surveys conducted by teaching unions in Northern Ireland consistently report that a large majority of teachers experience workload as unmanageable, with many considering leaving the profession if conditions do not improve.[249] In response to these concerns, the Northern Ireland Executive commissioned an Independent Review of Teacher Workload, signalling official recognition that workload and retention are linked system-level problems rather than individual failings from school leaders. Academic research reinforces this picture. A study of school leaders in Northern Ireland and Wales found high levels of stress, emotional exhaustion and reduced wellbeing, all of which are strongly associated in literature with intentions to leave teaching.[250]

248 Department of Education (Northern Ireland) (2025) 'Teacher workforce statistics 2024/25' [online] Available at: www.education-ni.gov.uk/publications/teacher-workforce-statistics-202425 (Accessed: 1 May 2026).

249 Department of Education (Northern Ireland) (2025) 'Independent Review of Teacher Workload – Final Report' [online] Available at: www.education-ni.gov.uk/publications/independent-review-teacher-workload-final-report (Accessed: 1 May 2026).

250 Marchant, E., Dowd, J., Bray, L., Rowlands, G., Miles, N., Crick, T., James, M., Dadaczynski, K. and Okan, O. (2024) 'The well-being and work-related stress of senior school leaders in Wales and Northern Ireland during COVID-19 "educational leadership crisis": A cross-sectional descriptive study' in *PLoS One*, 19(4), e0291278.

While intention to leave does not always translate directly into exit, it is a well-established predictor of attrition.

Media reporting about teacher retention has been incredibly emotive. The *Belfast Telegraph* claimed that 'Stormont has failed teachers during workload and retention crisis'[251] and the *Irish News* said that 'teachers' concerns over issues including pay and SEN must be addressed'.[252] Although this is not hard data on formal retention rates, it indicates a structural fragility within the workforce.

Retention

While England and Northern Ireland differ in governance, accountability structures and data transparency, there are striking similarities in the drivers of retention pressure. Both systems exhibit high workload and administrative burden, along with growing concerns about teacher wellbeing, and there is growing evidence of stress and burnout. Both have had policy responses that increasingly acknowledge retention as a system-level issue.

However, England has introduced explicit recruitment and retention strategies, including the Early Career Framework (ECF) and workload reduction initiatives, albeit with mixed success. Northern Ireland's approach has focused more on workload review and workforce stability, particularly through negotiations with unions and independent review processes. However, meaningful improvement depends on addressing the conditions under which teachers work and, like in England, without sustained attention to these factors, both England and Northern Ireland will continue to struggle to retain experienced teachers in the years ahead.

251 Bain, M. (2025) 'Stormont has failed teachers during workload and retention crisis, union claims' on *Belfast Telegraph* [online] Available at: www.belfasttelegraph.co.uk/news/education/stormont-has-failed-teachers-during-workload-and-retention-crisis-union-claims/a575109191.html (Accessed: 1 May 2026).

252 Ainsworth, P. (2025) 'Teachers' concerns over issues including pay and SEN must be addressed, union conference hears: The Irish National Teachers' Organisation's annual Northern Conference is taking place in Belfast' on *Irish News* [online] Available at: www.irishnews.com/news/northern-ireland/teachers-concerns-over-issues-including-pay-and-sen-must-be-addressed-union-conference-hears-3RQRV7WYIJFL5BM7QMOYRG6DXM (Accessed: 1 May 2026).

Wales

Background

Teacher retention is a live policy issue in Wales, but the evidence base suggests a more nuanced picture than in England. Wales does face recruitment and retention pressures, particularly in some secondary subjects and Welsh-medium provision, yet headline retention and attrition indicators are generally stronger than England's. Indeed, their retention pressures are not really characterised as a uniform 'retention crisis' across all phases and subjects. The Education Workforce Council (EWC), which maintains the Register of Education Practitioners, reports that 75.9% of teachers who were registered as school teachers in 2020 were still registered as school teachers five years later in 2025.[253] This is a comparatively strong five-year retention figure by UK standards!

However, Wales does experience uneven supply and retention challenges, especially in secondary shortage subjects such as maths, science, Welsh and modern foreign languages. The Association of School and College Leaders (ASCL) notes that the pandemic temporarily eased teacher-supply pressures, but warns that recruitment and retention challenges persist in shortage subjects, Welsh-medium schools and disadvantaged areas, and may intensify as labour-market conditions normalise.[254]

A separate Welsh Government-commissioned analysis of incentives and labour-market conditions reported that teacher attrition in Wales is around 4% per year, substantially lower than England's 9–10% annual leaver rate in comparable workforce data.[255] The same report suggests that Wales' lower exit rates may be partly explained by workforce composition; Wales has an older, more experienced teacher workforce on average, and experience is associated with stronger retention.[256]

253 Education Workforce Council (Wales) 'Education workforce statistics' [online] Available at: www.ewc.wales/site/index.php/en/about-us/policy-and-research/workforce-statistics (Accessed: 1 May 2026).

254 Association of School and College Leaders (2024) 'ASCL evidence to IWPRB 5th remit: March 2024' [online] Available at: www.ascl.org.uk/ASCL/media/ASCL/Membership/ASCL%20UK/ASCL%20Cymru/ASCL-evidence-to-IWPRB-5th-remit-March-2024-fv.pdf (Accessed: 1 May 2026).

255 Education Policy Institute (2024) 'Incentives to recruit and retain teachers in Wales' [online] Available at: https://epi.org.uk/publications-and-research/incentives-to-recruit-and-retain-teachers-in-wales (Accessed: 1 May 2026).

256 Education Policy Institute (2024) 'Incentives to recruit and retain teachers in Wales' [online] Available at: https://epi.org.uk/publications-and-research/incentives-to-recruit-and-retain-teachers-in-wales (Accessed: 1 May 2026).

Retention

Like England, Wales' approach has tended to combine workforce-planning, targeted incentives and system-level professional-learning reforms, rather than relying on a single flagship retention programme. A clear example is Wales' focus on Welsh-medium teacher supply. A Welsh Government evidence paper to the Senedd outlines the creation of a Welsh in Education Teacher Retention Bursary, offering £5000 to teachers who have achieved QTS since August 2020 and have completed three years teaching Welsh (or through the medium of Welsh) in the secondary phase.[257] The bursary is explicitly framed as both a retention lever and a way to generate evidence on whether financial incentives influence entry and staying behaviours. As this is a fairly recent initiative, there is not enough data available to measure the impact.

In England, bursaries have certainly helped to recruit teachers but direct evidence that bursaries improve retention is weak. This is due to most research to date focusing on recruitment, not long-term retention. While bursaries help more people start teaching, there is little robust evidence that they directly *increase* retention (that is, make teachers stay longer than they otherwise would). This is explicitly highlighted in the National Foundation for Educational Research (NFER) / Gatsby research, which recommended that future research is needed to assess cost-effectiveness fully.[258]

The same evidence paper to the Senedd mentioned earlier also describes pipeline initiatives, such as *Addysgu'r Dyfodol* (Future Teaching), which provides mentoring and school-experience opportunities to encourage entry into teaching, alongside efforts to develop Welsh language skills among the wider workforce.[259] More broadly, the Welsh Government commissioned a report that reviews the role of financial and non-financial levers in hard-to-staff areas and subjects, connecting retention

257 Welsh Government (2025) 'Teacher Recruitment and Retention – Evidence Paper for the Children, Young People and Education Committee' from Welsh Government written evidence to the Senedd, 11 September 2025, pp.12–13, outlining the Welsh in Education Teacher Retention Bursary.

258 Gatsby 'GATB Bursaries Evaluation Report Final' [online] Available at: www.gatsby.org.uk/app/uploads/sites/2/2025/07/gatb-bursaries-evaluation-report-final.pdf

259 Welsh Government (2025) 'Teacher Recruitment and Retention – Evidence Paper for the Children, Young People and Education Committee' from Welsh Government written evidence to the Senedd, 11 September 2025, pp.12–13, outlining the Welsh in Education Teacher Retention Bursary.

to local labour-market conditions, rural recruitment difficulties and subject-specific shortages.[260]

When analysing retention patterns in a really granular way, a strength in Wales is the availability of workforce intelligence via the EWC register. EWC produces annual workforce statistics and retention snapshots and submits evidence to national inquiries, helping to keep workforce sustainability on the policy agenda. This data infrastructure enables more responsive policy design and clearer identification of where retention is most fragile, such as specific sectors, subject areas or even geographical regions.

Wales' reforms have been tied to the implementation of the Curriculum for Wales, which has necessitated extensive professional learning. NFER argues that professional learning reform and curriculum reform are intertwined: the ability to retain and develop staff is part of delivering high-quality education during system change.[261] While professional learning is not always labelled as retention policy, research consistently links meaningful, high-quality CPD and supportive working conditions to teacher job satisfaction and reduced attrition intentions. This is an approach England has taken through the formulation of the ECF and revised National Professional Qualifications (NPQs).

Essentially, Wales appears to retain a higher proportion of teachers overall but still faces pressure points familiar to England. Its approaches to teacher retention, however, seem to be about keeping stability in the workforce and being more granular about what those specific pressure points are. The comparative lesson is not that Wales has solved retention, but that retention patterns and policy needs are uneven, and that building a stable workforce depends on both targeted incentives and the wider conditions of professional life in schools.

How is the picture different over the Channel?

260 Education Policy Institute (2024) 'Incentives to recruit and retain teachers in Wales' [online] Available at: https://epi.org.uk/publications-and-research/incentives-to-recruit-and-retain-teachers-in-wales (Accessed: 1 May 2026).

261 Worth, J. and Ghosh, A. (2022) 'Teacher Labour Market in Wales Annual Report 2022'. Slough: NFER.

France

Background

Starting with France, who exhibit a remarkably low teacher-attrition rate – an impressively low 0.4% in 2023–24.[262] The lower number of teaching positions in France means there is a huge amount of competition to become a teacher, and even the process of qualifying is extremely competitive. To be considered, candidates must take a series of competitive written and oral exams called the *concours*, which leads to becoming a certified teacher. The difference between this system and the PGCE is that prospective teachers are not just competing with themselves to achieve a pass score, but the score is also determined by the pool of candidates, all of whom are competing for a limited number of places. This is not uncommon in France, where almost all civil-service jobs are recruited via *concours*, some of which are more competitive than others.

The exams are organised into written and oral exams, which can be as long as six hours per exam. The written exams are based on a set programme, with five open-ended themes taken from the school curriculum on which the exam papers can be based. Candidates need to complete a synthesis of several documents and write an organised analysis comparing and contrasting the set of documents in relation to one of the themes of the programme. The documents can be literary extracts, primary or secondary source historical documents, speech transcripts, advertisements, photographs, paintings, and so on. Candidates then might be asked to translate two short passages from English to French and French to English. Two exercises of phonology / phonetics and linguistics are also included, where candidates must analyse and explain segments chosen from one of the given documents using technical linguistic terms to show their mastery of the language. One of the final written tasks involves prospective teachers writing a full unit plan for a given class in a high school or middle school, explaining and justifying the order in which they would present the documents to students, and the objectives, and then explain in detail the activities proposed in class, including some propositions of how they would evaluate it.

262 OECD (2025) 'Education at a Glance 2025: Chapter D8. How severe are teacher shortages across countries?' [online] Available at: www.oecd.org/en/publications/education-at-a-glance-2025_1c0d9c79-en/full-report/how-severe-are-teacher-shortages-across-countries_781f4a97.html (Accessed: 1 May 2026).

Remember: this is an outline of only the written test – candidates have to complete two oral tests in addition to this![263] Although the content of the exams themselves is not impossibly difficult, the way it is marked means that candidates must rank in the top portion of applicants owing to a limited number of available teaching positions, and this can be very competitive. An article in *Tes magazine* states that, a few years ago, there were 1500 applicants and just 570 positions.[264]

Teachers in England reading this may think 'no, thank you!' PGCEs here are tough, as candidates have to balance teaching with academic work, but this level of competition for teaching jobs has not existed in England for a while. When both authors of this book, Haili and Sam, trained almost 20 years ago, gaining a place on a PGCE to teach English was an incredibly competitive process and, as detailed in our teaching stories (Chapter 3), Haili did not even gain a place on the course the first time she applied. There is a growing sense, anecdotally at least, that recruitment pressures in recent years have made it harder to maintain consistent quality in new appointments – which is perhaps an inevitable consequence of the challenges schools face in filling posts. Indeed, only two years ago, civil servants at the Department for Education contacted Initial Teacher Training (ITT) providers to instruct that they needed to stop rejecting so many candidates,[265] which makes it seem like all standards needed to be thrown out.

If all competition has been taken out of becoming a teacher, it seems like anyone could do it, which doesn't exactly foster a sense of pride. In fact, it feeds into the national narrative about teachers with the joke I am sure every teacher has heard: 'those who can't, teach'. It may be tempting to think that the difficulty of training to teach in France means that people just don't bother; however, in a *Tes magazine* article, French teacher Cyril Guinet stated that the competitiveness of the *concours* process means

263 Donnelly, A. (2022) 'Everything you've ever wanted to know about the CAPES/CAFEP concours' on Present Perfect [online] Available at: https://presentperfectblog.com/2022/08/05/everything-youve-ever-wanted-to-know-about-the-capes-cafep-concours (Accessed: 1 May 2026).

264 Peirson-Hagger, E. (2024) 'Why is France so good at keeping its teachers?' on *Tes magazine* [online] Available at: www.tes.com/magazine/analysis/general/teacher-retention-why-france-so-good-keeping-its-teachers (Accessed: 1 May 2026).

265 Booth, S. (2023) 'Reject fewer teacher applicants, DfE tells trainers' on *SchoolsWeek* [online] Available at: https://schoolsweek.co.uk/reject-fewer-teacher-applicants-dfe-tells-trainers (Accessed: 1 May 2026).

those who go for it typically choose to stay in teaching for a lifetime.[266] In France, if a teacher leaves the state system, they also lose their *concours*, which makes the decision high stakes indeed. If they wanted to re-enter the profession, they would need to complete the process again, which seems to act as a deterrent.

Retention

Pay

While most teachers we interviewed for this book never mentioned pay at all, salaries frequently come up in discussions about teacher retention, with observations about teachers' pay not keeping up with the rate of inflation being mentioned. It might be natural, then, to surmise that French teachers have more attractive salaries, if it is more competitive to train and fewer leave. Yet, this isn't actually the case.

In England, teacher salaries rise relatively quickly, with annual increases on the Main Pay Scale (MPS) and then often bi-annually on the Upper Pay Scale (UPS), until teachers reach UPS3 and their final earnings reach £51,048 (correct as of January 2026). If teachers move through the pay scale in the expected time and don't pick up any extra payments for Teaching and Learning Responsibilities (TLR), they will reach their maximum earnings at between 12 and 14 years of teaching, with no opportunities for a higher salary, unless they wish to move into a leadership position.

According to the OECD,[267] the starting salary for primary-school teachers in France is roughly £30,311; it is around £32,916 in England, which is broadly comparable. Salaries in England rise much more quickly, with a primary teacher of 15 years in France earning around £35,000 and their English counterpart earning closer to £50,000. In France, the top end of the pay scale for primary practitioners is £55,000; meanwhile, in England, the top level remains £51,048 so, after 15 years, there is no financial incentive to stay longer in the same role, and many teachers are forced

266 Peirson-Hagger, E. (2024) 'Why is France so good at keeping its teachers?' on *Tes magazine* [online] Available at: www.tes.com/magazine/analysis/general/teacher-retention-why-france-so-good-keeping-its-teachers (Accessed: 1 May 2026).

267 OECD (2025) 'Education at a Glance 2025: Chapter D3. How much are teachers and school heads paid?' [online] Available at: www.oecd.org/en/publications/2025/09/education-at-a-glance-2025_c58fc9ae/full-report/how-much-are-teachers-and-school-heads-paid_5daf5678.html (Accessed: 1 May 2026).

into leadership positions, meaning the best teachers may leave the classroom in pursuit of a better salary.

However, teaching salaries in France are still considered to be poor. According to a 2024 OECD report, the real salaries of mid-career French teachers have stagnated, with only a 1% increase between 2015 and 2023, compared to a 4% average increase in other OECD countries.[268]

If it isn't pay, then, perhaps what helps France with their teacher attrition is the comparative lack of stress associated with teaching in England.

Stress

Stress regularly comes up as a key factor in why teachers are considering leaving the profession in England. The Education Support charity's 2023 Teacher Wellbeing Index reveals that 78% of education staff feel stressed, with 36% of teachers reporting experiencing burnout and half of staff reporting insomnia or difficulty sleeping.[269] A report by Headspace (2023) positions education as the most stressful career path in the UK, surpassing stress levels in sectors including financial services and insurance.[270]

Some of this stress undoubtedly comes from accountability measures, as highlighted by the Nuffield Foundation, who reveal that 68% of teachers in England experience stress related to these measures, compared to 45% in other countries.[271] This suggests that the emphasis on accountability in England adversely affects teachers' mental health. The OECD average for teachers experiencing high levels of stress is 18%;[272] 31% of teachers

268 Lecherbonnier, S. (2024) 'Les salaires réels des enseignants français en milieu de carrière stagnent, selon l'OCDE' on *Le Monde* [online] Available at: www.lemonde.fr/societe/article/2024/09/11/les-salaires-reels-des-enseignants-francais-en-milieu-de-carriere-stagnent-selon-l-ocde_6312842_3224.html (Accessed: 1 May 2026).

269 Education Support (2023) 'Twix 2023' [online] Available at: www.educationsupport.org.uk/media/0h4jd5pt/twix_2023.pdf

270 Headspace (2023) 'A Turn of the Tide: Employee Mental Health in 2023' [online] Available at: https://organizations.headspace.com/blog/a-turn-of-the-tide-employee-mental-health-in-2023 (Accessed: 1 May 2026).

271 Nuffield Foundation (2021) 'Teachers point towards school accountability as main driver of stress' [online] Available at: www.nuffieldfoundation.org/news/teachers-point-towards-school-accountability-as-main-driver-of-stress (Accessed: 1 May 2026).

272 OECD (2020) 'TALIS 2018 Results (Volume II): Chapter 2. Boosting the prestige and standing of the profession' [online] Available at: www.oecd.org/en/publications/talis-2018-results-volume-ii_19cf08df-en/full-report/component-7.html (Accessed: 1 May 2026).

in England report experiencing high levels of stress, which is significantly above that average.[273]

Although some accountability measures are internal, the majority of accountability stress comes from external factors such as Ofsted. In France, the inspection culture is vastly different from in England. Their system is characterised by a focus on individual teacher evaluations rather than whole-school assessments. It operates under the Ministry of National Education, and involves several key components:

- ***Inspecteurs Généraux* (General Inspectors):** These senior officials are responsible for overseeing specific subject areas or educational sectors at the national level. Their duties include evaluating curricula, advising on educational policies and ensuring consistency across the education system.
- ***Inspecteurs d'Académie* (Academic Inspectors):** Operating at the regional level within educational districts known as *académies*, these inspectors supervise schools and teachers, ensuring compliance with national educational standards and policies.
- ***Inspecteurs de l'Éducation Nationale* (National Education Inspectors):** Focusing primarily on primary education, these inspectors assess individual teachers, provide professional-development support and monitor the implementation of educational programs.[274]

The emphasis is very much on the evaluation of individual teachers, with inspectors observing classroom teaching, reviewing lesson plans and assessing pedagogical methods to ensure that teachers are meeting the required standards. This approach aims to enhance teaching quality directly by focusing on individual performance, rather than whole-school data. Inspections are undertaken by regional inspectors, and headteachers score teachers for 'punctuality', 'authority' and 'standing', but it is the inspector who scores the teacher's pedagogical performance. The teacher receives an overall score, 60% of which is accounted for by the inspector's assessment; the remaining 40% is contributed by the headteacher.

---

273 Nuffield Foundation (2021) 'Teachers point towards school accountability as main driver of stress' [online] Available at: www.nuffieldfoundation.org/news/teachers-point-towards-school-accountability-as-main-driver-of-stress (Accessed: 1 May 2026).

274 de Wolf, I.F. and Janssens, F.J.G. (2007) 'Effects and Side Effects of Inspections and Accountability in Education: An Overview of Empirical Studies' in *Oxford Review of Education*, 33(3), pp.379–396.

Primary-school teachers are usually inspected every three to four years; for secondary teachers, the gap between visits is six to seven years.[275] However, since 2010, there has been a shift towards a more Ofsted-like collective evaluation of the performance of primary schools, to analyse and understand the parameters likely to explain students' results. Some regional education authorities have adopted this approach, which results in an oral report delivered to the headteacher and teaching staff and a written report sent to the regional education office.

For secondary schools, inspection also involves various key performance indicators, including contextual value-added measures intended to show the school effect on student performance. Each school has objectives to be met within a specified timeframe and the indicators are used to evaluate these. The data is for school leaders and inspectors and is not made public – so there is much more of a focus on improvement than public scrutiny.

The French inspection system's focus on individual teacher evaluation reflects France's emphasis on teacher quality as a central component of educational excellence. Even the inspection process, which includes recommendations from inspectors on further training or professional-development opportunities to address specific teacher needs, ensures that teachers receive the necessary support to enhance their practice. Obviously, inspections are always stressful, but teachers in France are usually observed only at three points during their career, and teachers are given a month's notice ahead of their inspection: a far cry from the system in England.

Working hours

Perhaps the biggest difference between a teacher's work life in France and in England is working hours and the flexibility afforded to teachers. An average teacher in France spends 20 hours a week teaching, whereas teachers in England spend 24.[276] What most teachers in England might find remarkable is that teachers in the French system are not required to be in school outside of those hours. In a recent *Tes magazine* article, a

275 Pembroke, J. (2021) 'A comparison of assessment and accountability in the French and English school systems' on Sig+ [online] Available at: www.sigplus.co.uk/2021/03/a-comparison-of-assessment-and-accountability-in-the-french-and-english-school-systems (Accessed: 1 May 2026).

276 Department for Education (2025) 'School workforce in England' on Gov.uk [online] Available at: https://explore-education-statistics.service.gov.uk/find-statistics/school-workforce-in-england/2024 (Accessed: 1 May 2026).

teacher in France detailed how their 20 teaching hours were timetabled across four days and, on the other day, they were not required to go into school at all and could work from home.[277]

What is more, those non-contact times in France are not spent on admin tasks such as marking books, as teachers in France are expected only to mark exams. Both Haili and Sam are English teachers, and we have the absolute worst marking workload of any teachers – we said what we said! Marking only exams would take a considerable amount of work from teachers, making them much less stressed. As the Education Endowment Foundation said in 2017, in their 'Marked Improvement' report, excessive marking in different colour pens has very little impact on student results. Instead, verbal feedback with instantly actionable targets is much better.[278] This report was released over 10 years ago now and we still see leadership teams around the country insisting that teachers triple-mark books every week, in different colour pens, or use 'verbal feedback' stamps. It is no wonder that teachers are stressed.

According to teachers in France, though, the biggest contrast is perhaps their focus on concentrating on simply teaching, rather than on the other more pastoral work that teachers in England spend their time doing. Due to cuts to external services and more students with special educational needs being educated in mainstream schools, now more than ever teachers are providing students (and increasingly their families) with care beyond what is expected. More and more, teachers' jobs are becoming more akin to social workers or child psychiatrists because cuts have seen capacity in those areas significantly reduced. That teachers in France are just not expected to do this absolutely relieves pressure, as all they need to focus on is their teaching and subject knowledge. Quite simply, there are better frameworks and child services in France, so teachers can feel confident that they can just do their job and let other professionals do theirs.

---

277 Peirson-Hagger, E. (2024) 'Why is France so good at keeping its teachers?' on *Tes magazine* [online] Available at: www.tes.com/magazine/analysis/general/teacher-retention-why-france-so-good-keeping-its-teachers (Accessed: 1 May 2026).

278 Elliott, V., Baird, J.-A., Hopfenbeck, T.N., Ingram, J., Thompson, I., Usher, N., Zantout, M., Richardson, J. and Coleman, R. (2016) 'A marked improvement? A review of the evidence on written marking' on Education Endowment Foundation [online] Available at: https://educationendowmentfoundation.org.uk/education-evidence/evidence-reviews/written-marking (Accessed: 1 May 2026).

Conclusion

Of course, like any country, France has its own teacher-shortage issues and, although only 3000 of the 900,000 primary and secondary teachers resigned in 2022, this has increased 300% since six years earlier.[279] There has also been recent strike action, which saw teachers walking out in protest at the introduction of standardised assessment at primary-school level. Yet the context of that strike is telling: England has five statutory primary assessments, which generate significant workload and stress for teachers. It is worth reflecting on what that contrast reveals about the demands placed on the profession here.

Finland

Finland is renowned for its high teacher-retention rates, a success attributed to several key factors. Indeed, teaching was the first-choice career for 59% of teachers in Finland and for 67% in OECD countries and economies participating in the Teaching and Learning International Survey (TALIS).[280] In terms of why they joined the profession, at least 66% of teachers in Finland cite the opportunity to influence children's development or to contribute to society as a major motivation.[281] However, about one teacher out of three (35%) in Finland is aged 50 and above (the OECD average is 34%).[282] This means that Finland will have to renew about one out of three members of its teaching workforce over the next decade or so.

279 Trindade Pereira, I. and Can Yilmaz, M. (2025) 'How is the teacher shortage in the EU impacting the quality of education?' on Euro News [online] Available at: www.euronews.com/my-europe/2025/09/11/how-is-the-teacher-shortage-in-the-eu-impacting-the-quality-of-education (Accessed: 1 May 2026).

280 OECD (2019) 'TALIS 2018 Results (Volume I): Teachers and School Leaders as Lifelong Learners' from TALIS, OECD Publishing, Paris, https://doi.org/10.1787/1d0bc92a-en [online] Available at: www.oecd.org/content/dam/oecd/en/about/programmes/edu/talis/talis2018participantnotes/TALIS2018_CN_FIN.pdf (Accessed: 1 May 2026).

281 OECD (2019) 'TALIS 2018 Results (Volume I): Teachers and School Leaders as Lifelong Learners' from TALIS, OECD Publishing, Paris, https://doi.org/10.1787/1d0bc92a-en [online] Available at: www.oecd.org/content/dam/oecd/en/about/programmes/edu/talis/talis2018participantnotes/TALIS2018_CN_FIN.pdf (Accessed: 1 May 2026).

282 OECD (2019) 'TALIS 2018 Results (Volume I): Teachers and School Leaders as Lifelong Learners' from TALIS, OECD Publishing, Paris, https://doi.org/10.1787/1d0bc92a-en [online] Available at: www.oecd.org/content/dam/oecd/en/about/programmes/edu/talis/talis2018participantnotes/TALIS2018_CN_FIN.pdf (Accessed: 1 May 2026).

In terms of classroom environments, relations between students and teachers are positive overall, with 97% of teachers in Finland agreeing that students and teachers usually get on well with each other.[283] This is a far cry from the culture described by many teachers in England's schools, where behaviour is often described as a trigger for poor wellbeing.

Perhaps one of the biggest differences is that, in Finland, 58% of teachers 'agree' or 'strongly agree' with the statement that their profession is valued in society, which is higher than the average across OECD countries and economies participating in TALIS (26%). In Finland between 2013 and 2018, the percentage of teachers reporting that the teaching profession is valued in society has remained stable.[284] As we've discussed in previous chapters in this book, that sense of self-efficacy teachers get in having a higher status in society can really make the difference to those working in tough schools.

Professional development has a slightly different focus in Finland, with teachers reporting that they participate in collaborative professional learning at least once a month, and also have the opportunity to engage in team-teaching with the same frequency.[285] Many teachers in England might rarely get the opportunity to do this. A recent report from the Teacher Development Trust explicitly highlighted collaboration and collective professional learning as central to effective didagogical practice – that is, the practice of teaching teachers rather than teaching students.

Specifically, the report argues that teacher professional learning should be rooted in dialogue, reflection and collective sense-making, meaning that teachers learn best when they engage collaboratively with colleagues to make sense of evidence, share practice and reflect on how to improve

283 OECD (2019) 'TALIS 2018 Results (Volume I): Teachers and School Leaders as Lifelong Learners' from TALIS, OECD Publishing, Paris, https://doi.org/10.1787/1d0bc92a-en [online] Available at: www.oecd.org/content/dam/oecd/en/about/programmes/edu/talis/talis2018participantnotes/TALIS2018_CN_FIN.pdf (Accessed: 1 May 2026).

284 OECD (2019) 'TALIS 2018 Results (Volume I): Teachers and School Leaders as Lifelong Learners' from TALIS, OECD Publishing, Paris, https://doi.org/10.1787/1d0bc92a-en [online] Available at: www.oecd.org/content/dam/oecd/en/about/programmes/edu/talis/talis2018participantnotes/TALIS2018_CN_FIN.pdf (Accessed: 1 May 2026).

285 OECD (2019) 'TALIS 2018 Results (Volume I): Teachers and School Leaders as Lifelong Learners' from TALIS, OECD Publishing, Paris, https://doi.org/10.1787/1d0bc92a-en [online] Available at: www.oecd.org/content/dam/oecd/en/about/programmes/edu/talis/talis2018participantnotes/TALIS2018_CN_FIN.pdf (Accessed: 1 May 2026).

teaching. Effective didagogy requires conditions where collaboration is embedded in professional development, not simply isolated training events. This collaborative approach supports teachers to translate what they learn in training into their own classroom practice through shared discussion and collective problem-solving.[286] This is certainly something we could learn from Finland then.

Perhaps most strikingly, teachers in Finland enjoy significant autonomy in their classrooms, allowing them to tailor teaching methods to their students' needs. This trust in teachers' professional judgement enhances job satisfaction and reduces burnout, contributing to higher retention rates.[287] A study by Chung linked teacher autonomy in Finland to broader professional agency and decision-making in teaching practice, emphasising how the Finnish system entrusts teachers with autonomy at classroom, school and professional levels.[288] Many of the teachers in England we interviewed cited a lack of autonomy as one of their biggest frustrations, and many were able to say that they'd stayed in their schools long-term because leaders trusted their professionalism.

We will leave Europe now to head off to Singapore, which is often lauded as a place for England's policymakers to look to. How do they keep their talented teachers in the profession?

Singapore

Background

Singapore's Ministry of Education does not specifically publish attrition rates, but it does publish teacher-resignation rates. In a Parliamentary reply, the Ministry said the annual resignation rate has been stable at around 2% per year since 2018, that it is 2.5% on average in the first five years and 4% for teachers with three to five years' service (when training

286 Teacher Development Trust (2025) 'What is Didagogy? Exploring the Discipline of Teaching Teachers' [online] Available at: https://tdtrust.org/research/didagogy-the-discipline-of-teaching-teachers (Accessed: 1 May 2026).

287 OECD (2024) 'Results from TALIS 2024 – Country notes: Finland' [online] Available at: www.oecd.org/en/publications/results-from-talis-2024-country-notes_e127f9e2-en/finland_ab17fae3-en.html (Accessed: 1 May 2026).

288 Chung, J. (2023) 'Research-informed teacher education, teacher autonomy and teacher agency: the example of Finland' in *London Review of Education*, 21(1), 13.

bonds often end).[289] Remember: England's Department for Education (DfE) school workforce statistics show that only 67.7% of teachers are still teaching five years after qualification (that is, around a third have left state-funded teaching within five years). This is quite the contrast!

Retention

So, how do Singapore do it?

Professional development

It starts with a strong, structured professional pathway and heavy investment in the development of teachers. In fact, Singapore is widely noted for systematic professional development and career structures. In the OECD's TALIS 2024 reporting, Singapore highlights strong professional-development participation and system supports for teacher growth.[290] In a great series of blogs about this, Harry Fletcher-Wood calls this 'a careful approach to attracting, developing and retaining teachers'.[291] Research agrees. TALIS found Singaporean teachers to be 'some of the best trained teachers in the world'.[292]

This starts right at the beginning of a teacher's journey in initial teacher education. All new teachers are trained at the National Institute of Education, through a range of different routes. England too has different routes, with traditional university courses and school-based routes. However, the difference in Singapore is that teacher-training is in one national institute, so new recruits to the profession are getting the same diet of curriculum input, which has been tried in England with the introduction of the Core Content Framework in 2022.

289 Ministry of Education Singapore (2024) 'Data on resignation rates for teachers since 2018' [online] Available at: www.moe.gov.sg/news/parliamentary-replies/20240702-data-on-resignation-rates-for-teachers-since-2018 (Accessed: 1 May 2026).

290 Ministry of Education Singapore (2025) 'Singapore Teachers Embrace Digital Technologies and Benefit from Strong Professional Development: OECD TALIS 2024 Study' [online] Available at: www.moe.gov.sg/news/press-releases/20251007-singapore-teachers-embrace-digital-technologies-and-benefit-from-strong-professional-development-oecd-talis-2024-study (Accessed: 1 May 2026).

291 Fletcher-Wood, H. (2018) 'Education in Singapore: 7) The secret of Singapore's success' [online] Available at: https://improvingteaching.co.uk/2018/02/10/education-in-singapore-7-the-secret-of-singapores-success (Accessed: 1 May 2026).

292 Ng, P.T. (2007) 'Educational reform in Singapore: from quantity to quality' in *Educational Research for Policy and Practice*, 7(1), pp.5–15.

In many ways, the approach to training teachers is very familiar to what we do in England, with student teachers experiencing a combination of taught courses and placements in different schools. They also get the support of dedicated mentors and tutors. Perhaps the biggest difference is that all training is subject-specific and that mastery of teaching is the most important focus. This subject specificity is even key in primary, where primary teachers specialise in two subjects, so students are taught by subject specialists in Grades 5 and 6 (ages 10–12) and have three or four teachers in younger grades. Additionally, like in England, after qualification new teachers enter a two-and-a-half year 'Beginning Teacher' programme, which is led nationally (like the Early Career Framework / ITTECF in England), plus support in schools.[293] According to Fletcher-Wood, they have a 'clear and coherent national system for initial teacher-training and professional development in schools reinforces and builds on this foundation'.[294]

It seems like schools spend a lot of time and energy on professional development. This is largely co-ordinated by teachers and each school's teacher educators. Gongshang Primary School, for example, shares the direction and plan for their professional development with all staff, so teachers understand how professional-development activities connect to the school's vision and their own growth. Professional development activities are then planned systematically and collaboratively across departments to support teacher reflection and improve classroom practice. The focus is on collaboration, reflective practice, continuous improvement and alignment with the Singapore Teaching Practice model, which emphasises teachers as reflective practitioners who refine practice based on student outcomes.[295] Teachers often work as teams to plan, teach, observe and reflect on lessons. They also complete action research projects, where teachers investigate a classroom problem and test strategies, gathering data and sharing findings with colleagues.

Another common format is subject-specific pedagogy workshops, which cover instructional strategies specific to a discipline, often integrating

293 National Center on Education and the Economy [online] Available at: https://ncee.org/wp-content/uploads/2017/02/SingaporeCountryBrief.pdf

294 Fletcher-Wood, H. (2018) 'Education in Singapore: 7) The secret of Singapore's success' [online] Available at: https://improvingteaching.co.uk/2018/02/10/education-in-singapore-7-the-secret-of-singapores-success (Accessed: 1 May 2026).

295 Gongshang Primary School 'Staff Professional Development' [online] Available at: www.gongshangpri.moe.edu.sg/staff/pd (Accessed: 1 May 2026).

insights on how students learn complex concepts in mathematics or science, for example. There is also a real focus on collaborative reflection and collegial sharing, where teachers share case studies from their classrooms and discuss student outcomes, connecting practice with emerging evidence.[296] It is easy to think the grass is greener, but when teachers are offered such a variety of learning opportunities and this much collaboration, it seems like a far cry from the sitting in rows, everyone in the hall, one-and-done professional development teachers are sometimes subjected to in England.

In England, although we have the Education Endowment Foundation's report on the mechanisms that make professional development impactful, we do not have a national framework for professional development. Singapore, however, does and schools operate within a national professional-development framework that encourages:

- **100+ voluntary professional-development hours per year** for teachers across all Ministry of Education schools
- **facilitation by national providers** such as the National Institute of Education and the Academy of Singapore Teachers (AST), which offer structured programmes and networked learning communities in subjects and pedagogical areas
- **support for lesson study, action research, mentoring and collaborative inquiry** – all key components of teacher growth.

Together, these elements help Singapore schools design professional development that is ongoing, coherent with school goals, collaborative and grounded in practice.

Teacher Growth Model

Research on Singapore's professional-development landscape describes how professional development in schools is designed to be ongoing, connected to classroom practice, subject-specific and collaborative because it needs to align to the national Teacher Growth Model, which can be viewed on the Academy of Singapore Teachers website (search for 'teacher growth model'). This was designed by the Singapore's Ministry of Education in 2012 to guide how teachers grow, learn and build their careers across their whole working life. It's not a checklist or a set of standards.

296 Bautista, A., Wong, J. and Gopinathan, S. (2015) 'Teacher Professional Development in Singapore: Depicting the Landscape' in *Psychology, Society & Education*, 7, pp.311–326.

Instead, it's a shared mental model for what it means to become a better teacher over time, professionally, ethically and personally.

It frames teacher development around the idea that teachers grow best when learning is continuous, self-directed, collaborative and grounded in classroom practice. It also recognises that teacher quality is the key lever in Singapore's education system and that retaining teachers depends on giving them purpose, mastery and progression, not just pay.

The model is built around three inter-connected domains:

- **Professional Practice:** How teachers design, enact and reflect on teaching and learning – this includes subject and pedagogical knowledge; understanding how students learn; assessment literacy; use of evidence and reflection; and classroom decision-making
- **Professional Leadership:** How teachers contribute beyond their own classroom – this includes mentoring and coaching others; leading Professional Learning Communities; curriculum leadership; sharing practice and inquiry findings; and supporting school improvement – importantly, leadership is not limited to formal roles; classroom teachers are expected to exercise leadership through expertise
- **Personal Effectiveness:** How teachers sustain themselves professionally and ethically – this includes professional values and ethics; reflective habits; resilience and wellbeing; professional identity; and commitment to lifelong learning; this is a crucial retention lever because Singapore explicitly treats teacher wellbeing and moral purpose as part of professional growth, not as an optional extra.

Sounds amazing, doesn't it? Often, teachers who want to do the things in the 'Professional Leadership' domain in England have to leave the classroom. Yet, teachers grow within the Singaporean model because it is underpinned by three growth principles:

1. **Teachers own their learning and are expected to identify their own learning needs, set professional goals and seek feedback and development opportunities.** This sense of agency is central to why autonomy and retention are strong in Singapore.
2. **Growth happens through collaboration and schools operate as Professional Learning Communities.** This makes collaboration structural, not optional.
3. **Learning is career-long and differentiated because the model supports multiple career pathways, not a single 'up-or-out' route.**

This pathway model is one of the absolute strengths of the Singapore system, in our opinion. It gives teachers so many options to develop and progress that help them remain in schools and the classroom. There are three tracks:

1. The first is the **Teaching Track**, which takes teachers from Senior Teacher to Master Teacher. This is designed to keep the best teachers in classrooms while recognising and rewarding deep pedagogical expertise. What do these roles look like in practice?

    - **Senior Teachers** teach a full or near-full timetable and act as instructional coaches within departments. They model high-quality lessons (often observed by colleagues); lead lesson study, curriculum planning or assessment moderation; and mentor early career and struggling teachers. They also have a role in translating research into classroom practice – like Lead Practitioners in England, if they were utilised well.
    - **Master Teachers** are recognised as system-level experts in pedagogy. They still teach, but often with a reduced timetable, and they design and lead professional learning across schools. They work with the Academy of Singapore Teachers and the National Institute of Education, where they conduct classroom-based research and inquiry and shape national pedagogy. This is similar work to both Haili's and Sam's, but our roles are not common and we have very much had to carve out this niche!

When we think about the interviews we did, universally teachers had stayed because they were given similar opportunities by empowering leaders to be more involved in outwards-facing work and training, as well as development opportunities in their schools or Trusts. This stuff really matters for retention. In this system, promotion does not require leaving teaching. Status and pay rise are tied to instructional excellence, rather than climbing the greasy pole as quickly as possible, and teachers can pursue mastery without becoming managers. What a dream!

2. The next track is the **Leadership Track**, for Middle Leaders to Principals. It aims to develop leaders who understand teaching deeply and can lead schools as learning organisations.

    - **Middle Leaders** might be Heads of Department or Level Heads, and are responsible for curriculum coherence and assessment, observing teaching regularly and giving feedback, leading departmental professional development and inquiry cycles, using data diagnostically (not just for accountability and still teaching a meaningful timetable).

- **Senior Leaders (Vice-Principals / Principals)** focus on shaping school culture and professional learning, allocating time for collaboration and inquiry and developing staff through coaching, not just appraisal. They are very much expected to be instructional leaders, not just administrators. The key difference with leadership in England here is that this position is seen as pedagogical, not bureaucratic, and that leaders are credible because they were expert teachers.

3. The final track is the **Specialist Track** (Curriculum, Research, Policy). This helps to keep expert teachers inside the education system even if they want to step away from daily classroom teaching. In practice, these roles might be Curriculum Specialists, who are designing national syllabi and assessments, or supporting schools implementing new curriculum. They might work with subject communities and teachers, and pilot innovations and refine policy based on feedback. They might also work with universities to conduct applied educational research, or in policy, where they ensure policy is grounded in classroom realities. They are often former teachers with strong practice credentials. This track is really interesting as, in England, there is a strange nastiness between some serving teachers and leaders, who view anyone who has left the classroom as a 'grifter', who left as they couldn't hack it and now have nothing positive to add to the sector.

Education is a large ecosystem, with lots of stakeholders and, in the Singapore system, expertise is valued beyond the classroom, which means that the system avoids losing talent to consultancy or other sectors and teachers see long-term futures within education.

Even more interestingly, movement between tracks is very common. Teachers are not locked in and can move between the different tracks; this creates a career lattice, not a ladder. As we see in the thematic analysis (Chapter 5), too many teachers leave the profession due to pressures in their private lives. In Singapore, careers evolve with life stage and interests, burnout is reduced because change doesn't mean exit and professional growth feels long-term and humane.

Part 5
Putting it all together

CHAPTER ELEVEN:

A codified framework for teacher retention

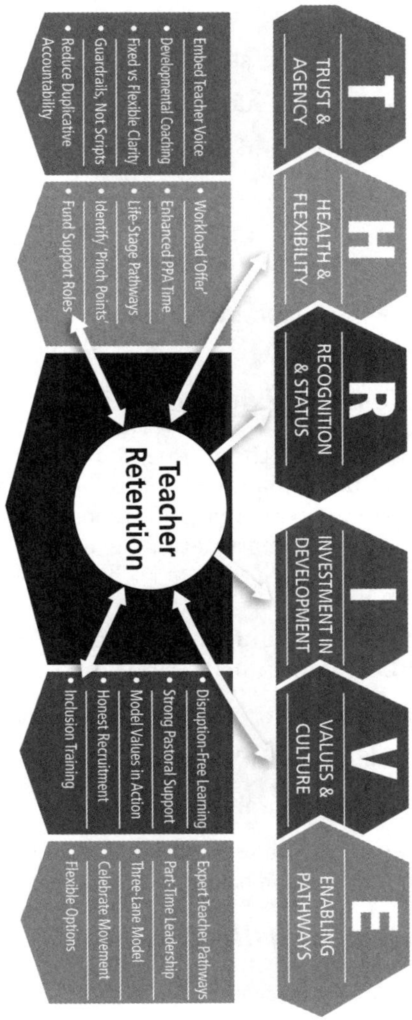

After two years of speaking to teachers and leaders, immersing ourselves in research from the last 30 years and consciously crafting people strategies in our own Trusts, we have created our teacher-retention framework THRIVE. After all, that is what we want for our teachers.

The THRIVE Framework for Teacher Retention in England stands for:

- **T:** Trust and professional agency
- **H:** Health, workload and life-stage flexibility
- **R:** Recognition, respect and status
- **I:** Investment in expertise and development
- **V:** Values, belonging and culture
- **E:** Enabling career pathways

This is designed to be used as a diagnostic and action framework at three levels: policy, Trust and school. In this chapter, we aim to codify what each of these looks like.

T: Trust and professional agency

In our interviews, veteran teachers repeatedly described staying when they were trusted, not micromanaged, especially when leaders shielded staff from performative pressures and teachers retained voice and autonomy in pedagogy and departmental decisions.

What does this look like?

- Teacher voice being structural: subject teams shaping curriculum / assessment (not being 'consulted' after)
- Low-stakes developmental observation and coaching
- Decision-making clarity: what's fixed versus what's flex?
- Central teams setting guardrails, not scripts
- Both policymakers and leaders educing duplicative accountability layers that teachers describe as corrosive.

H: Health, workload and life-stage flexibility

Teachers stay when leaders act early with practical workload supports and flexibility, especially at private-life pinch points, such as parenthood and caring responsibilities. They described retention as made possible by such actions as protected time, flexible timetables and leaders noticing strain before crisis.

What does this look like?

- Doubling planning, preparation and assessment (PPA) time or allowing staff to take PPA at home
- Extra planning days, personal days, flexible scheduling and structured support roles that reduce planning load
- Leaders identifying 'flight risk' pinch points in colleagues' lives, like in the NHS approach – support might include menopause-support clinics or evidence-based retention-planning tools for local contexts, rather than generic national approaches
- Publishing an internal 'workload offer', including marking expectations, meeting caps, email norms, cover protections
- A life-stage flexibility menu, including parttime pathways that don't kill career progression, phased returns, timetable protections
- Behaviour systems that protect teacher wellbeing, with clear, consistent protocols and support from dedicated pastoral colleagues
- Funding non-teaching support that genuinely removes workload, such as well-trained academic support assistants or non-teaching behaviour leads.

R: Recognition, respect and status

Teachers described staying when their contribution is visible and valued, including explicit celebration of experience, such as service badges, praise cultures and feeling that leaders' actions demonstrate their worth. Research links retention to the external environment. This includes media portrayal of teachers, societal respect and the way accountability narratives can erode professional pride.

What does this look like?

- Making expertise visible: internal 'expert teacher' roles, showcasing practice, honouring long service meaningfully
- Recognition that is professional, not patronising: 'we value your craft' + time / resources attached to demonstrate this

- Trust-wide expert roles and pay recognition for mentoring / teacher-education work
- National narrative reset: stopping discourse of derision dynamics and aligning reforms with teacher dignity
- Retention incentives by career stage
- Tracking returners to teaching and profiling their reasons for returning to avoid the 'grass is always greener' narrative.

I: Investment in expertise and development

Experienced teachers stay when they have development opportunities, including outwards-facing work, training roles and pathways that don't require leaving teaching to progress. This includes meaningful professional development, where possible, focused on subject specificity and the opportunity to collaborate in professional learning communities.

What does it look like?

- Making CPD job-embedded: lesson study / inquiry cycles, departmental practice development, coaching
- Protecting subject passion: reducing out-of-specialism teaching where possible and giving teachers the agency, time and resources to engage in developing their subject knowledge and pedagogical content knowledge in subject-specific ways
- Building in-house teacher educators, who are expert teachers who lead development with reduced timetables
- Creating outwards-facing roles that sustain identity (network leads, curriculum fellows, facilitators)
- CPD entitlement that is time-funded, not just more training piled onto workload
- Providing opportunities for sustained collaborative professional-development cycles.

V: Values, belonging and culture

Culture came through as the multiplier. Teachers said you can 'feel it within minutes'. They stay where culture aligns with values, where leaders act consistently under pressure and where behaviour and routines make teaching emotionally sustainable. Behaviour and routines are repeatedly linked to retention. Clear routines, consistent systems, strong leadership backing during incidents all matter, as they mean teachers can teach instead of firefight.

What does it look like?

- 'Right to disruption-free learning' operationalised: this means consistent routines, shared language, rapid support
- Clear values and educational philosophy, which is lived not laminated
- Pastoral systems that reduce teacher emotional load and rebuild belonging
- Culture due diligence in recruitment: showing candidates the real day to ensure a mutual fit
- Behaviour and inclusion support that is resourced not rhetoric, especially in high-challenge contexts
- Real, practical and actionable training for teachers on how to adapt teaching and meet students' needs.

E: Enabling career pathways

A recurring driver of staying is having routes to grow without having to leave the classroom and having options as life circumstances change.

What does it look like?

- Formal 'expert teacher' pathways with time and status, not just extra jobs for free
- Parttime leadership routes and stepping on / off Teaching and Learning Responsibilities (TLR) without stigma
- Creating a three-lane Trust workforce architecture: Craft (expert classroom), Lead (school leadership), System (curriculum / professional development / research)
- Making movement normal and celebrated, including return-to-classroom moves
- A national framework that legitimises expert teacher progression (not only management).

The following tables break these down into actionable, codifiable steps for school leaders, and include a self-evaluation red–amber–green (RAG) tool for leaders:

THRIVE Framework: school self-evaluation for teacher retention

T: Trust and professional agency

Goal: To reduce micromanagement and restore teacher agency by making trust structural, not rhetorical

Headline action	Actionable steps	RAG self-evaluation
Embed teacher voice in decision-making	• Subject teams have decision rights over curriculum and assessment • Delegated authority is documented and used • Outside consultation and expertise is replaced by genuine internal authority • Subject-led review points are scheduled	R / A / G
Developmental observation	• Appraisal is separate from coaching • Low-stakes observation focuses on teacher goals and mastery • Coaches are trained in non-judgemental feedback and helping teachers make better decisions • Coaching evidence is protected from inspection misuse	R / A / G
Clarify fixed vs flexible	• A Fixed versus Flexible charter is published • Statutory duties are clearly defined as fixed • Pedagogy and assessment are explicitly flexible through subject specificity • Charter is reviewed annually with staff	R / A / G

Headline action	Actionable steps	RAG self-evaluation
Guardrails not scripts	• Central guidance sets principles, not scripts • Central requirements are audited annually • Low-impact directives are removed • Non-negotiables have clear rationale, using robust research evidence	R / A / G
Remove duplicative accountability	• Inspection and appraisal evidence are aligned • Duplicate data drops are eliminated • Parallel lesson monitoring is removed • Unnecessary paperwork is reduced	R / A / G

H: Health, workload and life-stage flexibility

Goal: To make teaching doable across different life stages

Headline action	Actionable steps	RAG self-evaluation
Published workload offer	• Marking expectations are explicit • Meetings are capped • Email response norms are clear • Cover protections are enforced	R / A / G
Redesign time	• PPA is increased or reconfigured • Protected planning days exist • INSET is used for planning and collaboration • Low-impact tasks are removed	R / A / G
Life-stage flexibility	• Phased returns are offered • Timetable protections exist • Parttime roles allow progression • Flexible working is reviewed annually	R / A / G
Target retention pinch points	• Workforce data identifies flight-risk stages • Targeted support is offered • Mentoring or reduced load is provided • Impact on retention is reviewed	R / A / G

Headline action	Actionable steps	RAG self-evaluation
Workload-removing roles	• Support assistants are trained and deployed properly • Behaviour or pastoral leads are funded • Roles remove workload rather than redistribute it • Impact is monitored	R / A / G

R: Recognition, respect and status

Goal: To make professional expertise visible, valued and rewarded

Headline action	Actionable steps	RAG self-evaluation
Expert teacher recognition	• Expert roles exist with status • Time is allocated for expert work • Long service is meaningfully recognised	R / A / G
Recognition with resources	• Praise is linked to time or pay • Recognition avoids adding workload • Recognition aligns with professional values	R / A / G
Mentoring status	• Mentors are paid • Teaching load is reduced • Mentoring is recognised as expert work	R / A / G
Positive national narrative	• Reform language avoids blame • Inspection language affirms professionalism • Leaders and government officials model respect publicly	R / A / G
Use returners as evidence	• Returners are tracked • Reasons for return are shared • Insights inform retention strategy	R / A / G

I: Investment in expertise and development

Goal: To sustain experienced teachers through meaningful professional growth

Headline action	Actionable steps	RAG self-evaluation
Job-embedded CPD	• Lesson study or inquiry cycles are in place • Coaching is embedded • CPD occurs within directed time	R / A / G
Protect subject expertise	• Out-of-specialism teaching is minimised • Subject-specific CPD is funded • Departments have protected development time for intellectual preparation	R / A / G
In-house teacher educators	• Expert teachers lead development • Teaching load is reduced • Role is recognised as a career route	R / A / G
Outwards-facing roles	• Teachers act as network or system leads • School attachment is maintained • Time is funded	R / A / G
Time-funded CPD entitlement	• Protected CPD time exists • CPD time is audited annually • Low-impact CPD is removed	R / A / G

V: Values, belonging and culture

Goal: To create cultures where teachers feel safe and supported

Headline action	Actionable steps	RAG self-evaluation
Disruption-free learning	• Consistent routines are implemented • Leadership response to incidents is rapid • Behaviour systems protect staff	R / A / G
Values in action	• Leaders back staff under pressure • Policies align with stated values • Contradictory policies are removed	R / A / G

Headline action	Actionable steps	RAG self-evaluation
Strong pastoral systems	• Non-teaching pastoral staff are funded • Teacher emotional labour is reduced • Escalation routes are clear	R / A / G
Honest recruitment	• Candidates see the real school day • Mutual fit is prioritised • Retention of new hires is tracked	R / A / G
Practical inclusion training	• Training is classroom-focused • SEND and behaviour support accompany training • Impact is reviewed • SENDCos teach and allow teachers in to see best practice in making adaptations and meeting needs	R / A / G

E: Enabling career pathways

Goal: To create a career lattice that allows growth without exit

Headline action	Actionable steps	RAG self-evaluation
Expert teacher pathways	• Progression routes reward classroom excellence • Time, pay and status are attached • Unpaid add-ons are avoided	R / A / G
Flexible leadership	• Parttime leadership is available • TLR allows step on / off • Stigma-free role changes are normalised	R / A / G
Three-lane workforce model	• Craft, Lead and System pathways are defined • Movement criteria are published • Transitions are supported	R / A / G
Celebrate movement	• Return-to-classroom moves are valued • Career fluidity is modelled • Retention after movement is tracked	R / A / G
National expert teacher framework	• Expert teacher progression is legitimised nationally • Parity with leadership pay exists • Impact on retention is evaluated	R / A / G

Part 6
Key learnings

CHAPTER TWELVE:

Schools and Trusts that have got it right: case studies

Earlier in this book (Chapter 2), we make the case that experienced teachers are not a luxury or a legacy feature of the system – they are central to its quality and stability. If that is true, then retention cannot be treated as a background issue. It becomes a practical leadership question: What do schools and Trusts actually do that make experienced teachers want to stay?

This chapter looks directly at practice. It brings together case studies of schools and Trusts where leaders have made deliberate choices about culture, workload, flexibility and professional growth. These are not models to lift and copy. They are grounded examples of how leaders think and act when they take retention seriously.

Case studies

Bingley Grammar School

> Bingley Grammar School is a large, coeducational 11–18 secondary school serving a diverse demographic in West Yorkshire. Over recent years, the school has been on a very positive improvement journey, with a focus on enhancing staff wellbeing and retention, reducing workload and building a supportive, collaborative culture.

How is the school approaching teacher retention?

- **Intentional culture-building:** The school has fostered a culture of trust, support and long-term staff loyalty. Leaders understand that purpose and respect are intrinsic motivators, and small acts of kindness build goodwill and commitment. Staff feel valued in multiple ways – not just financially.
- A strong focus on positive behaviour: **Building respectful, positive relationships with students is prioritised.** The Headteacher says: 'We're not a "shouty" school. We work really, really hard on relationships

with the students and that definitely does tie into retention... There is a strong behaviour policy... most of the time, the kids don't cross [the lines].'

- Workload: Leaders acknowledge that teaching is high pressure, but support staff practically. **Wellbeing is treated as meaningful support**, not superficial messaging.
- **Flexible working conditions:** A high proportion of staff work parttime, and there is flexible scheduling to support work–life balance across all roles. Staff are given paid time off for personal / family emergencies.
- **Trust and autonomy:** Leaders say that 'we allow teachers to teach. We trust them to do their job and that freedom makes a difference'. There is a **high value placed on teachers' professional judgement**, and a focus on engagement and progress of students over compliance and tick-box approaches.
- **Meaningful professional development:** Frequent, structured, in-house CPD is tailored to staff needs. Staff have input and autonomy over their development focus, and professional learning supports both subject-specific and career-stage needs.
- Customised retention strategies: **A tailored, individualised approach to staff retention**, based on deep leadership knowledge of staff circumstances, avoids generic, one-size-fits-all solutions.
- **A low-stakes environment:** Quality assurance is developmental, not judgemental, and trust underpins all performance management.
- **Leadership by example:** Leadership credibility stems from real classroom engagement – senior leaders teach demanding classes and exam groups.

What impact are they having?

High retention rates, with **around two-thirds of staff who have stayed over 15 years**. Leaders say: 'We break every government statistic for retention. We are so far out of the statistical norm, it's unreal. We have a lot of people who've done teacher-training with us, or do the SCITT pathway and stay with us. Eight or nine people have returned from other jobs almost immediately after leaving.'

Leader perspective

Luke Weston, Headteacher, and Alex Dean, Senior Deputy Headteacher

It's a big family. It's the world's craziest family, but it's ours.

This is a proper comprehensive school. We have kids here from some tough areas. It's not an easy school by any stretch of the imagination, but there is something about the way that things are done here that keeps people here.

We're not a 'shouty' school. We work really, really hard on relationships with the students and that definitely does tie into retention because people are not coming here and having massive battles. It's not always easy. We've got a really mixed cohort but, most of the time, the vast majority of kids are an absolute pleasure to be with, compared to perhaps some other schools where you feel like you're going in for a fight every day. Genuinely speaking, the relationship we have with kids is definitely something that keeps our staff in. There is a strong behaviour policy that underpins it, with really clear stages of choice and conversation. There are lines we've got, and most of the time, the kids don't cross them. We will exclude if we need to, but the vast majority of those exclusions happen for a one-off event. It's a big family. It's the world's craziest family, but it's ours.

A while back at Friday leaving speeches, we asked staff how many people have been here 15 years or above. A good two-thirds of the staff put their hands up. We break every government statistic for retention. We are so far out of the statistical norm, it's unreal. We have a lot of people who've done teacher-training with us, or do the SCITT pathway and stay with us. Eight or nine people have returned from other jobs almost immediately after leaving.

Do we have a deliberate retention policy? Yes. Is it different for every single member of staff? Yes. It's horses for courses and dependent on what that member of staff needs at any particular time, and on the wider staff body. I think it helps that I've [Luke] been immemorial. I've been Head for 15 years. And that level of intelligence on the ground is the bit you need – I literally know everyone. I always joke: I've got people everywhere! You need to know people because 'one size fits all' does not work by any stretch of the imagination, or otherwise any of those DfE recruitment or retention policies would have worked.

We give two days a year for what we call 'child ill day'. So, if you've got a problem with your fridge or your kid's ill, you can take two of them off that. That makes a difference. We've got 56% of the staff population parttime. That makes a difference. The national average is 43 at the moment. We have parttime senior leaders. And 99% of the time, folks will get the day off that they want as well.

Once you start to interleave all of these things, that's the approach. It's having 30 things on deck that you're doing with any one person at one time. We've got two staff joining us as new starters and they were absolutely amazed. They want to take their kids for their first day at school and I'm like, yeah, put a blue form. Not a problem. And it's things like that, quite small things, they do have a cost. But they make a huge difference as well. It's goodwill, isn't it?

We've done a fair bit around workload – we've done the work on understanding that it's a high-pressure job for those 10 weeks. Yes, there are times when we just need to pitch in. And I'm always very careful with wellbeing because that's just the umbrella under it. There's a lot of other stuff going on underneath, and standing up and preaching about wellbeing really doesn't help anybody.

We allow teachers to teach. We trust them to do their job and that freedom makes a difference. We just get the best people you can and let them crack on because most people do a damn good job. We have certain things we ask people to do, such as shared learning intentions, most important knowledge. We definitely don't have, 'you must start like this'. We ask people to do some sort of settling activity, often recall-based, but we don't have, 'you must do this, followed by this, followed by this, followed by this'.

Our senior team have a heavy teaching load and the credibility of teaching difficult classes. That makes a huge difference and the whole senior team teach, apart from our behaviour deputy, because he gets dragged away, so it's unfair on the kids. We've all got examination groups and things, not just dabbling with a bit of PSHE and saying that you teach.

When we do quality assurance, there isn't a set checklist. It's absolutely okay for something not to be seen or not to be applicable within a context. You don't go in expecting to see X, Y, Z. Really fundamental is: Are the kids engaged? Are they making learning progress? Is the behaviour allowing them to make that progress? There is a degree of flexibility. Some subjects do have bought-in schemes and it works for them. It's their decision, not forced down to people. If there's a problem or an issue, our staff understand that doesn't mean it's a death knell. It's developmental. It's, okay, a bit of an issue here, what we're going to do is fix it – work together, put coaching in. So, you've got that trust there, which is super important – that people know if they're having a bad day and somebody sees that, it isn't going to be the end of the world. It's not high stakes, it's developmental. Trust is, in the end, the bit that makes everything else work here.

Most of our CPD is internal. Every other week we have a bespoke PD session where the school shuts early. That's a massive financial and timetabling cost that people don't see, but we have a hugely bespoke system here. We work really hard to have a curriculum, for want of a better word. We wouldn't put children in a classroom without a scheme of work, so I don't do that with professional development. There's a scheme of work, so to speak. So, at the moment, we tend to have focuses that run. We had a massive focus on Rosenshine at one point, cold-calling, post-Covid. We had quite a lot of stuff about getting children back engaged.

We're currently working with the SSAT on the Embedding Formative Assessment programme. That is bespoke because it's giving strategies, but people then pick the strategies they believe are going to work for them, their classes, their career stage. It's been really good getting people in and out watching each other. We are trying within the PD curriculum to make sure it's as relevant as it possibly can be and offering people what they need career-stage-wise, whether that's professional qualifications, or memberships of the Chartered College, or an HR course someone is interested in. It's trying to let people have a degree of autonomy about what they're spending PD time on.

A fair bit of the professional-development time is given over to subjects. Middle leaders take a steer on that, in terms of what their subject needs to take professional development forwards. Sometimes we do stuff that's whole school, sometimes we do stuff that's subject-based. We change it up across the programme, across the year, to try and make sure that everything's hit, and we keep whole-school things to a minimum, because they're generally the least useful, unless it's safeguarding, and I think people value that too.

When experienced teachers leave the profession, we're losing that teaching and learning expertise. People who know exactly how to work their way through what needs to be done to get those learning outcomes to get children through exams. Because no matter how hard an ECT works, they just don't have that subject knowledge. They don't have the toolkit fully developed. And the children, potentially, the provision they're getting can be reduced at points. The children like to know their teacher's the expert. And, as leaders, we've stayed the game. The reason why our school is different from others is because of the level of knowledge that we both have about this place.

With Bridget Phillipson as the new Secretary of State, if she delivers on a lot of the stuff she's talking about, she will go a long way to sorting out education. Trying to stop the rot of people leaving is the answer. She does seem to have listened, doesn't she? So, it starts off with not demonising the profession – and value. People feeling valued, and everyone's got their own motivators of value, whether that's their family, monetary, or whether it's wellbeing, or whether it's high regard. It's not just about the money. We've got to the point in education where anybody can say whatever they want, like on social media, and there's no right of reply. And I think for senior-leader retention and recruitment, that's where your big problem is, where people are just being deluged by negativity.

The Education Alliance (TEAL)

TEAL is a Multi-Academy Trust based in East Yorkshire and Hull. Formed in 2012, the Trust comprises four secondaries, seven primaries and an alternative provision, serving 6700 young people. TEAL also run their own SCITT, Yorkshire Wolds Teacher Training, which trains around 60 trainees each year.

How is the Trust approaching teacher retention?

- A **clear organisational purpose**, aligned to a public statement of service: we are here to make great schools and happy, strong communities so people have better lives
- A **focus on leadership behaviours** at the heart of healthy school cultures, underpinned by an ethical leadership charter
- School-improvement strategy – to have a great teacher in every classroom – drives **significant focus on recruitment, retention and development**
- **Strong commitment to reducing workload** through a charter and stripping away tasks that do not directly contribute to the core mission
- Recognition of the crucial importance of the early career years and a **more flexible approach to mentoring ECTs**
- Professional-development strategy underpinned by an understanding of the **importance of teachers having mastery, autonomy and purpose** in their work

- A strong PD offer, which includes **multiple opportunities for teachers to work in their departments and to collaborate across the Trust**, to improve quality and reduce the duplication of effort
- **Enhanced benefits,** including maternity leave in line with the NHS, policy improvements for kinship carers and improved parental and adoption leave
- **Removal of traditional systems and processes that inhibit retention and progression,** including PRP, threshold and the need to apply for parttime or flexible working.

What impact are they having?

- Recruitment and retention data from 2024 shows that leavers are down by over 25%, and applications are up by over 20%.
- Survey data shows significant impact on staff satisfaction with a range of measures:
    - Staff who agree 'I can achieve a good work–home balance': all staff up from 59% to 76%; teachers up from 36% to 72%
    - ECT retention after two years 100%; ECT retention after three years 100%.

Leader perspective

Jonny Uttley, CEO

At TEAL, we developed our core purpose – what we sometimes now call our North Star – which is that we are here to make great schools and happy strong communities so that people have better lives. It's about public service; it's about making the lives of others better. We're very, very clear about that purpose. We're very clear about our values, about how we lead, and we have an ethical leadership framework. So, we ask a lot of leaders, not in terms of systems and processes, or onerous workload and long hours, but in terms of the standards that they set around behaviour – because leadership behaviour has to be at the core of a healthy culture.

We are very much a people-focused organisation, so we recognise that through a school-improvement perspective. The best thing we can do is to have a good teacher in every classroom, which means that we have to be really strong on recruitment, retention and development – that's where we put so much of our energy.

We have a SCITT, where we train about 60 trainees a year. And we are serious about having a culture that's based around developing great teachers. To do that, you need to be heavily committed to ITT, whether that's being fortunate enough to have a SCITT or whether it's playing a key role in another organisation. But teacher-training is absolutely the heart of what we do. We recognise that those first three years – the first year being the training year, and then ECT1 and ECT2 – are absolutely key years. If you've got staff still working in the profession at the end of that second year, then I think you're in a strong position as a group of schools and as a Trust moving forwards.

I think we've got a really good CPD offer, which helps to retain more experienced staff. So, although we've put a lot into the early career years, we recognise that you have to have high-quality CPD for everyone. We have got rid of one-target performance management. I think that, the longer that people are in the profession, the less useful that was. We call it Professional Quality Improvement – it's a single goal. We've changed our pay policy so people have automatic pay progression. We've got rid of the threshold. So, what we've tried to do is get rid of a lot of the stupid, pointless stuff that's been going on for too long in schools, and strip the job right back, to allow people to focus on just planning and delivering great lessons for kids.

We take workload very seriously. About five / six years ago or so, we developed a workload charter, which is a kind of expression of culture. Professional trust is our starting point rather than professional suspicion. And we publicly commit to saying that people should not have to choose between being seen as good at their job or being a good mum or dad or family member.

And I think all of those things together have helped us to have really strong retention data from early career, right through to more experienced staff.

All Saints Catholic College

All Saints Catholic College is a Roman Catholic coeducational secondary school located in a high-deprivation area in North Kensington, London. The school is part of a cluster of Catholic institutions in the area and serves approximately 828 students. All Saints has been on a significant journey of improvement over the last 10 years, under the leadership of Headteacher Andrew O'Neill. In 2022, it was rated Outstanding in all areas by Ofsted.

How is the school approaching teacher retention?

- Intentional culture building – open, transparent communication to foster a **strong sense of community and shared purpose**, for staff to feel appreciated, supported and part of a team
- An **innovative approach to extended school provision** – structured after-hours study support and enrichment activities for students, such as sport, arts and oracy, with meals included; staff benefit from reduced homework and behaviour friction, better-prepared students in class and stronger relationships built outside the classroom
- **Reduced contact time** – the average non-contact time for a teacher is 35% (teaching around 20 out of 30 lessons weekly)
- **Reduced class size** of around 22 at KS4 to reduce marking load for staff
- **Flexible working** opportunities
- **Weekly later start time** of 10:50am for teachers, achieved by removing tutor time and registering students during lesson 1
- **Academic support assistants** who are graduates in the subject area **provide capacity for teachers** and are a recruitment pipeline – they adapt lesson resources for student need and support in lessons
- **Developmental approach to CPD** prioritises professional and personal growth – CPD is relevant, planned around what is specifically being taught to make a tangible difference to classroom practice and delivered through department meetings; for staff on the Upper Pay Spine (UPS), the focus is on developing others.

What impact are they having?

- Weekly late start for staff has **reduced sickness absence and increased morale**
- **Sustained staffing stability** identified by the Headteacher as a central driver of whole-school turnaround and performance
- **School improved** from near closure and lowest popularity locally to Outstanding in all areas, with staff retention and stability described as foundational to that improvement
- Centralised behaviour systems **enable teachers to teach successfully** and consistently after years of disruption

- Retention of experienced teachers provides **relational credibility with students and cultural continuity** during improvement phase
- Deliberate mix of experienced and early-career staff **strengthens both performance and sustainability**
- Increased recruitment of experienced middle leaders used intentionally to **sustain standards** post-Outstanding judgement
- Reduced contact time and smaller KS4 class sizes **lower marking and planning load**
- Flexible late-start structure widely valued by staff and associated with **improved wellbeing and work–life balance**
- Staff-care culture contributes to **recruitment attractiveness and staff loyalty**.

Leader perspective

Andrew O'Neill, Headteacher

We've got to treat teachers like they're elite athletes.

I often describe All Saints as a school that exists on the extremes. The school is located 500 metres from Grenfell Tower, so we exist very close to the tragedy that happened. Roughly 50% of our students receive pupil premium funding. This year, across the school, 25% of our pupils have SEND, 10% of which have EHCPs. So, we're more than five times the national rate for EHCPs. When I joined the school, it was on the brink of closure and it was the least popular school in the whole of London – probably one of the least popular in the country. My job was to try and keep the school open.

Across the last nine years, we've transformed the school. We're now one of the most popular schools in the country – and I think we're the most popular Catholic school in the country now. So, it's going well – and I would say that our approach to staffing and our leadership of staffing has been the fundamental driver in being able to transform the school, hold on to staff and introduce that level of stability, but also high performance at the same time.

At the start, the culture we effectively created was, 'this school hasn't been great, it hasn't been well led, but we're in this together, everybody – we're going to transform it together'. There was no high-handed behaviour. It was very much me as the Headteacher saying, 'I'm going to roll up my sleeves. I'm going to be in the playground. I'm going to be in classrooms. I'm going to be serving dinner.' And service is one of the key parts of our motto: prayer, work and service. We probably talk about service the most – about serving children and about teaching being a vocation. We've always talked about that up front and openly, that this is what we're about. We are about transforming lives, and you need to be all in to do that.

I'm obsessed with staffing. I would say it's the number one thing that has fundamentally changed this school. So, I'm obsessed with recruiting staff and keeping staff. You see so many headteachers who go into schools that need transforming and what they do is decide that the adults have got it all wrong. They start getting rid of people. But my approach was, it's so obvious that this school has not been well led, that I cannot blame all the teachers. We changed the systems overnight so that people could be successful. We brought in centralised detentions. We were trying to teach the staff, here's what consistency looks like – and if we support you then actually there's a chance for you to feel happy in your job and to thrive in your job and be able to actually teach for the first time in years. That's where we started. It was very much about looking after people because, if they left at that point, I knew I'd struggle to recruit. So, I take care of people.

The most experienced teachers were the safest pair of hands, in that they had the cachet in the bank with some of the kids. To some degree, they were the harder ones in terms of shifting their mindset. So we recruited new, younger staff that we were able to bring in to be the real shape-shifters, the ones to demonstrate that it could be done – and then the older ones brought the experience and the knowledge and the expertise to the table. And it was a really interesting dynamic. Some of them have retired now, but there's still five or six of those staff who are at the school who just love the school so much.

Since getting Outstanding, one of the issues we've had is, how do we sustain it? The youngsters were a real driving force behind it because of the levels of energy – but they don't have the longevity and experience to know how you keep something going. So last year, I said, 'right, we are taking in another 40 or 50 kids – I need to start bringing in more experience'. Quite a number of the staff I recruited last year are middle leaders who've got more than 10 years of experience. Sometimes you do need people who bring that gravitas in and can take some of the younger staff and go, 'here's where we're going to go next'. So, it has been an active and conscious decision to bring in experience, which is counterintuitive to the way school funding is currently working and going.

The thing we started with was trying to reduce people's timetables. I've always managed to hold on to that level of empathy around what it's like to mark and what it's like to plan. I think so many headteachers really easily forget, and they look back on teaching with rose-tinted glasses when they're out of the classroom, whereas I've always been, no, we need to just assume it's really, really, really difficult and we need to default to what it's like for a teacher who's got no responsibility and has been teaching for three years, and therefore they're not afforded the benefits of having a TLR and some sort of timetable reduction.

My good friend Fran works with elite athletes. She worked with the British cycling team, and I remember talking to her about Eliud Kipchoge – he's the greatest marathon runner that's ever existed. She told me how they looked after them – like going to their hotel rooms and bringing them beds and pillows and all the creature comforts, so when they got there it was all ready for them just to go to bed. And I was like, wow – they really do look after those athletes.

And if we think about teaching, teaching is the absolute converse of that. What we do is we tell teachers to go off and do their job, but then we tend to just add loads to their job every single day. 'Oh, by the way, can you do this? Can you do that? And you need to make these phone calls.' We're just constantly stacking what they've got to try and do. We've got to flip the narrative around this and actually treat teachers like they're elite athletes, because parents want them to perform, kids need them to perform. It is about performance, and support – how do I support the performance and make the conditions as good as possible for you? So, I've been trying to decrease contact time and increase PPA. And we have reduced class sizes.

We have got rid of tutor time in the morning – the roll call is done from Lesson 1, so I don't have to have everybody on the school site. So every teacher has one morning a week where they can come in by about 10:40. The reason I went for mornings is, if you put a teacher on to a school site and they're already here, out of pure guilt, they'll remain and do work. And then, over a period of time, you'll find that they'll be like, 'I see no benefit from this'. Whereas, if they're in their bed and they've got a decision to make – 'do I go in, or do I stay in bed, or do I have a slower morning?' – the decision is all theirs, and they have full agency and autonomy. They genuinely love it. They get more sleep, some are going to the gym.

Some of our more experienced staff with young kids are taking their child to school. I never took my kids to school, and you miss out. As schools, we talk about the importance of family and the importance of children – and we criticise families who don't spend time with their children. Yet we create a system where that's not available for teachers. So, we're hypocrites in the sense that we will advocate the value of it, but then we'll demonstrate that we don't actually value it – and that's not okay.

I provide so many opportunities to bring everybody together. I make sure that we humanise the profession because, yes, teaching's hard – and we need to be careful about saying that because people then go, 'teaching is impossible'. It's not that it's not possible – it just takes up a lot of energy, because it's a performance profession. You are going at it all day long, you're really busy and time is short, and you can be short with people and fire off messages. And, actually, sometimes you just need to bring people back together to remind them that, you know what, we're actually friends! Let's talk about that. Let's have a laugh. Let's talk about something different. So sometimes we get the table-tennis tables out or we play hide and seek around the school. We have a proper laugh. Then everyone might head off down to the pub. That culture still exists. And when new staff join, it's very much, 'this is the best place to work… everyone gets on with each other and we look out for each other'.

We do loads of stuff that are creature comforts. We buy expensive coffee, we buy the milk; every Friday, we take a delivery of two massive boxes of oranges so staff get freshly squeezed orange juice. We do a full breakfast in the staffroom in winter every Monday – me and the SLT go down to the kitchens and we make bacon and sausage sandwiches for the staff that we bring up. If there's an event, we buy in the food – pizzas or whatever, so the staff are fed. You've got to actually take care of people – and people appreciate the fact that you just think about them. It has always been about bringing people together, feeling that they're part of something.

Lots more teachers would stay if they worked in an environment where people were human with them. I have heard of cases where headteachers have had formal meetings with teachers who have been off because someone in their family died – and I think, don't make it into a formal meeting in which you take them to task. Then it becomes not just about them – it becomes about every member of staff who hears that you're heartless. What we've got to is this position where headteachers are not trained to empathetically deal with complex HR decisions and they don't know how to do it and they don't know how to be human. They think that, 'oh, I'm a headteacher and I must do this in my job' and it's just so wrong and so perverse. I tell my SLT: talk to people. Make the time to explain why we're doing things rather than being really high-handed and trying to make out you're important. You're no more important than someone who's teaching in the classroom.

So, back to my obsession with staffing – it's always been about looking after people and holding on to people, because it is about having that sense of team.

Sir William Perkins's School

Sir William Perkins's School is an independent coeducational secondary school in Surrey, serving students aged 11–18. The school has a strong academic tradition and a broad co-curricular programme, with a sustained focus on teaching quality, student wellbeing and world readiness. In recent years, the school has placed increased emphasis on professional trust and organisational clarity as part of its approach to sustaining high performance and staff retention.

How is the school approaching teacher retention?

- Leadership culture built explicitly on **professional trust** – leaders communicate belief in staff expertise and capability and position their role as enabling great work rather than controlling it
- Active **leader sponsorship of professional development** – leaders identify potential in staff and personally encourage them to pursue qualifications, programmes and career-development opportunities
- **Professional development is personalised and career-stage aligned** – subject mastery, research engagement, chartered status, leadership programmes and coaching are supported based on individual pathway rather than generic entitlement
- Subject expertise and subject identity are treated as retention drivers – teachers are encouraged to deepen subject knowledge and shape curriculum, preserving **professional passion**
- **Administrative-workload reduction** – leaders have reviewed and simplified operational systems through staff consultation, approval processes and trip procedures to remove duplication
- **Flexible working culture** developing through leadership decisions – family-critical moments such as a child's first day at school are supported as standard practice rather than exceptional permission.

What impact are they having?

- **Strong long-service culture** evident – multiple staff with over 20 years' tenure demonstrate deep institutional loyalty and connection to the school
- **High voluntary engagement** from experienced staff – long-serving colleagues are first to volunteer for committees, social initiatives and culture-building activity

- **Increased staff perception of being heard** – administrative simplification followed direct staff feedback, strengthening trust
- **Professional-development uptake** increases when leaders actively sponsor individuals – encouragement and endorsement lead directly to participation
- **Support-staff retention** is notably strong where contract flexibility exists – flexible-working structures correlate with long tenure.

Leader perspective

Steve Berryman, Senior Deputy Headteacher

I've been really privileged. In every job I've ever had, I've worked with leaders who afforded trust. They believed in you. They said it openly: 'I trust you, I believe you know what you're doing, here are the resources, go and do the job well'. That thread runs through every role I've had. I think that's why I've stayed in the profession.

Professional development isn't just programmes. Sometimes it's someone saying, 'you'd be great at this, you should go for it'. Every person I've nudged has succeeded. People deserve that belief.

As a profession, we make teachers do really stupid things administratively. When you map the processes, you realise how much professional time is wasted. We've normalised it – but it's not normal. It's disrespectful of expertise.

The longer you've taught, the more time you need outside the classroom, not less. More expertise should mean more thinking time, more mentoring time, more development time. We've got that the wrong way round.

Flexible working retains great people. I've seen it work. The resistance is cultural, not operational.

Experienced teachers carry wisdom and memory – but they also need to stay future-focused. The balance is respecting experience while keeping curiosity alive.

If you want to retain experienced teachers, give them space to grow and space to contribute – not just more classes.

People stay where they feel trusted, where their time is respected and where leadership is human.

Thornden School

Thornden School is a large coeducational secondary school in Hampshire, serving a diverse comprehensive intake across the 11–16 age range. The school has a long-standing reputation for strong academic outcomes and a rich cultural and creative offer, particularly in the arts and music. Under the leadership of Headteacher Caroline Lowing, the school has focused on sustaining high standards through investment in staff development, leadership pathways and a collaborative professional culture.

How is the school approaching teacher retention?

- **Strong culture of belonging and relational trust** – staff stay long-term because they feel supported, respected and part of a community, not because of formal retention schemes
- **Multiple staff-voice mechanisms** – regular staff clinics, open forums and structured feedback routes are used to surface concerns and ideas
- **Active focus on retention and recruitment as a leadership priority** – recognised as a live strategic risk, not an HR side issue
- Use of **flexible career pathways** within Trust structures – opportunities in school improvement, teaching school hub work and cross-Trust roles broaden career options without leaving the profession
- Expectation that experienced teachers contribute as mentors – **mentoring framed as professional legacy work**, with timetable recognition and reciprocal support
- **Workload reduction** through system design – focus on slick, simplified processes so teachers can focus on core teaching work
- **Consistent centralised approaches** to behaviour and curriculum-resourcing reduce individual teacher burden.

What impact are they having?

- **Long staff tenure** – significant numbers of experienced teachers remaining long-term due to culture, relational leadership and role variety
- Improved **internal trust** – staff-engagement structures increase perception of being heard

- **Mentoring pipeline strengthened** – experienced staff transferring practice to early career teachers
- **Culture-led retention** – staff report staying because they enjoy the school and feel supported, not because of incentives
- **Recruitment stabilised** through culture messaging – values and mission used as attraction strategy where market conditions are tight
- **Workload pressure** partially mitigated through system simplification – operational friction reduced
- **Leadership pipeline** supported through shadowing and staged responsibility.

Leader perspective

Caroline Lowing, Head of School

You have to be resilient because the job is genuinely hard. Moral purpose – that core – is what sustains you. Without it, I don't know how people stay. Every step I've taken in leadership has been about impact rather than status. I've moved forwards because it meant I could help more children.

Schools are joyful places, and we don't say that often enough. Young people are funny. Staff teams are funny. There isn't a day when something doesn't make me laugh out loud. That matters – joy is part of sustainability in this work.

Being a woman of colour in school leadership can be isolating. I have walked into leadership spaces where I am the only non-white leader in the room – sometimes across a whole area. That is why networks matter so much. Professional support matters. Representation matters. You need people who understand your experience and who you can speak to honestly.

As a profession, we haven't always done professional development well. It has improved, but leadership preparation is still too shallow for the size of the step people are being asked to take. The move from deputy to headship is enormous. Proper shadowing and staged responsibility should be normal, so that people are not making that jump unsupported.

People don't stay because of policies – they stay because they like the place and they like the people. Kindness and respect retain staff more effectively than most formal strategies. Culture is what holds people.

We also have to be honest about mission creep. Schools care deeply, so we keep picking more up – social, emotional, family and community responsibilities – but not everything should sit with schools. If leaders do not draw boundaries, workload becomes unsustainable very quickly.

When experienced teachers leave, the loss is significant. They carry professional judgement and instinct that others are still developing. They see things early and prevent problems before they surface. You cannot replace that quickly.

We need to talk the profession up more. Public respect matters. Young people – especially young people of colour – need to see teaching as a credible and respected career. Visibility matters for the future workforce.

I won't play recruitment games that damage culture. You cannot build a values-led school by being held to ransom. Long-term culture matters more than short-term fixes.

Retention and recruitment are what keep school leaders awake at night now. This is not a side issue – it is core business.

Harrogate Grammar School

Harrogate Grammar School is a large coeducational secondary school and sixth form in North Yorkshire, serving a broad comprehensive intake across the Harrogate area. The school has a strong academic reputation alongside a wide co-curricular offer and established partnerships across its local community and Trust network. In recent years, the school has focused on sustaining high standards through investment in teaching quality, staff development and organisational culture.

How is the school approaching teacher retention?

- **Flexible working embedded** as a strategic retention lever – parttime working has expanded significantly, rising from around 25 to around 60 parttime teachers through deliberate leadership mindset and timetable design; hybrid and compressed hours for support staff
- **Off-site PPA** option introduced – teachers can complete PPA time off site, giving greater control over when and where work is completed
- **'Trading to Flex' model** implemented – teachers can exchange additional cover hours into a central bank in return for approved personal days for significant life events or opportunities

- **Strong belonging culture** intentionally cultivated – regular staff briefings designed with celebration, humour and recognition built in
- **Structured recognition systems** – long-service awards, celebration events and personal acknowledgement of staff milestones embedded
- Pipeline leadership roles created – temporary and associate leadership roles used to give **development opportunities** and prevent stagnation
- Trust-wide lateral **career pathways** – staff released to work across Trust schools and hubs to gain broader influence without leaving
- **Professional-development investment prioritised** – leaders say yes to development opportunities where possible, including qualifications and programmes.

What impact are they having?

- High proportion of experienced teachers retained – **significant share of staff with over 20 years' experience remain in post**
- Strong staff-survey feedback on flexible working – flexibility initiatives produced unusually **positive staff-culture survey responses**
- Increased perception of **professional trust** – off-site PPA and flex arrangements signal leadership confidence in staff professionalism
- **Reduced supply-cover reliance** through flex-cover bank – internal cover-exchange model reduces external staffing pressure.

Leader perspective

Neil Renton, Headteacher

If a school of over 2000 students with a broad curriculum can make flexible working function, then it can be done. It starts with mindset. You begin from yes, and then you work out how to make it possible.

We made a deliberate decision to expand parttime working as a retention strategy. We moved from around 25 parttime teachers to roughly 60. That didn't happen by accident – it was designed. The goal was to keep good people in the profession by making work fit their lives more sustainably.

Small elements of professional control make a big difference. Allowing staff to take PPA off site, for example, has had a significant impact on how people feel about their work and their trust in leadership. It signals that we see them as professionals who can manage their time.

We introduced a system where staff can place cover hours into a central bank and draw them back for important life events. We are deliberately value-neutral about what those events are. If something matters to a member of staff, then it matters. That principle builds trust and fairness.

Belonging is built through communication and language. I am careful to say *our* school, not *my* school. That isn't cosmetic – it reflects how leadership should work. People need to feel collective ownership.

Culture has to be constructed intentionally. We build celebration into regular briefings – humour, recognition, everyday hero moments. Those small acts accumulate. Positive culture does not appear by accident.

Experienced teachers carry forms of wisdom that cannot be quickly replaced. They have seen cycles, they understand nuance and they handle complex situations instinctively. That professional judgement is built over time.

Parttime pathways allow us to retain that expertise for longer. If I can keep 0.8 of an experienced teacher, then later 0.6 or 0.5, I have kept something precious in the profession that would otherwise be lost entirely. Gradual transitions also allow knowledge to be passed on rather than walking out of the building all at once.

Creating pipeline roles and sideways opportunities across the Trust gives people ways to grow without leaving. Not every development pathway has to be upwards. Lateral movement and specialist roles are important retention tools.

Professional development should not depend on chance or individual advocacy. It should be designed into the system so that growth is expected and supported.

Funding certainty would significantly improve retention decisions. It is difficult to invest long-term in people when budgets are unclear or unstable. Stability in funding enables stability in staffing.

Flexible working is not a perk. It is a retention necessity.

Saint Stephen's Primary School

Saint Stephen's Primary School is a standalone Church of England primary school in Bradford, serving a highly deprived and transient inner-city community with significant social need. The school operates in a complex context but has sustained strong staff retention and organisational stability over time.

How is the school approaching teacher retention?

- **Strong, explicit moral purpose** – staff are recruited and retained through clarity that the school's work is emotionally demanding but deeply meaningful
- Highly **relational leadership culture** – open-door access to the headteacher and senior leaders, with multiple communication routes and regular direct contact
- Treating staff explicitly as professionals – **high-trust, high-expectation** model rather than compliance culture
- Individualised **professional-growth pathways** – appraisal used to stretch and challenge staff around personal intellectual and professional interests
- **Funded advanced study** – school funding used to support Masters and planned PhD study for research-engaged staff
- **Staff-led curriculum development** – teachers designing schemes, resources and subject models rather than relying solely on commercial packages
- **Personal crisis support** – leadership actively supports staff through illness, bereavement and family crisis; there is a broad definition of compassionate leave, including emotionally significant relationships beyond narrow policy definitions
- External **professional exposure** – staff encouraged and funded to engage with conferences, research and other schools.

What impact are they having?

- **Very high staff retention** – minimal voluntary departures; vacancies arise mainly through international moves or life changes; multiple teachers with over 20 years' service at the school; low internal attrition despite high-context challenge – deprivation and transience do not translate into staff turnover
- **Internal progression pipeline** – staff are developed into leadership and specialist roles within the school
- Recovery and retention of previously struggling teachers – staff who failed elsewhere have become highly effective in **supportive culture**

- **High professional engagement** – teachers actively leading curriculum innovation and research-informed practice
- **Strong psychological safety** – staff willing to propose ideas, challenge practice and admit mistakes
- **High staff loyalty** – flexibility and personal support produce reciprocal commitment.

Leader perspective

Paul Ury, Headteacher

Retention has to be deliberate. Nothing happens by osmosis. If you want people to stay, you design for it. You make choices every day that show staff they matter and that their work is valued.

If you treat people as professionals, they respond as professionals. If you infantilise them, they disengage. Professional trust is not a soft extra; it is the foundation. That means giving people space to think, to question, to develop and to try new approaches without fear.

I build intellectual stretch into appraisal and development conversations. I introduce challenge – research projects, new areas of thinking, unfamiliar directions – because professionals want to grow. Many of our staff are engaged in Masters-level work, research and subject innovation. That keeps people alive professionally. It keeps the work fresh and purposeful.

Care has to be personal and visible. Every member of staff here – teachers and support staff – knows that, at some point, I will have helped them through something difficult. That isn't accidental. Loyalty is built through human moments. If something matters deeply to a member of staff, then it matters to me. Policy might say no; leadership sometimes needs to say yes. You only get one chance at certain life events, and leaders should recognise that.

The work can be emotionally demanding, and pretending otherwise is dishonest. We fund counselling because staff see and carry difficult things. There is a cost to that, and responsible leadership acknowledges it.

Consistency matters. Staff should never wonder which version of me is going to walk through the door. Predictability builds safety. What is said in my office stays there. In public, I back my staff. That clarity of stance strengthens trust across the organisation.

Professional respect also means permission to explore. I encourage teachers to test ideas – new curriculum models, different pedagogical approaches, emerging tools – because stagnation weakens schools. Schools become stale when they stop being challenged. I want ideas flowing outwards and inwards, with staff exposed to difference and new thinking.

I invest heavily in bringing people together and in keeping the culture intellectually and morally alive. A good school is not defined by a score or a headline measure. It is defined by whether it changes life chances and serves its community well.

People do not stay because of perks. They stay because they are valued, stretched, trusted and supported. That is the work of leadership – and it has to be intentional.

Co-op Academy Belle Vue

Co-op Academy Belle Vue is a rapidly growing free school in Manchester serving a highly disadvantaged community. Now in its fourth year, the school has expanded quickly, serving a diverse intake with high levels of deprivation, SEND and limited mobility.

How is the school approaching teacher retention?

- Retention built through **predictable systems** – highly consistent routines, behaviour expectations and classroom structures reduce cognitive and emotional load for staff
- **Codified teaching model** – 'Teach Like a Belle Vue Champion' handbook with defined techniques, shared language and video exemplars reduces ambiguity and supports staff confidence
- Behaviour systems designed for **disruption-free classrooms** – leaders commit explicitly that teachers will not be left alone with persistent disruption
- **Vulnerability lens** applied to staff decisions – leadership repeatedly asks what policies feel like for the most vulnerable member of staff (for example ECTs, single parents, new joiners)
- **All CPD delivered within directed time** – no after-school CPD requirement; daily morning professional learning embedded in timetable

- Two to two-and-a-half hours' weekly CPD – **structured, deliberate practice** model combined with **subject and curriculum development time**
- **Senior leaders actively participate in CPD** – modelling credibility and maintaining instructional alignment
- **Coaching model** replaces formal lesson observations – drop-ins used for agreed coaching goals rather than judgemental evaluation
- Early and frequent **staff-voice** collection – feedback gathered within first month of term to adjust systems quickly
- **Culture of belonging and shared language** – values embedded in daily vocabulary and systems
- Structured **celebration and recognition culture** – regular appreciation rituals for staff and support teams
- **Meeting clustering** – all after-school meetings and events scheduled on the same day each week to support childcare planning
- **Timetabled PPA at end of day** – allows teachers to complete PPA at home and leave site earlier
- **Early finish built into timetable** – staff have regular 2:40pm finishes and a 2:15pm Friday finish
- **Directed-time duty design** – lunch supervision built into directed time so duties are not additional burden
- **Free breakfast and lunch for staff** – removes stigma and supports staff facing financial pressure without disclosure
- **Career acceleration opportunities** – rapid leadership and responsibility pathways available in growing school structure
- Experienced teachers given **coaching and leadership** roles – responsibility used as retention and motivation lever.

What impact are they having?

- Strong **early-career retention** – multiple teachers have remained and progressed rapidly into leadership roles
- **High CPD engagement** – staff participation and enthusiasm sustained through in-day delivery model

- **Reduced workload friction** – timetable and meeting design lowers structural stressors
- **Increased staff-belonging signals** – shared language and rituals strengthen identity and attachment.

Leader perspective

Scott Fletcher, Principal

If a classroom is predictable, it protects the most vulnerable learner – and it also protects the most vulnerable teacher. That principle sits underneath our design decisions. We look at systems through the lens of the most vulnerable member of staff and the most vulnerable student, and we build from there.

Our commitment to staff is disruption-free classrooms. Teachers should be able to teach. That means behaviour systems have to work, routines have to be consistent and leadership has to follow through. You cannot talk about retention if teachers are firefighting all day.

We codified our teaching model to reduce cognitive load and ambiguity. Clarity reduces stress. When expectations are shared, named and modelled, teachers don't have to guess. That frees up energy for teaching rather than interpretation.

Professional development happens during the school day. If something matters, it deserves directed time. We do not bolt learning onto the edges of people's lives. Experienced teachers lead and coach within that model, and we place them deliberately in CPD groups so that expertise is shared and everyone grows.

Belonging is built through shared language and daily habit. Words like 'community', 'ambition' and 'care' are not slogans; they are part of how we speak and act every day. Culture is constructed through repetition.

We are transparent in recruitment. Candidates experience the real school day when they visit. We have to be right for them and they have to be right for us. That honesty improves fit and reduces early attrition.

We design workload structurally wherever we can. Meetings are clustered onto one day so childcare and family logistics are predictable. That is a small operational decision with a big human impact. Everyone has PPA at the end of the day and can leave site. That is a signal of trust and professionalism.

Flexibility matters at life moments. If someone needs to take their child to school on the first day, we make it work. You don't get that moment back. These decisions communicate values more clearly than policies ever can.

We remove quiet barriers where we can. Staff receive breakfast and lunch. I don't need to know who might be struggling financially – I remove the obstacle for everyone. Universal provision protects dignity.

I don't think in terms of how to make people stay forever. I think about how to make this a place where people grow and thrive while they are here. If people develop well, contribute well and feel well supported, retention follows.

Experienced teachers are gold. They bring judgement, stability and wisdom. When we lose them, we lose more than capacity; we lose professional memory. Retention is not a poster or a slogan. It is timetable design, behaviour design and culture design, working together.

Chiltern Learning Trust

Chiltern Learning Trust is a Multi-Academy Trust based in the East of England, serving a diverse student population across primary and secondary schools in areas of significant socioeconomic disadvantage. The Trust has grown steadily over recent years and is recognised for its strong emphasis on inclusion, leadership development and community partnership. Chiltern has developed a people-centred improvement model that places staff belonging, professional growth and internal progression at the heart of its strategy.

How is the Trust approaching teacher retention?

- Chiltern Learning Trust approaches retention long before appointment – leaders describe recruitment as **relational and intentional**.
- The Trust takes a long-term view and does not believe there is a silver bullet for retention – particularly the retention of teachers from marginalised ethnic groups – and addresses diversity at the very top of school leadership. They have spent a lot of time and effort cultivating and crafting a culture where belonging is key.
- Professional learning is deliberately social and humane, designed around teachers' lives. **Belonging is treated as a strategy.** This, again, is particularly key for teachers from marginalised ethnic groups, who need to see themselves as able to belong in school as leaders. The Trust recognises that, traditionally, teachers from this background have found it difficult to thrive and, instead, just survived.

- Staff are trained at every level on racial literacy. This includes what racism looks like and what institutional bias is; policies, processes and systems are fixed so that prejudice is minimised through blind applications.
- Communities are created so that people can see others like them. This celebrates communities and what binds them. These have been made to be more inclusive, such as 'Chai and Chat'. Staff are encouraged to be part of associations such as BAMEed or the Somali Educator's Association.
- Social opportunities have been created for people to network, such as the Racial Equity Network Dinner. This brings people together to break bread in an inclusive environment.
- **Autonomy with alignment** allows schools to retain identity while benefiting from **shared learning**. **Professional judgement** is respected.
- Line management is decisive. Leaders invest in **humane leadership**, codifying what it means to be 'good eggs'.
- An in-house talent-development programme exists for future leaders. Initially, headteachers were given assistance to help them identify teachers from marginalised ethnic groups to do this pathway. This has focused on meritocracy, not mirror-tocracy.
- The Trust focuses on diversity in National Professional Qualification (NPQ) candidates, using scholarship funding.

What impact are they having?

- **Retention is strengthened** through the relational-recruitment approach.
- **Cross-Trust role mobility** retains high-performing staff through internal progression rather than exit.
- Social CPD formats increase **voluntary engagement and professional community**.
- Leadership accessibility increases staff perception of being **known and valued**.
- A belonging-led culture **reduces non-financial attrition drivers**.
- More diverse leaders at all levels mean staff see leaders at all levels who look like them. In fact, three of the last five headteacher appointments came from marginalised ethnic groups. This was not through positive discrimination – it was through recognising talent.

Leader perspective

Sufian Sadiq, Chief Talent and Transformation Officer

Our retention journey ironically starts before people join us. And that's the interesting part, because there's no point thinking about retention once they're with you. First impressions count, and first impressions leave a lasting impression.

We're very local, and locality plays a key role. We want schools to have their own identity. We want them to retain that identity, because it matters to the community. But what we do want them to do is work together, collaboratively.

We've got people who move between the organisation. You might be a second in department in one school, a head of department in another, then an assistant head somewhere else. And there are people who've worked in three or four of our schools. They're some of our highest performers.

Our social CPD plays a massive part. We're big on social CPD. Last night, we were in a café. We've done CPD in a jazz club. We all know how people react to CPD during the day in school. But CPD in a jazz club? People choose to be there.

We're very accessible. We don't say, 'Oh, I'm too busy, speak to my PA'. If you want to meet us, we meet you. We're out in the community. That recruitment, that social element, that's part of the retention offer.

People don't leave us because of money. We know that. What makes the biggest difference is what we're calling being 'good eggs'.

I've got a page of notes where I write things down about people. Because when you walk away, you forget. So I'll write it down. And then when I see them, I can say, 'How was Andrew's operation?' And those things have made the biggest difference. People feel seen.

When people leave, it's the small things. When you unpack it, that's what it is. The culture gets eroded from lack of human empathy. That's what makes people want to leave.

You could strip everything else away. If you just kept the fact that we treat people well, and we're good to them on a human level, you'd still see higher retention.

And that's right from the top. You'll see our CEO, you'll see me. We're not an ivory tower. We're normal. And that effort to be normal, accessible and supportive with people is a massive, massive part of it.

CHAPTER THIRTEEN:
Key findings for leaders

Introduction

As we have heard from the voices of teachers and leaders throughout this book, high retention in schools is not explained by perks, slogans or one-off wellbeing initiatives. In every case, it is explained by leadership behaviour and intentional organisational design. Experienced teachers stay where their daily experience feels professionally respectful, structurally sustainable, intellectually alive and humanly possible. They leave where trust is low, workload is unmanaged, leadership is brittle and culture is performative rather than relational. The strongest retention settings are not perfect schools, but their leaders make deliberate choices about culture, time, flexibility, development and dignity. What follows here are the key findings for leaders that emerge consistently from the evidence and lived experience we have gathered.

Behaviour

The first and most consistent finding is that leadership behaviour significantly outweighs leadership policy. Teachers do not stay because a retention strategy exists on paper; they stay because of how they are treated in everyday moments. Experienced teachers, in particular, are often highly sensitive to tone, fairness and consistency. They notice whether leaders explain decisions or hide behind process; whether they listen or deflect; whether they show steadiness under pressure or transmit anxiety downwards. In high-retention settings, leaders are described as predictable, accessible and direct. They have difficult conversations openly and answer requests clearly, even when the answer is no. They are transparent and do not allow silence to breed resentment. These leaders treat professional disagreement as dialogue and feedback, not disloyalty. In schools where leaders are relationally steady, there is psychological safety, and psychological safety is a retention condition.

Behaviour culture is also repeatedly identified as a staff-retention issue; not only a student-outcome issue. Predictable, well-supported behaviour systems reduce teacher stress and protect classroom joy. Leaders in high-retention schools design behaviour systems that remove repeated burden from individual teachers. They follow through, and do not leave staff isolated with persistent disruption. Many teachers we spoke to described this as one of the strongest signals that leadership has their back. Where behaviour support is inconsistent, exhaustion accelerates, regardless of other strengths.

Closely connected is the centrality of professional trust. Experienced teachers stay where they are treated as experts rather than operatives, where accountability is intelligent and developmental and where observation and coaching are used to improve practice not to make judgements. Leaders assume professionalism first and intervene proportionately when needed. Teachers are given room to exercise judgement about pedagogy, curriculum and classroom decisions within clear shared frameworks. Where leaders over-specify method, over-monitor compliance and reduce teaching to script-following, experienced teachers disengage or leave. Trust is not a soft preference – it is a structural retention lever.

Workload

A second major finding is that workload must be engineered, not merely acknowledged. Every teacher in our case studies distinguishes between leaders who talk about workload and leaders who redesign work. The difference is practical. High-retention schools and Trusts change timetable structures, meeting patterns, marking expectations, behaviour systems and administrative processes. They remove tasks; they don't just add tools. Meetings are clustered to support family life, CPD is part of directed time and behaviour systems are centralised. Leaders understand that teacher time and energy is finite, and they design systems accordingly to reduce duplication of effort. Planning time is protected and curriculum resources are co-created and shared. But, where leaders leave workload to individual resilience, experienced staff steadily drain away.

Flexibility emerges as one of the most powerful and underused retention strategies. In our interviews, teachers repeatedly identify life-stage inflection points – early parenthood, caring responsibilities, health challenges, midlife strain – as moments when rigid structures push people out. The strongest leaders normalise flexible working rather than treating it as an exception. Parttime roles, job shares, phased late-career transitions, hybrid professional roles and compassionate-leave decisions appear repeatedly in high-retention contexts. Importantly, flexibility is not framed as an indulgence, but as stewardship of expertise. Leaders who say 'How can we make this work?' retain people that other schools lose. Leaders who say 'policy won't allow it' often do not. Many teachers we spoke to recalled a leader who had supported them to work flexibly at a key time in their life and had, in turn, inspired long-term loyalty well beyond the cost of their actions.

Belonging

Another clear finding is that belonging is built intentionally. High-retention schools curate belonging, not by posters and mission statements, but through repeated signals of inclusion and value – rituals, recognition and shared language. Staff contributions are celebrated, milestones are marked, routine gatherings are made meaningful through warmth and humour. Belonging is signalled as early as induction, where new staff are welcomed relationally, not just procedurally. Many of the teachers we interviewed described small but significant gestures made by leaders: a handwritten thank-you note, a good wish for their ill child, a birthday card. These things are not trivial. They counterbalance the emotional load of teaching, building identity and loyalty. In these schools, belonging is treated as infrastructure.

Development

Professional growth and development across the full career span are other significant factors. Experienced teachers do not stay because learning stops; they stay because it continues. The strongest leaders reject the idea that professional development is only for early career teachers or aspiring senior leaders. They create pathways for expert classroom practitioners to deepen their craft, lead subject work, mentor others, engage in research and contribute across schools. Development is often personalised and sometimes sponsored – leaders actively encourage individuals towards qualifications, networks and new responsibilities. Just as important, development is not always tied to promotion. Several experienced teachers we spoke to were clear that they want growth without management responsibility. Where mastery pathways exist, retention strengthens.

Subject

Subject and intellectual vitality matter more to teachers than leaders sometimes assume. Teachers who remain long-term often describe subject passion as a sustaining force. High-retention schools and Trusts protect subject identity and subject community. They enable subject-specific professional learning, external networks and cross-school collaboration. They allow teachers to keep thinking, not just delivering, by avoiding reducing teaching to generic techniques detached from disciplinary depth. Where subject value is marginalised – particularly in creative and practical disciplines – experienced teachers are more likely to leave the classroom.

Our case studies show that role variety and mobility retain people. Leaders who redesign roles around evolving strengths and interests keep experienced staff energised and enthusiastic. Hybrid roles, cross-Trust work, mentoring positions, subject leadership, community partnerships and research projects provide renewal without requiring exit. Trusts, in particular, can use lateral movement as a retention strategy. Where career pathways are rigid, stagnation leads to attrition.

Recognition

Recognition and dignity also emerged as central. Experienced teachers do not expect constant praise, but they do expect to be seen. Many describe mid- and late-career invisibility as a risk factor – early career teachers receive coaching and encouragement, while veterans are assumed to cope. Strong leaders counter this by naming expertise, inviting contribution and acknowledging impact. They understand that professional dignity – being treated as someone whose judgement matters – is a retention condition. These leaders see experience as an asset, not a cost.

Leadership

A further finding is that humane leadership during a crisis has a long memory. Teachers do not forget how they were treated during illness, bereavement, pregnancy, family emergency or professional setback. Several of the longest-serving teachers we spoke to trace their retention to one leader who made a compassionate decision at a critical moment. Conversely, several near-exits are traced to moments of bureaucratic rigidity or coercive leadership during vulnerability. Crisis response is not marginal to retention; it is formative.

Finally, leaders who retain experienced teachers are honest about constraints but intentional about choices. They acknowledge funding pressure and accountability demands, but they still choose to invest in people where it counts. They design for sustainability, understanding that retention is cheaper, educationally and financially, than constant replacement. Mostly, they know that, when experienced teachers leave, the loss is not just numerical but cultural and instructional, and they act accordingly.

Conclusion

The central message from experienced teachers is clear. They stay in schools where professionalism is trusted, workload is designed, flexibility is normalised, development is continuous, belonging is cultivated and leadership is humane. These are not soft factors, but strategic ones. We do not need governments to design policy to mandate these things: they are all within our control. Leaders who deliberately build them create schools where expertise remains – and where both teachers and students benefit from that continuity.

CHAPTER FOURTEEN: Key findings for policymakers

Introduction

If England is serious about improving educational quality, equity and system stability, it must urgently shift its centre of gravity from recruitment alone to the retention of experienced teachers. The evidence is clear, the moral case is strong and the consequences of inaction are already visible in classrooms across the country. What this book demonstrates, unequivocally, is that retention is not a marginal workforce issue but a core lever of system performance. Experienced teachers are not simply a 'nice to have'; they are the connective tissue of schools, the carriers of professional knowledge and the quiet guarantors of educational continuity. Policy must now be designed with that reality firmly in view.

For too long, retention policy in England has been framed narrowly around early-career attrition. While this focus is understandable, it has obscured a deeper and more damaging pattern: the steady erosion of the middle and later career workforce. Teachers with 10, 15 or 20 years of experience are leaving in significant numbers, often not because they have lost their commitment to students or to teaching itself, but because the system has made it increasingly difficult for them to continue with dignity, autonomy and professional pride. This book shows that experienced teachers typically do not leave suddenly. They leave after long periods of erosion: of trust, of flexibility, of recognition and of belief that their expertise still matters.

The snowball effect

The first and most important message for policymakers is that retention is cumulative. Teachers rarely leave because of one reform, one inspection or one difficult year. They leave because multiple pressures stack up over time. Excessive workload, performative accountability, lack of agency, poor behaviour support and rigid career structures interact in ways that make even deeply committed professionals question whether staying is sustainable. Policy responses that treat retention as a short-term incentive problem, solvable through bonuses or one-off initiatives, will continue to fall short.

Autonomy

Also central to the findings of this book is the role of trust and professional agency. Experienced teachers stay when they are trusted to exercise judgement, not when they are tightly managed through scripts, checklists and surveillance. Over successive decades, policy has increasingly substituted professional trust with compliance mechanisms, often in the name of standards or consistency. The result has been a form of micromanagement that corrodes professional identity.

Teachers interviewed for this book consistently described feeling most settled, effective and motivated when leaders and, by extension, policy frameworks, create space for autonomy within clear guardrails. For policymakers, this means recognising that accountability systems must distinguish between assurance and control. Inspection, appraisal and performance management should not duplicate or reinforce one another in ways that amplify fear and workload. Where they do, experienced teachers are often the first to disengage or exit.

Workload

In addition, workload emerged not as an abstract complaint, but as a lived reality shaped by policy decisions. Teachers do not object to hard work; they object to wasted work. Administrative duplication, excessive data demands and constant policy churn create a sense of futility that experienced teachers find particularly dispiriting. Many interviewees described reaching a point where they felt their expertise was being drowned out by bureaucracy. Effective retention policy therefore requires ruthless clarity about what genuinely improves teaching and learning, and what exists primarily to signal compliance. Policymakers must take responsibility for reducing the cumulative burden generated by overlapping accountability systems and frequent reform cycles. Without this, school-level efforts to reduce workload will always be undermined.

Flexible working

A particularly important finding concerns life-stage flexibility. Teaching policy in England has historically been designed around an implicitly young, unencumbered workforce. Yet many of the teachers the system most needs to retain are those navigating parenthood, caring responsibilities, health changes or simply the desire for a more balanced life after decades of service.

The evidence here is stark: experienced teachers are far more likely to stay when flexibility is real rather than rhetorical. This includes access to parttime work without career penalty, phased returns after absence, protected timetables at points of personal strain and leadership roles that do not assume fulltime availability as a default. Policymakers should note that flexibility is not a concession; it is a retention strategy. Other public services, most notably the NHS, have begun to plan explicitly for workforce 'pinch points'. Education policy would benefit from adopting a similar lens.

Recognition

Recognition and professional status also loom large in teachers' decisions to stay or go. This book documents a persistent sense among experienced teachers that their contribution has become increasingly invisible. While early-career support has rightly expanded, many mid- and late-career teachers feel overlooked, taken for granted or reduced to delivery agents. This is compounded by a broader cultural narrative in which teaching is too often framed as failing, resistant to change or in need of constant correction. Policymakers should understand that rhetoric matters. Public discourse, inspection language and reform-framing all shape teachers' sense of professional worth. Where teachers feel consistently denigrated, even implicitly, retention suffers.

Crucially, recognition must be material as well as symbolic. Teachers are acutely sensitive to performative appreciation that is not backed by time, influence or pay. This book makes a compelling case for formalising expert teacher roles that allow experienced practitioners to contribute through mentoring, curriculum leadership, professional development and system work, without having to leave the classroom entirely. This is not simply about creating titles, but about legitimising expertise as a career endpoint in its own right. At present, policy frameworks continue to privilege leadership progression over pedagogical mastery. This has the unintended effect of pushing excellent teachers out of classrooms, or out of the profession altogether, when leadership roles do not fit their skills or life circumstances.

Development

Investment in professional development is another decisive factor in retention. Teachers with long careers behind them do not stay because they have nothing left to learn. On the contrary, they stay when they are still learning, still growing and still connected to their subject and craft. This book highlights the importance of job-embedded, collaborative professional learning, led by expert practitioners and grounded in classroom reality. Policymakers should be wary of professional-development models that are heavily centralised, generic or detached from teachers' day-to-day work. Equally, the expansion of mentoring and training responsibilities must be accompanied by proper resourcing. The evidence here suggests that when experienced teachers are asked to mentor, coach or train others without time or recognition, retention is actively harmed rather than helped.

Perhaps the most strategic message for policymakers concerns career pathways. This book argues convincingly that the traditional career ladder no longer reflects how teachers want, or indeed need, to work. Linear progression towards senior leadership, fulltime and irreversible, does not align with the realities of modern professional lives. What retains experienced teachers is not constant upwards movement, but the ability to move sideways, pause, return or refocus without stigma. A career lattice, rather than a ladder, allows teachers to adapt their roles as their interests and circumstances change. Policy can either enable this fluidity or block it. At present, national frameworks tend to do the latter.

Behaviour

The cultural dimension of retention cannot be overstated. Teachers in this study spoke powerfully about the feel of a school – something they could sense almost immediately. While culture is shaped locally, it is not immune to national policy signals. Behaviour policy is a clear example. Where national frameworks and guidance fail to support schools to establish consistent, staff-protective behaviour systems, the emotional toll on teachers increases. Experienced teachers, often relied upon to manage the most challenging classes, can quickly find themselves exhausted. Retention policy must therefore attend not only to workforce structures, but to the conditions under which teaching is emotionally sustainable.

Finally, policymakers must recognise that retention is a justice issue as well as a workforce one. The loss of experienced teachers disproportionately affects schools serving disadvantaged communities, where turnover is already high and stability is hardest to achieve. When experienced teachers leave, it is often these students who lose first. Retention policy that fails to account for this risks entrenching inequality. Conversely, a system that actively values, supports and retains experienced teachers is one that invests in long-term improvement, not short-term fixes.

Conclusion

The central lesson of this book is simple but profound. Teachers stay when they are trusted, supported, recognised and able to live sustainable professional lives. None of these conditions is beyond the reach of policy. But achieving them requires a shift in mindset: from seeing retention as an individual resilience problem, to understanding it as a structural design challenge. The experienced teachers of England have shown extraordinary commitment over decades of change. The question now is whether policy will finally be designed to deserve their loyalty.

If the aim is a stable, expert and confident teaching workforce, the path forwards is clear. Retain those who have already chosen, time and again, to stay.

Part 7
Closing words

CHAPTER FIFTEEN:
Call to action

This book began with a simple but uncomfortable truth: England does not have a teacher-recruitment problem alone. It has a retention problem and, specifically, a crisis of losing its most experienced teachers. As we have shown, this loss is not inevitable. It is not the natural endpoint of a demanding career. It is the consequence of choices: cultural, structural and political. These choices have made it harder and harder for experienced teachers to remain.

Across decades of reform, accountability cycles and workforce initiatives, one thing has remained strikingly consistent. Teachers do not leave because they stop caring. They leave because the system stops caring for them. Again and again, in interviews, in data and in lived experience, the same story emerges: teachers stay when they feel trusted, valued, supported and able to live a life alongside their work. They leave when these conditions are eroded, slowly and persistently, until staying becomes an act of personal sacrifice rather than professional commitment.

This final chapter is, therefore, not a summary, but a call to action. Because what is required now is not more diagnosis, but courage. The courage to name what is broken. The courage to stop doing what we know does not work. And the courage to design a system that deserves the loyalty of those who have already given it decades of their lives.

If we are serious about educational improvement, we must be serious about stability. Experienced teachers are not simply better teachers in a narrow technical sense; they are the carriers of professional memory, relational expertise and institutional knowledge. They are the mentors who make early-career support meaningful. They are the colleagues who hold schools steady through crisis. They are the ones who know which reforms are worth embedding and which will quietly pass. When they leave, schools do not just lose capacity. They lose continuity, confidence and culture.

Yet, for too long, policy has treated experience as incidental. The dominant narrative has been one of constant renewal: new frameworks, new standards, new teachers. Experience has been implicitly framed as something to be managed, monitored or refreshed, rather than something to be protected and invested in. This has led to a profound imbalance. We pour resources into getting teachers in, while failing to create the conditions that make them want to stay / be able to stay.

One of the clearest lessons of this book is that retention is structural, not individual. Teachers do not lack resilience. They respond rationally to the environments they work in. When workload is excessive and poorly prioritised, when accountability is duplicative and punitive, when autonomy is stripped away in the name of consistency and when professional growth requires leaving the classroom, experienced teachers make understandable choices. They step back, step sideways or step out altogether.

Crucially, many of those who leave would have stayed. That is perhaps the most painful finding of all. These are not teachers who fell out of love with teaching. They are teachers who loved it enough to recognise when the cost had become too high.

The evidence presented here shows that when schools and systems get retention right, they do so by design. They make trust real by embedding teacher voice in decision-making. They reduce performative accountability and invest instead in developmental cultures. They recognise that workload is not just about hours, but about meaning. They build flexibility around the realities of adult lives. They create career pathways that honour expertise without forcing exit from the classroom. And they cultivate cultures where teachers feel safe to teach well, rather than constantly braced for judgement.

None of this is radical. Much of it is already happening in pockets of the system. What is missing is coherence and commitment at scale.

For policymakers, the implications are clear. Retention cannot sit on the margins of workforce strategy, addressed through one-off incentives or early-career-only interventions. It must be central to how the system is governed. This means aligning inspection, appraisal and professional development so that they reinforce, rather than undermine, professional trust. It means resisting the urge to introduce new initiatives without first removing old ones. It means recognising that flexibility, autonomy and dignity are not 'soft' issues, but essential conditions for a sustainable workforce.

It also means changing the narrative. The way teachers are spoken about matters. Decades of derision, suspicion and blame have taken their toll. When teachers are portrayed as obstacles to reform rather than agents of it, the message received is clear: your experience is a problem to be fixed, not an asset to be valued. Rebuilding retention requires a public and political commitment to professional respect.

For school and Trust leaders, the call is equally urgent. Retention is leadership work. It is shaped by the daily decisions leaders make about priorities, protection and pressure. Leaders cannot control national policy, but they can control how it lands. They can choose to shield staff from unnecessary demands. They can make workload visible and manageable. They can notice when valued colleagues are approaching breaking point and act before they leave. They can ensure that experienced teachers are not only relied upon but replenished.

This is not about nostalgia or resisting change. Experienced teachers are not asking for a return to some imagined golden age. They are asking for conditions in which their expertise can continue to grow, matter and be shared. They want to learn, to contribute and to leave the profession better than they found it. When we fail to create those conditions, we do not just lose individuals, we squander collective capacity.

The future of the profession depends on the choices we make now. England cannot recruit its way out of this crisis. Even if targets are met, a system that continues to haemorrhage experience will remain fragile. Retention is not the opposite of recruitment; it is its foundation. New teachers thrive where experienced teachers stay. Improvement accelerates where knowledge accumulates. Equity advances where stability endures.

This book has been an act of listening to those who stayed, often quietly, without recognition or reward. They did not stay because teaching was easy. They stayed because something mattered enough to hold them. Our task now is to ensure that staying is no longer an act of endurance, but a viable, respected and life-affirming choice.

The question facing the system is therefore not whether we can afford to invest in retaining experienced teachers. It is whether we can afford not to. The teachers who have stayed have already shown us what commitment looks like. It is time for the system to show its commitment in return. We wanted to show our commitment to them too by filling this book with their words. Their stories nurture the soul – it is them we can really learn from about how to remain in love with the profession.

REFERENCES

Ainsworth, P. (2025) 'Teachers' concerns over issues including pay and SEN must be addressed, union conference hears: The Irish National Teachers' Organisation's annual Northern Conference is taking place in Belfast' on *Irish News* [online] Available at: www.irishnews.com/news/northern-ireland/teachers-concerns-over-issues-including-pay-and-sen-must-be-addressed-union-conference-hears-3RQRV7WYIJFL5BM7QMOYRG6DXM (Accessed: 1 May 2026).

Alhamdan, B., Al-Saadi, K., Baroutsis, A., Du Plessis, A., Hamid, O.M. and Honan, E. (2014) 'Media representation of teachers across five countries' in *Comparative Education*.

Allen, R. (2019) *Teacher Supply in England: A Review of the Evidence*. London: Education Policy Institute.

Allen, R. and Sims, S. (2018) *The Teacher Gap*. London: Routledge.

Allen, R., Jerrim, J. and Sims, S. (2022) 'How did the COVID-19 pandemic affect educational inequality?' in *Oxford Review of Education*.

Alsup, J. (2006) *Teacher Identity Discourses: Negotiating Personal and Professional Spaces*. New York: Routledge.

Ariza-Montes, A., Muniz R.N.M., Leal-Rodríguez, A.L. and Leal-Millán, A.G. (2016) 'Workplace Bullying Among Teachers' in *Journal of Occupational and Environmental Medicine*.

Arksey, A.M. and Greidanus, E.J. (2022) '"I Could Hardly Breathe": Teachers' Lived Experiences of Bereavement After the Violent Death of a Student' in *Canadian Journal of Counselling and Psychotherapy*.

Association of School and College Leaders (2024) 'ASCL evidence to IWPRB 5th remit: March 2024' [online] Available at: www.ascl.org.uk/ASCL/media/ASCL/Membership/ASCL%20UK/ASCL%20Cymru/ASCL-evidence-to-IWPRB-5th-remit-March-2024-fv.pdf (Accessed: 1 May 2026).

Bain, M. (2025) 'Stormont has failed teachers during workload and retention crisis, union claims' on *Belfast Telegraph* [online] Available at: www.belfasttelegraph.co.uk/news/education/stormont-has-failed-teachers-during-workload-and-retention-crisis-union-claims/a575109191.html (Accessed: 1 May 2026).

Baker, M. (2022) 'Post-Pandemic Teacher Retention: A National Crisis' in *Educational Review*, 74(2).

Ball, S. (1993) 'Education Markets, Choice and Social Class: The Market as a Class Strategy in the UK and the USA' in *British Journal of Sociology of Education*.

Ball, S.J. (1990) *Politics and Policy Making in Education: Explorations in Sociology*. London: Routledge.

Ball, S.J. (2003) 'The teacher's soul and the terrors of performativity' in *Journal of Education Policy*.

Bandura, A. (1982) 'Self-efficacy mechanism in human agency' in *American Psychologist*.

Bandura, A. (1997) *Self-efficacy: The exercise of control*. New York: W.H. Freeman.

Bautista, A., Wong, J. and Gopinathan, S. (2015) 'Teacher Professional Development in Singapore: Depicting the Landscape' in *Psychology, Society & Education*.

Bazeer, N., Rocks, S., Rachet-Jacquet, L., Shembavnekar, N., Kelly, E. and Charlesworth, A. (2022) 'How many NHS workers will we need over the coming decade?' on The Health Foundation [online] Available at: www.health.org.uk/reports-and-analysis/working-papers/how-many-nhs-workers-will-we-need-over-the-coming-decade (Accessed: 30 April 2026).

Belger, T. (2021) 'UCAS teacher training applications data: 7 things we learned' on *SchoolsWeek* [online] Available at: https://schoolsweek.co.uk/teacher-training-apply-ucas-applications-rise (Accessed: 30 April 2026).

Bennett, T. (2017) 'Creating a Culture: How school leaders can optimise behaviour' [online] Available at: https://assets.publishing.service.gov.uk/media/5a7506e4ed915d3c7d529cec/Tom_Bennett_Independent_Review_of_Behaviour_in_Schools.pdf (Accessed: 30 April 2026).

Berry, B., Bastian, K.C., Darling-Hammond, L. and Kini, T. (2019) 'How Teaching and Learning Conditions Affect Teacher Retention and School Performance in North Carolina' [online] Available at: https://learningpolicyinstitute.org/sites/default/files/product-files/Leandro_Working_Conditions_REPORT.pdf (Accessed: 30 April 2026).

Biesta, G., Priestley, M. and Robinson, S. (2015) 'The role of beliefs in teacher agency' in *Teachers and Teaching*.

Blair, A. (2002) *The courage of our convictions: why reform of the public services is the route to social justice*. London: Fabian Society.

Blair, T. (2005) 'Speech on Education to City of London Academy, 12 September, Downing Street' [online] Available at: www.pm.gov.uk/output/Page8181.asp

Blatchford, P. (2018) 'The Teacher's Salary Dilemma: Why Pay Does Not Reflect the Value of Teaching' in *Teacher Education Quarterly*.

Bloom, A. (2022) 'Improving Teachers' Pay: 1980's Campaign' on 175 Years Strong / The Educational Institute of Scotland [online] Available at: https://175.eis.org.uk/improving-teachers-pay/improving-teachers-pay-1980s-campaign (Accessed: 30 April 2026).

Booth, S. (2023) 'Reject fewer teacher applicants, DfE tells trainers' on *SchoolsWeek* [online] Available at: https://schoolsweek.co.uk/reject-fewer-teacher-applicants-dfe-tells-trainers (Accessed: 1 May 2026).

Borman, G.D. and Dowling, N.M. (2008) 'Teacher attrition and retention: A meta-analytic and narrative review' in *Review of Educational Research*.

Brown, I. (2001) 'F.E.A.R.' from *Music of the Spheres*. London: Polydor.

Bubb, S. and Earley, P. (2020) *The Impact of Educational Accountability on Teachers: A Longitudinal Study*. London: Routledge.

Buchan, Prof J., Charlesworth, A., Gerschlick, B. and Seccombe, I. (2019) 'A critical moment: NHS staffing trends, retention and attrition' on The Health Foundation [online] Available at: www.health.org.uk/sites/default/files/upload/publications/2019/A%20Critical%20Moment_1.pdf (Accessed: 30 April 2026).

Cambridge (2016) 'The average age of teachers in secondary schools' [online] Available at: www.cambridgeassessment.org.uk/our-research/data-bytes/the-average-age-of-teachers-in-secondary-schools (Accessed: 30 April 2026).

Cannata, M. (2010) 'Understanding the Teacher Job Search Process: Espoused Preferences and Preferences in Use' in *Teachers College Record*.

Caring Times (2024) 'As care worker visas drop 81%, Martin Green calls situation "untenable"' [online] Available at: https://caring-times.co.uk/as-care-worker-visas-drop-81-martin-green-calls-situation-untenable/#:~:text=As%20care%20worker%20visas%20drop,situation%20'untenable'%20%7C%20Caring%20Times (Accessed: 1 May 2026).

Carlo, A., Michel, A., Jean, C.C., Bucheton, D., Demougin, P., Gordon, J., Sellier, M., Udave, J.P. and Valette, S. (2013) 'Study on Policy Measures to Improve the Attractiveness of the Teaching Profession in Europe' on International Task Force on Teachers for Education 2030 [online] Available at: https://teachertaskforce.org/knowledge-hub/study-policy-measures-improve-attractiveness-teaching-profession-europe-final-0 (Accessed: 30 April 2026).

Chung, J. (2023) 'Research-informed teacher education, teacher autonomy and teacher agency: the example of Finland' in *London Review of Education*.

Cohen, J., McCabe, E., Michelli, N.M. and Pickeral, T. (2009) 'School Climate: Research, Policy, Teacher Education and Practice' in *Teachers College Record*.

Cohen, R.M. and Scheer, S. (eds.) (1997) *The Work of Teachers in America: A Social History Through Stories*. London: Routledge.

College of Policing (2026) 'Police leadership programme' [online] Available at: www.college.police.uk/career-learning/leadership (Accessed: 1 May 2026).

Cook, L., Carder, S. and Zschomler, D. (2025) '"Being a Social Worker… It's in My DNA": Retaining Experienced Child and Family Social Workers: The Role of Professional Identity' in *Child & Family Social Work*.

Cuervo, H. (2025) 'Teacher job satisfaction and retention in small rural schools: A theory of recognition approach' in *International Journal of Educational Research*.

Cumiskey, L. (2024) 'Hinds admits mentor workload "too high" as ECF reforms unveiled' on *SchoolsWeek* [online] Available at: https://schoolsweek.co.uk/hinds-admits-mentor-workload-too-high-as-ecf-reforms-unveiled (Accessed: 30 April 2026).

Cumiskey, L. (2024) 'School teacher trainers reveal ITTECF mentor workload doubts' on *SchoolsWeek* [online] Available at: https://schoolsweek.co.uk/school-teacher-trainers-reveal-ittecf-mentor-workload-doubts (Accessed: 30 April 2026).

Cunningham, P. (1992) 'Teachers' professional image and the Press 1950–1990' in *History of Education*.

Dabrowski, A. (2020) 'Teacher Wellbeing During a Pandemic: Surviving or Thriving?' in *Social Education Research*.

Daily Mail (2012) '900,000 toil for ten hours a week unpaid'

Daily Mail (2012) 'By the way… Why teachers deserve more respect than doctors'

Daily Mail (2012) 'Teachers and lawyers put in the most overtime'

Daily Mail (2020) 'Suspended for telling the truth' on X [online] Available at: trib.al/TwMQUxa (Accessed: 13 May 2026).

Daily Mail (2020) 'Teaching unions put pressure on Government to delay school reopenings' [online] Available at: www.dailymail.co.uk/wires/pa/article9094261/Teaching-unions-pressure-Government-delay-school-reopenings.html

Day, C. (2002) *Developing Teachers: The Challenges of Lifelong Learning*. London: Routledge.

Day, C. and Gu, Q. (2010) *The New Lives of Teachers*. London: Routledge.

Day, C. and Gu, Q. (2014) *Resilient teachers, resilient schools*. London: Routledge

Day, C., Sammons, P., Stobart, G., Kington, A. and Gu, Q. (2007) *Teachers Matter: Connecting Work, Lives and Effectiveness*. Maidenhead: Open University Press.

De Wet, C. (2014) 'Educators' understanding of workplace bullying' in *South African Journal of Education* [online] Available at: https://files.eric.ed.gov/fulltext/EJ1136350.pdf

de Wolf, I.F. and Janssens, F.J.G. (2007) 'Effects and Side Effects of Inspections and Accountability in Education: An Overview of Empirical Studies' in *Oxford Review of Education*.

Deb, H.C. (1985) 'Teachers' Dispute (England and Wales)' on UK Parliament [online] Available at: https://api.parliament.uk/historic-hansard/commons/1985/oct/22/teachers-dispute-england-and-wales (Accessed 30 April 2026).

Department for Education (2018) 'Diversity of the teaching workforce: statement of intent' on Gov.uk [online] Available at: www.gov.uk/government/publications/diversity-of-the-teaching-workforce-statement-of-intent (Accessed: 1 May 2026).

Department for Education (2021) *School workforce in England: November 2020*. London: DfE.

Department for Education (2023) 'Teachers' Standards: An Overview' [online] Available at: https://assets.publishing.service.gov.uk/government/uploads/system/uploads/attachment_data/file/665522/Teachers_standard_information.pdf (Accessed: 13 May 2026).

Department for Education (2024) 'Education Secretary begins push to recruit 6,500 new teachers' on Gov.uk [online] Available at: www.gov.uk/government/news/education-secretary-begins-push-to-recruit-6500-new-teachers (Accessed: 30 April 2026).

Department for Education (2024) 'School workforce in England' on Gov.uk [online] Available at: https://explore-education-statistics.service.gov.uk/find-statistics/school-workforce-in-england (Accessed 30 April 2024).

Department for Education (2025) 'Teacher and leader development: ECF and NPQs' on Gov.uk [online] Available at: https://explore-education-statistics.service.gov.uk/find-statistics/teacher-and-leader-development-ecf-and-npqs (Accessed: 30 April 2026).

Department for Education (2025) 'Working lives of teachers and leaders: wave 4' on Gov.uk [online] Available at: www.gov.uk/government/publications/working-lives-of-teachers-and-leaders-wave-4 (Accessed: 7 May 2026).

Department for Health and Social Care (2024)

Department of Education (Northern Ireland) (2025) 'Independent Review of Teacher Workload – Final Report' [online] Available at: www.education-ni.gov.uk/publications/independent-review-teacher-workload-final-report (Accessed: 1 May 2026).

Department of Education (Northern Ireland) (2025) 'Teacher workforce statistics 2024/25' [online] Available at: www.education-ni.gov.uk/publications/teacher-workforce-statistics-202425 (Accessed: 1 May 2026).

Department of Health and Social Care (2023) 'Over 50,000 extra nurses in NHS – hitting government target early' on Gov.uk [online] Available at: www.gov.uk/government/news/over-50000-extra-nurses-in-nhs-hitting-government-target-early (Accessed: 1 May 2026).

Donnelly, A. (2022) 'Everything you've ever wanted to know about the CAPES/CAFEP concours' on Present Perfect [online] Available at: https://presentperfectblog.com/2022/08/05/everything-youve-ever-wanted-to-know-about-the-capes-cafep-concours (Accessed: 1 May 2026).

Dreer-Göthe, B. (2025) 'How appreciation predicts teachers' job satisfaction, emotional exhaustion, and quitting intentions' in *Educational Studies*.

Dunkley, E. and Shearing, H. (2021) 'TikTok abuse "is pushing teachers over the edge" on BBC [online] Available at: www.bbc.co.uk/news/education-59264238 (Accessed: 30 April 2026).

Dyfed-Powys Police Federation (2024) 'Poor pay and treatment pushing officers towards resignation' [online] Available at: https://polfed.org/dyfedpowys/news/2024/pay-and-morale-2023-results (Accessed: 1 May 2026).

Dyson, J. (2025) 'Fewer teachers quit and more return: 10 key workforce findings: Data suggests recruitment and retention pressures may be easing' on *SchoolsWeek* [online] Available at: https://schoolsweek.co.uk/fewer-teachers-quit-and-more-return-10-key-workforce-findings (Accessed: 1 May 2026).

Education Endowment Foundation (2023) 'Three takeaways from the evidence on improving teacher recruitment and retention' [online] Available at: https://educationendowmentfoundation.org.uk/news/eef-blog-three-takeaways-from-the-evidence-on-improving-teacher-recruitment-and-retention (Accessed: 30 April 2026).

Education Policy Institute (2024) 'Incentives to recruit and retain teachers in Wales' [online] Available at: https://epi.org.uk/publications-and-research/incentives-to-recruit-and-retain-teachers-in-wales (Accessed: 1 May 2026).

Education Support (2023) 'Twix 2023' [online] Available at: www.educationsupport.org.uk/media/0h4jd5pt/twix_2023.pdf

Education Workforce Council (Wales) 'Education workforce statistics' [online] Available at: www.ewc.wales/site/index.php/en/about-us/policy-and-research/workforce-statistics (Accessed: 1 May 2026).

Educational Institute of Scotland, The 'Workload Research' [online] Available at: www.eis.org.uk/Content/images/Campaigns/QualityEducation/WorkloadResearch.pdf

Elliott, S., Brown, A. and Jones, H. (2017) 'Teacher Workload: Causes, Consequences, and Solutions' in *Journal of Education Policy*.

Elliott, V., Baird, J.-A., Hopfenbeck, T.N., Ingram, J., Thompson, I., Usher, N., Zantout, M., Richardson, J. and Coleman, R. (2016) 'A marked improvement? A review of the evidence on written marking' on Education Endowment Foundation [online] Available at: https://educationendowmentfoundation.org.uk/education-evidence/evidence-reviews/written-marking (Accessed: 1 May 2026).

Fielding, M. (2001) 'OFSTED, Inspection and the Betrayal of Democracy' in *Journal of Philosophy of Education*.

Fletcher-Wood, H. (2018) 'Education in Singapore: 7) The secret of Singapore's success' [online] Available at: https://improvingteaching.co.uk/2018/02/10/education-in-singapore-7-the-secret-of-singapores-success (Accessed: 1 May 2026).

Frenzel, A.C., Daniels, L. and Burić, I. (2021) 'Teacher emotions in the classroom and their implications for students' in *Educational Psychologist*.

Fullan, M. (2001) *Leading in a Culture of Change*. San Francisco: Jossey-Bass.

Fullard, J. (2021) 'Local pay and teacher retention in England' on Education Policy Institute [online] Available at: https://epi.org.uk/publications-and-research/local-pay-and-teacher-retention-in-england (Accessed: 30 April 2026).

Furlong, J. (2022) 'Universities, Research, and Initial Teacher Education in England and Wales: Taking the Long View' in *The Palgrave Handbook of Teacher Education Research*. Cham: Palgrave Macmillan [online] Available at: https://doi.org/10.1007/978-3-030-59533-3_12-1 (Accessed: 30 April 2026).

Gatsby 'GATB Bursaries Evaluation Report Final' [online] Available at: www.gatsby.org.uk/app/uploads/sites/2/2025/07/gatb-bursaries-evaluation-report-final.pdf

General Teaching Council for Scotland, The (2024) 'The GTC Scotland Register – Registration Snapshot report: Leaving the Register' [online] Available at: www.gtcs.org.uk/documents/pages/registration-snapshot-report-2024-09-leaving-the-register (Accessed: 1 May 2026).

General Teaching Council for Scotland, The (2025) 'GTC Scotland publishes registration report 2025 and makes recommendations to improve teacher supply' [online] Available at: www.gtcs.org.uk/news/news-and-updates/gtc-scotland-publishes-registration-report-2025-and-makes-recommendations-to-improve-teacher-supply (Accessed: 1 May 2026).

Gillborn, D. and Youdell, D. (2000) *Rationing Education: Policy, Practice, Reform and Equity*. London: Open University Press.

Goddard, R., Hoy, W. and Hoy, A. (2000) 'Collective Teacher Efficacy: Its Meaning, Measure, and Impact on Student Achievement' in *American Educational Research Journal*.

Gongshang Primary School 'Staff Professional Development' [online] Available at: www.gongshangpri.moe.edu.sg/staff/pd (Accessed: 1 May 2026).

Gorard, S., Chen, W., Tan, Y., Huat See, B., Gazmuri, C., Tereshchenko, A., Demie, F. and Siddiqui, N. (2023) 'The disproportionality of ethnic minority teachers in England: trends, patterns, and problems', *Routledge Open Res*.

Gov.uk (2024) 'What is a mentor?' [online] Available at: https://becoming-a-teacher.design-history.education.gov.uk/manage-school-placements/what-is-a-mentor (Accessed: 30 April 2026).

Gove, M. (2013) 'Michael Gove speech on academies' [online] Available at: www.gov.uk/government/speeches/michael-gove-speech-on-academies (Accessed: 12 May 2026).

Gove, M. (2013) 'Michael Gove: The civil rights struggle of our time' [online] Available at: www.gov.uk/government/speeches/the-civil-rights-struggle-of-our-time (Accessed: 12 May 2026).

Gu, Q. and Day, C. (2007) 'Teachers' resilience: A necessary condition for effectiveness' in *Teaching and Teacher Education*.

Guardian, The (2008) 'Today's lesson: brilliant teachers: Awards celebrate the humble talent of those who dedicate themselves to Britain's pupils' [online] Available at: www.theguardian.com/theguardian/teaching-awards-2008 (Accessed: 12 May 2026).

Hall, R. and Pulsford, M. (2019) 'Neoliberalism and primary education: Impacts of neoliberal policy on the lived experiences of primary school communities' in *Power and Education*.

Hansen, A. (2009) 'Researching "teachers in the news": the portrayal of teachers in the British national and regional press' in *Education 3–13: International Journal of Primary, Elementary and Early Years Education*.

Hargreaves, A. and Fullan, M. (2012) *Professional Capital: Transforming Teaching in Every School*. New York: Teachers College Press.

Hattie, J. (2003) 'Teachers Make a Difference: What is the research evidence?' from Australian Council for Educational Research.

Headspace (2023) 'A Turn of the Tide: Employee Mental Health in 2023' [online] Available at: https://organizations.headspace.com/blog/a-turn-of-the-tide-employee-mental-health-in-2023 (Accessed: 1 May 2026).

Helman, Z. and Gibbs, S. (2022) *The Trouble With English and How To Address It: A Practical Guide to Designing and Delivering a Concept-Led Curriculum*. London: Routledge.

Henehan, K. (2021) 'Uneven steps: Changes in youth unemployment and study since the onset of Covid-19' on Resolution Foundation [online] Available at: www.resolutionfoundation.org/publications/uneven-steps (Accessed: 30 April 2026).

Henry, J. (2020) 'Missing out on school is disaster that lasts forever – as the huge damage inflicted on youngsters by a long break from the classroom is laid bare by several new studies' on *Daily Mail* [online] Available at: www.dailymail.com/news/article-8607983/Missing-school-disaster-lasts-forever.html (Accessed: 13 May 2026).

Home Office (2025) 'Police workforce, England and Wales: 31 March 2024' on Gov.uk [online] Available at: www.gov.uk/government/statistics/police-workforce-england-and-wales-31-march-2024/police-workforce-england-and-wales-31-march-2024 (Accessed: 1 May 2026).

Hoot, The (2026) '"Ofsted must help, not hinder" – Sir Martyn Oliver on the new framework' [online] Available at: https://thehoot.news/topics/ofsted-must-help-not-hinder-sir-martyn-oliver-on-the-new-framework (Accessed: 30 April 2026).

Houghton, A. (1974) 'Report of the Committee of Inquiry into the pay of Non-University Teachers' London: HMSO [online] Available at: https://education-uk.org/documents/houghton1974/index.html (Accessed: 7 May 2026).

Hughes, H. (2021) *Preserving Positivity*. Woodbridge: John Catt Educational.

Hughes, H. (2022) *Humans in the Classroom*. London: McNidder and Grace.

Hutchings, M. (2011) 'What impact does the wider economic situation have on teachers' career decisions? A literature review' from Institute for Policy Studies in Education, London Metropolitan University [online] Available at: https://assets.publishing.service.gov.uk/media/5a7b14e140f0b66a2fc05055/DFE-RR136.pdf (Accessed: 7 May 2026).

Id-Deen, L. and Nalu, N. (2026) 'Belonging Matters: Amplifying Teachers' Voices in Schools' in *Mathematics Teacher Educator* on National Council of Teachers of Mathematics [online] Available at: https://pubs.nctm.org/view/journals/mte/12/3/article-p185.xml (Accessed: 1 May 2026).

Ingersoll, R. (2001) 'Teacher turnover and teacher shortages' in *American Educational Research Journal*.

Ingleby, E. (2021) *Neoliberalism Across Education: Policy And Practice From Early Childhood Through Adult Learning*. London: Palgrave.

Jeffrey, B. and Woods, P. (1998) *Testing Teachers: The Effects of Inspections on Primary Teachers*. London: Routledge.

Karasova, J. and Nehyba, J. (2025) 'Novice teachers' classroom behaviour management: Situations, responses and impact on student behaviour' in *British Educational Research Journal*.

Keese, J., Thompson, C.G., Waxman, H.C., McIntush, K. and Svajda-Hardy, M. (2023) 'A Worthwhile Endeavor? A meta-analysis of research on formalized novice teacher induction programs' in *Educational Research Review*.

Kelchtermans, G. (2005) 'Teachers' emotions in educational reforms' in *Journal of Educational Change*.

Kim, L.E. and Asbury, K. (2020) 'Like a rug had been pulled from under you: The impact of COVID-19 on teachers in England' in *British Journal of Educational Psychology*.

Kim, L.E., Oxley, L. and Asbury, K. (2022) 'My brain feels like a browser with 100 tabs open: A longitudinal study of teachers' mental health and well-being during the COVID-19 pandemic' in *British Journal of Educational Psychology*.

Kim, L.E., Owusu, K. and Asbury, K. (2024) 'The ups and downs in perceived societal appreciation of the teaching profession during Covid-19: A longitudinal trajectory analysis' in *British Educational Research Journal*.

Kini, T. and Podolsky, A. (2016) 'Does Teaching Experience Increase Teacher Effectiveness? A Review of the Research' on Learning Policy Institute [online] Available at: https://learningpolicyinstitute.org/product/does-teaching-experience-increase-teacher-effectiveness-review-research (Accessed: 30 April 2026).

Kirby, D. (2016) 'The Influence of Teacher Media Images on Professional Teacher Identities' [online] Available at: https://discovery.ucl.ac.uk/id/eprint/1519713/1/Kirby_The%20Influence%20of%20Teacher%20Media%20Images%20on%20Professional%20Teacher%20Identities_Fin al_Davina_Kirby_2016.pdf

Kõlves, K., Ross, V., Hawgood, J., Spence, S.H. and De Leo, D. (2017) 'The impact of a student's suicide: Teachers' perspectives' in *Journal of Affective Disorders*.

Kraft, M.A., Blazar, D. and Hogan, D. (2018) 'The effect of teacher coaching on instruction and achievement: A meta-analysis of the causal evidence' in *Review of Educational Research*.

Kyriacou, C. and Zuin, A. (2014) 'It's the permanence of online abuse that makes cyberbullying so damaging for children' on The Conversation [online] Available at: http://theconversation.com/its-the-permanence-of-online-abuse-that-makescyberbullying-so-damaging-for-children-29874 (Accessed: 30 April 2026).

Lawson, D. (2020) 'Pitiful "can't do" attitude of union that puts teachers firmly before pupils' on *Daily Mail* [online] Available at: https://www.dailymail.com/debate/article-8610315/DOMINIC-LAWSON-Pitiful-attitude-union-puts-teachers-firmly-pupils.html (Accessed: 13 May 2026).

Lecherbonnier, S. (2024) 'Les salaires réels des enseignants français en milieu de carrière stagnent, selon l'OCDE' on *Le Monde* [online] Available at: www.lemonde.fr/societe/article/2024/09/11/les-salaires-reels-des-enseignants-francais-en-milieu-de-carriere-stagnent-selon-l-ocde_6312842_3224.html (Accessed: 1 May 2026).

Leithwood, K., Harris, A. and Hopkins, D. (2008) 'Seven strong claims about successful school leadership' in *School Leadership & Management*.

Lennert da Silva, A.L. and Mølstad, C.E. (2020) 'Teacher autonomy and teacher agency: a comparative study in Brazilian and Norwegian lower secondary education' in *The Curriculum Journal*.

Liddle, R. (2020) 'Covid has made heroes of many of our frontline workers... but not teachers' on *The Sun* [online] Available at: www.thesun.co.uk/news/13432637/covid-frontline-heroes-not-teachers-rod-liddle (Accessed: 12 May 2026).

London Innovation and Improvement Alliance (2023) 'Big Listen Report' [online] Available at: www.liia.london/wp-content/uploads/2023/06/29.06.23-Big-Listen-Report.pdf

Long, R. and Bridges, E. (2026) 'Teacher recruitment and retention in England' [online] Available at: https://commonslibrary.parliament.uk/research-briefings/cbp-7222/#:~:text=Postgraduate%20teacher%20training%20recruitment,(64%25%20below%20target) (Accessed: 30 April 2026).

Macdonald, D. (2022) 'Memories of 1980s pay strikes show why teachers must get a fair deal' on *Tes magazine* [online] Available at: www.tes.com/magazine/analysis/general/memories-1980s-pay-strikes-show-why-teachers-must-get-fair-deal (Accessed: 30 April 2026).

Macdonald, M.A. (2025) 'National Workload Action Group Final Report' on Department for Education [online] Available at: https://assets.publishing.service.gov.uk/media/68d51a8030734bac9ba0fcbc/National_Workload_Action_Group_Final_Report_September_2025.pdf (Accessed: 1 May 2026).

Mahony, P. and Hextall, I. (2000) *Reconstructing Teaching: Standards, Performance, and Accountability*. Falmer: Routledge.

Maisey, R. (2024) 'A deep dive into behaviour in schools' on Nuffield Foundation [online] Available at: www.nuffieldfoundation.org/news/a-deep-dive-into-behaviour-in-schools (Accessed: 30 April 2026).

Marchant, E., Dowd, J., Bray, L., Rowlands, G., Miles, N., Crick, T., James, M., Dadaczynski, K. and Okan, O. (2024) 'The well-being and work-related stress of senior school leaders in Wales and Northern Ireland during COVID-19 "educational leadership crisis": A cross-sectional descriptive study' in *PLoS One*.

Martin, M. (2024) 'Have new teacher training reforms helped retention?' on *Tes magazine* [online] Available at: www.tes.com/magazine/news/general/have-new-teacher-training-reforms-upped-retention (Accessed: 30 April 2026).

Martin, M. (2024) 'We need a teacher "propaganda parade", says Carter' on *Tes magazine* [online] Available at: www.tes.com/magazine/news/general/we-need-teacher-propaganda-to-tackle-recruitment-crisis-says-andrew-carter (Accessed: 30 April 2026).

Marufu, T.C., Collins, A., Vargas, L., Gillespie, L. and Almghairbi, D. (2021) 'Factors influencing retention among hospital nurses: systematic review' in *British Journal of Nursing*.

Maslach, C. and Leiter, M.P. (2016) 'Burnout' in *Stress: Concepts, cognition, emotion, and behaviour*. Cambridge: Academic Press.

Maslach, C. and Leiter, M.P. (2016) 'Understanding the burnout experience: recent research and its implications for psychiatry' in *World Psychiatry*.

McAdams, D.P. (1985) *Power, intimacy, and the life story: Personological inquiries into identity*. Homewood: Dorsey Press.

Mcculloch, G. and Ben-Peretz, M. (2009) 'International perspectives on veteran teachers: Introduction' in *Teachers and Teaching*.

McLean, D., Worth, J. and Smith, A. (2024) 'Teacher Labour Market in England Annual Report 2024', Slough: NFER [online] Available at: www.nfer.ac.uk/publications/teacher-labour-market-in-england-annual-report-2024 (Accessed: 30 April 2026).

Measuring Quality in Initial Teacher Education 'Teacher Retention' on General Teaching Council Scotland [online] Available at: www.mquite.scot/teacher-retention (Accessed: 1 May 2026).

Ministry of Education Singapore (2024) 'Data on resignation rates for teachers since 2018' [online] Available at: www.moe.gov.sg/news/parliamentary-replies/20240702-data-on-resignation-rates-for-teachers-since-2018 (Accessed: 1 May 2026).

Ministry of Education Singapore (2025) 'Singapore Teachers Embrace Digital Technologies and Benefit from Strong Professional Development: OECD TALIS 2024 Study' [online] Available at: www.moe.gov.sg/news/press-releases/20251007-singapore-teachers-embrace-digital-technologies-and-benefit-from-strong-professional-development-oecd-talis-2024-study (Accessed: 1 May 2026).

Mr Teece (2024) on X [online] Available at: https://x.com/MrTeece_/status/1864426065457824197 (Accessed: 1 May 2026).

MTPT Project, The (2021) 'Doing the Washing Up Badly' [online] Available at: www.mtpt.org.uk/light-research (Accessed: 13 May 2026).

Myatt, M. 'Humans first, professionals second' [online] Available at: www.marymyatt.com/blog/humans-first-professionals-second (Accessed: 30 April 2026).

NASUWT 'Violence and Abuse of Teachers on the Rise' [online] Available at: www.nasuwt.org.uk/article-listing/violence-and-abuse-of-teachers-on-the-rise.html

National Audit Office (2014) 'Training new teachers' [online] Available at: www.nao.org.uk/wp-content/uploads/2016/02/Training-new-teachers-Summary.pdf

National Center on Education and the Economy [online] Available at: https://ncee.org/wp-content/uploads/2017/02/SingaporeCountryBrief.pdf

National Children's Bureau (2024) 'Outcomes of CSC Provision' [online] Available at: www.ncb.org.uk/sites/default/files/uploads/files/Outcomes%20of%20CSC%20provision_Full%20Report_Final%20January%202024.pdf

National Police Chiefs Council (2025) 'Police Uplift Programme' [online] Available at: www.npcc.police.uk/our-work/police-uplift-programme (Accessed: 1 May 2026).

New Britain Project, The (2024) 'Missing Mothers' [online] Available at: www.newbritain.org.uk/missing-mothers (Accessed: 30 April 2026).

NFER (2020) 'Teacher autonomy: how does it relate to job satisfaction and retention?', Slough: NFER [online] Available at: www.nfer.ac.uk/media/r1ubcb4s/teacher_autonomy_how_does_it_relate_to_job_satisfaction_and_retention.pdf (Accessed: 30 April 2026).

Ng, P.T. (2007) 'Educational reform in Singapore: from quantity to quality' in *Educational Research for Policy and Practice*.

NHS England (2023) 'NHS retention drive expanded across the country with thousands fewer staff leaving frontline roles' [online] Available at: www.england.nhs.uk/2023/12/nhs-retention-drive-expanded-across-the-country-with-thousands-fewer-staff-leaving-frontline-roles (Accessed 1 May 2026).

NHS England 'Our NHS People Promise' [online] Available at: www.england.nhs.uk/our-nhs-people/online-version/lfaop/our-nhs-people-promise (Accessed: 1 May 2026).

Nicholas, K. (2025) 'Evidence Brief: Nursing Attrition, Recruitment and Retention' from UK: Workforce, Training and Education Knowledge Management Team [online] Available at: www.ewin.nhs.uk/sites/default/files/Nursing%20Attrition%2C%20Recruitment%20and%20Retention_Evidence%20Brief.pdf (Accessed: 1 May 2026).

Nuffield Foundation (2021) 'Teachers point towards school accountability as main driver of stress' [online] Available at: www.nuffieldfoundation.org/news/teachers-point-towards-school-accountability-as-main-driver-of-stress (Accessed: 1 May 2026).

Nursing & Midwifery Council (2025) 'Sharp drop in international recruitment slows overall growth of UK Register' [online] Available at: www.nmc.org.uk/news/news-and-updates/sharp-drop-in-international-recruitment-slows-overall-growth-of-uk-register (Accessed: 30 April 2026).

O'Reilly, P.E. (2014) 'Teachers at Work: Factors Influencing Satisfaction, Retention and the Professional Well-Being of Elementary and Secondary Educators', City University of New York [online] Available at: https://academicworks.cuny.edu/cgi/viewcontent.cgi?article=1087&context=gc_etds& (Accessed: 30 April 2026).

OECD (2019) 'TALIS 2018 Results (Volume I): Teachers and School Leaders as Lifelong Learners' from TALIS, OECD Publishing, Paris, https://doi.org/10.1787/1d0bc92a-en [online] Available at: www.oecd.org/content/dam/oecd/en/about/programmes/edu/talis/talis2018participantnotes/TALIS2018_CN_FIN.pdf (Accessed: 1 May 2026).

OECD (2020) 'TALIS 2018 Results (Volume II): Chapter 2. Boosting the prestige and standing of the profession' [online] Available at: www.oecd.org/en/publications/talis-2018-results-volume-ii_19cf08df-en/full-report/component-7.html (Accessed: 1 May 2026).

OECD (2020) 'Teachers & educators' [online] Available at: https://gpseducation.oecd.org/revieweducationpolicies/#!node=41728&filter=Secondary (Accessed: 30 April 2026).

OECD (2020) 'TALIS 2018 Results (Volume II): Teachers and School Leaders as Valued Professionals' from TALIS. OECD Publishing: Paris [online] Available at: www.oecd.org/en/publications/talis-2018-results-volume-ii_19cf08df-en.html (Accessed: 12 May 2026).

OECD (2024) 'Education Policy Outlook 2024: Reshaping Teaching into a Thriving Profession from ABCs to AI' [online] Available at: www.oecd.org/en/publications/education-policy-outlook-2024_dd5140e4-en.html (Accessed: 1 May 2026).

OECD (2024) 'Results from TALIS 2024 – Country notes: Finland' [online] Available at: www.oecd.org/en/publications/results-from-talis-2024-country-notes_e127f9e2-en/finland_ab17fae3-en.html (Accessed: 1 May 2026).

OECD (2025) 'Education at a Glance 2025: Chapter D3. How much are teachers and school heads paid?' [online] Available at: www.oecd.org/en/publications/2025/09/education-at-a-glance-2025_c58fc9ae/full-report/how-much-are-teachers-and-school-heads-paid_5daf5678.html (Accessed: 1 May 2026).

OECD (2025) 'Education at a Glance 2025: Chapter D8. How severe are teacher shortages across countries?' [online] Available at: www.oecd.org/en/publications/education-at-a-glance-2025_1c0d9c79-en/full-report/how-severe-are-teacher-shortages-across-countries_781f4a97.html (Accessed: 1 May 2026).

Ofsted (2022) 'Education recovery in schools: summer 2022' on Gov.uk [online] Available at: www.gov.uk/government/publications/education-recovery-in-schools-summer-2022/education-recovery-in-schools-summer-2022 (Accessed: 30 April 2026).

Ofsted (2023) 'The Annual Report of His Majesty's Chief Inspector of Education, Children's Services and Skills 2022/23' [online] Available at: https://assets.publishing.service.gov.uk/media/655f2551c39e5a001392e4ca/31587_Ofsted_Annual_Report_2022-23_WEB.pdf (Accessed: 30 April 2026).

Onyefulu, C., Madalinska-Michalak, J. and Bavli, B. (2022) 'Teachers' motivation to choose teaching and remain in the profession: A comparative mixed methods study in Jamaica, Poland and Turkey' in *Power and Education*.

Peirson-Hagger, E. (2024) 'Why is France so good at keeping its teachers?' on *Tes magazine* [online] Available at: www.tes.com/magazine/analysis/general/teacher-retention-why-france-so-good-keeping-its-teachers (Accessed: 1 May 2026).

Pembroke, J. (2021) 'A comparison of assessment and accountability in the French and English school systems' on Sig+ [online] Available at: www.sigplus.co.uk/2021/03/a-comparison-of-assessment-and-accountability-in-the-french-and-english-school-systems (Accessed: 1 May 2026).

Podolsky, A., Kini, T. and Darling-Hammond, L. (2019) 'Does Teaching Experience Increase Teacher Effectiveness? A Review of US Research' in *Journal of Professional Capital and Community*.

Poliscope 'Helping Nottinghamshire Police make the most of the Police Uplift Programme' [online] Available at: www.poliscope.org.uk/case-study-nottinghamshire (Accessed: 1 May 2026).

Pountney, R., Rata, E. and Swift, D. (2025) 'Exploring curriculum coherence and professional knowledge' in Wyse, D., Baumfield, V., Mockler, N. and Rearden, M., (eds.) *The BERA-SAGE Handbook of Research-Informed Education Practice and Policy*. London: BERA / Sage.

Pressley, T. (2021) 'Factors contributing to teacher burnout during COVID-19' in *Educational Researcher*.

Provenzo, E.F., McCloskey, G.N., Kottkamp, R.B. and Cohn, M.M. (1989) 'Metaphor and meaning in the language of teachers' in *Teachers College Record*.

Rajendran, J., Santhi, J. and Kumar Chauhan, R.K. (2023) 'The Impact of Continuous Professional Development on Teacher Retention and Performance' in *Journal of Harbin Engineering University*.

Rigby, A. (2026) 'What we learned from four Ofsted report card inspections' on *SchoolsWeek* [online] Available at: https://schoolsweek.co.uk/what-we-learned-from-four-ofsted-report-card-inspections (Accessed: 30 April 2026).

Roberts, K. (2007) 'Non-specialist teachers on course' on Royal Society of Chemistry [online] Available at: https://edu.rsc.org/news/non-specialist-teachers-on-course/2020716.article (Accessed: 30 April 2026).

Ronfeldt, M., Loeb, S. and Wyckoff, J. (2012) 'How Teacher Turnover Harms Student Achievement' from National Center for Analysis of Longitudinal Data in Education Research [online] Available at: https://caldercenter.org/sites/default/files/2024-11/Ronfeldt-et-al.pdf?utm_ (Accessed: 30 April 2026).

Ronfeldt, M., Loeb, S. and Wyckoff, J. (2013) 'How Teacher Turnover Harms Student Achievement' in *American Educational Research Journal*.

Ryan, R.M. and Deci, E.L. (2000) 'Self-determination theory and the facilitation of intrinsic motivation, social development, and well-being' in *American Psychologist*.

Sam, C.H. and Gupton, J. (2024) 'Reconceptualizing Teachers as First Responders' in *Practitioner & Theoretical Perspectives Journal of Trauma Studies in Education*.

Samuel, M. (2026) 'Social work vacancies increased at Cafcass last year, amid drop in practitioner numbers' on CommunityCare [online] Available at: www.

communitycare.co.uk/content/news/social-work-vacancies-increased-at-cafcass-last-year-amid-drop-in-practitioner-numbers (Accessed: 1 May 2026).

Save the Children (2024) 'Thousands of teachers reveal "deep problems" in classrooms four years on from school lockdown' [online] Available at: www.savethechildren.org.uk/news/media-centre/press-releases/2024/teachers-reveal-deep-problems-in-schools-4-years-on-from-covid-lockdown (Accessed: 30 April 2026).

Schutz, P.A. and Zembylas, M. (2009) *Advances in Teacher Emotion Research: The Impact on Teachers' Lives*. New York: Springer.

Schutz, P.A., Hong, J. and Cross Francis, D. (eds.) (2018) *Research on Teacher Identity: Mapping Challenges and Innovations*. New York: Springer.

Scottish Government (2025) 'Pupil and teacher characteristics 2025 published' [online] Available at: www.gov.scot/news/pupil-and-teacher-characteristics-2025-published (Accessed: 1 May 2026).

Scottish Government (2025) 'Teacher numbers and the teacher workforce planning process: FOI release' [online] Available at: www.gov.scot/publications/foi-202400439555 (Accessed: 1 May 2026).

Scottish Liberal Democrats (2024) '1,300 teachers have quit within five years of starting work' [online] Available at: www.scotlibdems.org.uk/news/article/1300-teachers-have-quit-within-five-years-of-starting-work? (Accessed: 1 May 2026).

Scutt, C. and Peacock, A. (2024) 'Today's proposals are crucial for a CPD entitlement that works' on *SchoolsWeek* [online] Available at: https://schoolsweek.co.uk/todays-proposals-are-crucial-for-a-cpd-entitlement-that-works (Accessed: 30 April 2026).

Shanshan, L. (2023) 'The effect of teacher self-efficacy, teacher resilience, and emotion regulation on teacher burnout: a mediation model' in *Frontiers in Psychology* [online] Available at: www.frontiersin.org/journals/psychology/articles/10.3389/fpsyg.2023.1185079 (Accessed: 30 April 2026).

Sharp, C. and Aston, K. (2024) 'Ethnic diversity in the teaching workforce: evidence review', Slough: NFER [online] Available at: www.nfer.ac.uk/publications/ethnic-diversity-in-the-teaching-workforce-evidence-review (Accessed: 30 April 2026).

Sharp, C. and Aston, K. (2024) 'Ethnic diversity in the teaching workforce: evidence review', Slough: NFER [online] Available at: https://mission44.org/wp-content/uploads/2024/10/ethnic_diversity_in_the_teaching_workforce-1.pdf (Accessed: 1 May 2026).

Siddiquei, M.I. and Kathpal, S. (2021) 'Challenges of online teaching during COVID-19: An exploratory factor analysis' in *Human Behaviour and Emerging Technologies*.

Skaalvik, E.M. and Skaalvik, S. (2017) 'Teacher Stress and Teacher Self-Efficacy: Relations and Consequences' in McIntyre, T.M., McIntyre, S.E. and Francis, D.J. (eds.) *Educator Stress: An Occupational Health Perspective*. Cham: Springer.

Slater, E. (2018) 'Fight for Education: A Black Paper. Edited by C.B. Cox and A.E. Dyson. London: The Critical Quarterly Society. 1969. P.80. Price 5s' in *British Journal of Psychiatry*.

Social Work England (2026) 'Social worker survey results 2024' [online] Available at: www.socialworkengland.org.uk/about/publications/social-worker-survey-results-2024 (Accessed: 1 May 2026).

Sokal, L., Trudel, L.E. and Babb, J. (2020) 'Canadian Teachers' Attitudes toward Change, Efficacy, and Burnout during the COVID-19 Pandemic' in *International Journal of Educational Research Open*.

Spalding, C. (2016) 'I have seven tattoos, but I agree with my school policy that says you should hide them in class' on *Tes magazine* [online] Available at: www.tes.com/magazine/archive/i-have-seven-tattoos-i-agree-my-school-policy-says-you-should-hide-them-class (Accessed: 30 April 2026).

STV News (2024) 'Hundreds of new teachers quit profession within five years, figures show: The General Teaching Council for Scotland said 1,337 teachers had left the register within five years' [online] Available at: https://news.stv.tv/scotland/hundreds-of-new-teachers-quit-profession-within-five-years-figures-show? (Accessed: 1 May 2026).

Sullivan, A., Johnson, B., Simons, M. and Tippett, N. (2020) 'When performativity meets agency: how early career teachers struggle to reconcile competing agendas to become "quality" teachers' in *Teachers and Teaching*.

Sutton Trust, The (2011) 'Improving the impact of teachers on pupil achievement in the UK – interim findings' [online] Available at: www.suttontrust.com/our-research/improving-impact-teachers-pupil-achievement-uk-interim-findings (Accessed: 27 May 2025).

Teacher Development Trust (2025) 'What is Didagogy? Exploring the Discipline of Teaching Teachers' [online] Available at: https://tdtrust.org/research/didagogy-the-discipline-of-teaching-teachers (Accessed: 1 May 2026).

Teaching Commission (2025) 'Shaping the future of teaching' [online] Available at: https://teachingcommission.co.uk/report (Accessed: 30 April 2026).

Tereshchenko, A., Mills, M. and Bradbury, A. (2020) 'Making progress? Employment and retention of BAME teachers in England', London: UCL Institute of Education [online] Available at: https://discovery.ucl.ac.uk/id/eprint/10117331/1/IOE_Report_BAME_Teachers.pdf (Accessed: 13 May 2026).

Trindade Pereira, I. and Can Yilmaz, M. (2025) 'How is the teacher shortage in the EU impacting the quality of education?' on Euro News [online] Available at: www.euronews.com/my-europe/2025/09/11/how-is-the-teacher-shortage-in-the-eu-impacting-the-quality-of-education (Accessed: 1 May 2026).

Tripp, D. (1994) 'Teachers' lives, critical incidents, and professional practice' in *International Journal of Qualitative Studies in Education*.

Tschannen-Moran, M. and Hoy, A.W. (2001) 'Teacher efficacy: Capturing an elusive construct' in *Teaching and Teacher Education*.

UK Government (2025) 'Government evidence to the STRB – data annexes – September 2025' [online] Available at: https://assets.publishing.service.gov.uk/media/6900daff84b816d72cb9aa97/STRB_26_data_annex.xlsx (Accessed: 7 May 2026).

UK Parliament (2016) 'Police and Crime Commissioners: here to stay: Government response to the Committee's Seventh Report of Session 2015–16' [online]

Available at: https://publications.parliament.uk/pa/cm201617/cmselect/cmhaff/822/82204.htm (Accessed: 1 May 2026).

UK Parliament (2024) 'Teacher recruitment, training and retention' [online] Available at: https://publications.parliament.uk/pa/cm5804/cmselect/cmeduc/119/report.html (Accessed: 30 April 2026).

UK Parliament 'Continuing professional development' [online] Available at: https://publications.parliament.uk/pa/cm201617/cmselect/cmeduc/199/19909.htm (Accessed: 30 April 2026).

UK Parliament 'The Macpherson Report: Twenty-two years on' [online] Available at: https://publications.parliament.uk/pa/cm5802/cmselect/cmhaff/139/13907.htm (Accessed: 1 May 2026).

University of Southampton (2024) 'Choice and consistent shift patterns could improve nurses' work-life balance' [online] Available at: www.southampton.ac.uk/news/2024/02/nurses-shifts.page (Accessed: 13 May 2026).

Vähäsantanen, K., Paloniemi, S., Hökkä, P.K. and Eteläpelto, A. (2017) 'An agency-promoting learning arena for developing shared work practices' in Goller, M. and Paloniemi, S. (eds.) *Agency at work: An agentic perspective on professional learning and development*. Springer International Publishing / Springer Nature.

Very Big Brain (2025) 'The Neuroscience of Storytelling: Why Your Brain Loves a Good Plot' [online] Available at: https://verybigbrain.com/professions-interests/the-neuroscience-of-storytelling-why-your-brain-loves-a-good-plot (Accessed: 30 April 2026).

Walker, M. (2024) 'The Early Career Framework: Key findings for policymakers and school leaders from the early roll-out evaluation', Slough: NFER [online] Available at: www.nfer.ac.uk/blogs/the-early-career-framework-key-findings-for-policymakers-and-school-leaders-from-the-early-roll-out-evaluation (Accessed: 1 May 2026).

Walker, M., Worth, J. and Van den Brande, J.: National Foundation for Educational Research (2019) 'Teacher workload survey 2019' on Department for Education [online] Available at: https://assets.publishing.service.gov.uk/media/5e12fcb7e5274a0f9e82e4fd/teacher_workload_survey_2019_main_report_amended.pdf (Accessed: 30 April 2026).

Welsh Government (2025) 'Teacher Recruitment and Retention – Evidence Paper for the Children, Young People and Education Committee' from Welsh Government written evidence to the Senedd, 11 September 2025.

Wilshaw, M. (2012) 'High expectations, no excuses' (a speech to the London Leadership Strategy's Good to Great conference) [online] Available at: https://webarchive.nationalarchives.gov.uk/ukgwa/20141107034501/http://www.ofsted.gov.uk/news/high-expectation-no-excuses-sir-michael-wilshaw-hmci-outlines-changes-ofsted-inspection-drive-delive-0 (Accessed: 12 May 2026).

Worth, J. (2022) *Early career teacher retention after COVID-19*. London: NFER.

Worth, J. and Faulkner-Ellis, H. (2022) 'Teacher Labour Market in England – Annual Report 2022', Slough: NFER [online] Available at: www.nfer.ac.uk/publications/teacher-labour-market-in-england-annual-report-2022 (Accessed: 30 April 2026).

Worth, J. and Ghosh, A. (2022) 'Teacher Labour Market in Wales Annual Report 2022'. Slough: NFER.

Worth, J. and Van den Brande, J. (2020) 'Teacher autonomy: how does it relate to job satisfaction and retention?', Slough: NFER [online] Available at: www.nfer.ac.uk/publications/teacher-autonomy-how-does-it-relate-to-job-satisfaction-and-retention (Accessed: 30 April 2026).

Worth, J. and Van den Brande, J. (2020) *Teacher workload and retention*. London: NFER.

Worth, J., Del Pozo Segura, J.M. and Kuhn, L. (2026) 'What helps to improve teacher retention? A pathway analysis of factors affecting retention', Slough: NFER [online] Available at: www.nfer.ac.uk/media/3stjkeac/what_helps_to_improve_teacher_retention.pdf (Accessed: 20 April 2026).

Worton 'The role of capital in the field of initial teacher education in England' [online] Available at: https://discovery.ucl.ac.uk/id/eprint/10110984/1/Worton_The_role_of_capital_in_the_field_of_initial_teacher_education_in_England_Main_FINAL.pdf (Accessed: 30 April 2026).

www.inquest.org.uk/blog/my-sister-ruth-perry